Elusive Reform: The French Universities, 1968-1978

Westview Replica Editions

This book is a Westview Replica Edition. The concept of Replica Editions is a response to the crisis in academic and informational publishing. Library budgets for books have been severely curtailed; economic pressures on the university presses and the few private publishing companies primarily interested in scholarly manuscripts have severely limited the capacity of the industry to properly serve the academic and research communities. Many manuscripts dealing with important subjects, often representing the highest level of scholarship, are today not economically viable publishing projects. Or, if they are accepted for publication, they are often subject to lead times ranging from one to three years. Scholars are understandably frustrated when they realize that their first-class research cannot be published within a reasonable time frame, if at all.

Westview Replica Editions are our practical solution to the problem. The concept is simple. We accept a manuscript in camera-ready form and move it immediately into the production process. The responsibility for textual and copy editing lies with the author or sponsoring organization. If necessary we will advise the author on proper preparation of footnotes and bibliography. We prefer that the manuscript be typed according to our specifications, though it may be acceptable as typed for a dissertation or prepared in some other clearly organized and readable way. The end result is a book produced by lithography and bound in hard covers. Initial edition sizes range from 400 to 600 copies, and a number of recent Replicas are already in second printings. We include among Westview Replica Editions only works of outstanding scholarly quality or of great informational value, and we will continue to exercise our usual editorial standards and quality control.

Elusive Reform: The French Universities, 1968-1978
Habiba S. Cohen

In no Western country was student uprising as dramatic as in France in the late 1960 s; in none were university reforms as sweeping. The student revolt of May 1968 threatened the downfall of the French Fifth Republic. Six months later, the Orientation Act of Higher Education was passed. The new law called for a total revamping of structures and methods of governance, curriculum, and finance in all French universities.

The sweeping overhaul of the system caused confusion and discouragement, and the uniformity of application prevented individual experimentation, hampered university autonomy, and preserved the government's centralized control. Continued student unrest led to a conservative interpretation of some of the law's crucial articles. This study traces the development of the new French universities in the critical decade 1968-1978 as it became apparent that ambitious reforms of the new law were to fall far short of the high standards and the goals set by its proponents.

Habiba S. Cohen, assistant dean in the College of Arts and Sciences, Indiana University, received her Ph.D. from Indiana University. She lived and studied in France during several of the years covered by this study.

L'enseignement en France est à l'image de la société française: rigoureusement égalitaire en apparence, fortement hierarchisé en realité.

—Frédéric Gaussen, 1978

. . . democratization has created financial, political, social and pedagogical difficulties, and no modern society has been able to master the tensions and contradictions of its educational system.

—Roger Masters, 1971

Elusive Reform: The French Universities, 1968-1978

Habiba S. Cohen

Westview Press / Boulder, Colorado

A Westview Replica Edition

Published in 1978 in the United States of America by
  Westview Press, Inc.
  5500 Central Avenue
  Boulder, Colorado 80301
Frederick A. Praeger, Publisher

Library of Congress Catalog Card Number: 78-19677
ISBN: 0-89158-195-2

Printed and bound in the United States of America

301359

For William, Natalie, and Leslie

CONTENTS

xi

LIST OF TABLES

LIST OF GRAPHS

LIST OF APPENDICES

PREFACE

On May 3, 1968, a student revolt broke out in the courtyard of the Sorbonne. It triggered widespread unrest and nearly brought down the regime of Charles de Gaulle. Order was restored only when the government promised workers and students sweeping reforms. After meeting the workers' demands, de Gaulle turned his attention to the students. He selected a capable minister of education, Edgar Faure, who helped draft the Orientation Act of Higher Education, passed by parliament in October and promulgated on November 12, 1968. This study is an examination of that law and its effects on French universities. Chapter one treats the state of higher education prior to 1968; chapter two, the May crisis; chapter three, the emergence of the Faure law with consideration of its intellectual origins, the political conflicts over its passage, and, finally, an examination of its main provisions with regard to university governance, curriculum, and finance. Once the passing of the law has been studied, the focus changes. The three most important provisions of the law — governance and structures, curriculum, and finance — are separately considered in chapters four, five, and six, respectively. The chapters examine the development in each field from the passage of the law in 1968 until 1978. The concluding chapter presents an overview of the developments in the French university and attempts to draw a balance sheet of the reform effort a decade later.

This book examines the extent to which the 1968 law has been effective; has the promise born of the student revolt and the law been realized? It is at the same time an historical account of a crucial decade in French higher education which formed the contemporary French university.

This study was made possible by the generous help of many individuals: the librarians of the Centre de documentation at the ministry .ducation, rue de Grenelle, of the Paris institut d'études politiques, the Centre de sociologie européene, the Institut national de recherche et de documentation pédagogiques (INRDP), the Maison des sciences de l'homme and the Bibliothèque nationale, the Hoover Institution on War, Revolution and Peace, Stanford, California, especially Ms. Agnes Peterson and Ms. Helen Berman. I wish also to thank Mme Bergounioux, director of the Centre régional de recherche et de documentation pédagogiques in Paris (INRDP), Mme Delclaux of the Institut national d'administration scolaire et universitaire (INAS). Mr. E. J. Vergnes of the ministry of education service des études informatiques et satistiques spent much of his valuable time in 1975 and again in 1977 assisting me in tracking down statistics. Mention should also be made of the officials of the secretariat of state of universities who generously received me and answered interminable questions. Faculty members who selflessly assisted me were: Georges Oppenheim (Paris V), Claudine Viano (Paris X), Jean Sommers (Strasbourg I), Claire and Marc Dupuis (Strasbourg I). Presidents Jean-Marc Bischoff of Strasbourg III (Law), and Etienne Trocmé of Strasbourg II (Letters) took time out of their busy schedules to answer questions and share with me their special insight into the French university.

The sources for this study included published government documents, interviews with university personnel and officials at the secretariat of state of universities, and newspaper and journal articles. The latter two were often authored by participants, public officials, professors, and students, thus giving an inside view of the university.

The value of the French franc has varied in the last decade. For purposes of convenience I have calculated it at $.20. Also it should be noted that until June 1974, the central organ in charge of higher education was the ministry of education, then until 1978 the secretariat of state of universities and thereafter the ministry of universities.

Higher education in France is a complex topic for research especially when the researcher's formal studies had been in Anglo-Saxon institutions. I have tried to overcome the snares of ethnocentrism; only the reader can decide if I have succeeded.

Originally this study was written as a dissertation at Indiana University. I wish to express my deepest gratitude to Professor Robert Shaffer who guided me patiently throughout. It is difficult to thank him enough for his thoughtfulness, concern and example over the years. I am indebted to Georgina Frank, Mollie Ducket, and Susan Wladaver, for help in typing and editing.

I cannot sufficiently thank my family. My husband, William B. Cohen, was always supportive, spent many hours over the various drafts and provided useful criticism. My parents, Sophie and Nassim Reuben Suleiman know how much I owe them. My daughters, Natalie Rachel and Leslie Rebecca helped keep life in perspective.

INTRODUCTION

Campus protest in Europe and the United States was a common phenomenon in the 1960s. Protests in the U.S., unlike those in Europe, had traditionally been apolitical, except for the 1930s. But in the 1960s, students on both sides of the Atlantic found political reasons for protest. In France, the Algerian war of the 1950s polarized the university community, as it did society. In the early 1960s, the Vietnam war and the civil rights movement galvanized American students. Political agitation paralleled a general discontent with the structure and role of the university.

In the late 1960s the baby boom generation reached college age. Universities expanded to meet this need, but in some countries, such as France, the expansion was started too late. Students balked at the lack of adequate facilities, the bureaucratic nature of the modern university, and the curriculum, which they viewed as irrelevant. They questioned the role of the university in society denouncing it as an ivory tower and a class-bound institution.

The idealism of youth made itself felt in all societies by a youth group which was demographically larger than it had ever been. Young people experienced a sense of power and solidarity as their culture was embraced by the media. Their program included the demand for reforms of the university, especially its democratization. The university, it was felt should be a mirror of society and should prepare people with a relevant education in tune with the modern technological world. Universities should shed their authoritarian mode of governance and involve students and other members of the university community in matters of common concern. Those who clung to the traditional university as a center of research and learning were outnumbered by zealous young faculty and students, who called for innovations in the curricula and an opening up of the university to the masses.

A number of countries experienced student uprisings, but the most dramatic one occurred in France. Although changes had been demanded in the 1960s, reformers were unable to interest the government in their cause. The serious nature of the student revolt, however, convinced the government that sweeping measures would promptly have to be taken. University reform in many industrial countries took place as a result of student agitation, but in none was the pressure stronger or the reform so apparently precipitous as in France.

A dramatic chapter in the history of higher education began in France

1

following the events of May 1968. What appeared to be a revolution was ignited by student protest, occupation of buildings, marches in the streets, and the throwing of cobblestones and molotov cocktails. Fighting with the police and the national guard escalated the conflict and touched off not only a student uprising but a social revolt as well. French workers joined the bands of student strikers and gradually the entire nation was brought to a standstill. The survival of the French Fifth Republic was threatened. The government had to salvage the regime by making peace with the workers and then with the students. This was accomplished by the end of June 1968 after an election confirmed Charles de Gaulle's power, presumably giving him a mandate to act. Once the government negotiated with the workers, he promised educational reform and turned his attention toward the universities.

From May through October, a period of feverish discussion began within the French university community. For those involved it was an exhilarating period, during which they promoted ideas which they hoped would be incorporated in the reform bill that the government promised. In Anglo-Saxon universities, similar discussions took place regarding governance, curriculum innovation, democratization, and the role of the university in society. But these discussions went on inside distinct institutions and were aimed at adapting them to the perceived needs of society. In France the university community worked for a national reform bill; all universities were to be similarly structured. While an individual university in the U.S. debated the type of governance structure and participation pertinent to itself and its student body, in France the debate centered around what would be best incorporated in a law for the entire university system of the nation. Methods of participation in elections, types of examination systems and university regulations were discussed in terms of across-the-board policies for all universities. Autonomy and participation were key concepts embraced by reformers. Some were aware of the irony in their position; autonomy and participation were to be dictated by a national law enacted in Paris. Such contradictions often stalked the reformers.

The law passed in November 1968 called for an "audacious reconstruction" of the universities, which would force them to take a "leap into the unknown," as Edgar Faure, the Minister of Education, described it. In order to allay the fears of the conservatives and to keep the extremists at bay, the law proved to be less audacious than Faure had originally proposed. If it had been liberally interpreted and carried out in the spirit of the reformers, the universities could have undergone an "audacious

2

reconstruction" in the decade that followed. But, as will be shown, it was an elusive reform. The bill was increasingly interpreted with a narrowness of spirit that vitiated much of its meaning.

The tradition of a centralized system of education in France created particular problems for the reformers and even shaped their own thinking; no matter how deeply in revolt against the existing power structure, they tried to find a central, national solution to the short-comings of French universities. In spite of all the reforms, ultimate power has remained with the minister of universities. In Anglo-Saxon countries, higher education has recently moved toward centralization. The move toward state-controlled education has been strengthened by the public demand for accountability. In the early 1970s when it became apparent that resources were limited, central planning of resource alloca-tion came to be seen as necessary. In Germany, where universities are dependent on the länder governments for support, the call has been for more federal involvement in the division of resources. And in France, the move toward university autonomy and decentralization from the ministry has failed, resulting in a full circle return to centralization.

Thus, educational systems on both sides of the Atlantic have been shifting toward greater centralization. While in France centralization has been a tradition, this is a recent phenomenon in the U.S. Centralization or co-ordination by a central bureau has recently been viewed in the U.S. as a positive, efficacious method of controlling educational institutions. The example of the French system would suggest, however, that ineffi-ciencies exist within a centralized system as well; the loss of autonomy is detrimental to diversity, and to the ability of universities to adjust in a flexible manner to changing educational needs.

Financial resources and the size of an educational enterprise are important factors in understanding some of the problems facing all educational institutions. In the 1960s seemingly limitless resources were available in the U.S. In Europe, impressive expansion took place; for a time, education was the largest single item in the French national budget, larger than the budget for defense. In the late 1970s, it became evident that resources were not limitless, that expansion of universities could not go unchecked, and that student enrollment would eventually level off. The utopian ideals of the 1960s — open universities — could not become a reality. The loosely structured curricula that evolved from the protest of the 1960s could not produce educated graduates with the basic skills that modern society demanded: writing, mathematics, the liberal arts, and technical tool skills.

3

The unprecedented technological and social changes which have occurred in modern industrial states have made it nearly impossible for educational planners to predict change or to prepare curriculum and teaching methods in anticipation of needs for the 1980 and 1990s. Universities are torn between the commitment to greater universality of recruitment and a concern for quality education. With limited funds, hard choices undoubtedly will have to be made.

The French reforms of 1968 reveal the ambitious efforts of one nation to make far-reaching changes. They tried to decentralize the system of higher education, introduce a participatory democracy in the governance of what had become autonomous universities, provide relevancy in the curriculum, open the universities to the masses, and transform a highly structured, hierarchical system of authority into a more cooperative, relaxed, free, egalitarian community. The system would henceforth show a greater regard for students and student life, a hitherto neglected area of concern in European universities.

The French university provides a rare example of a centralized system of education that within a period of three months achieved a law restructuring the university system. The reforms were shaped by a mixture of goals set by university administrators, faculty, students, politicians, and various utopians. The goals of the change were limited by the values of the culture. The French staunchly cling to the principle of equality. This value, however, clashed with the adoption of university autonomy, for autonomy implied the development of diverse and competitive institutions; valuing equality, the French were compelled to forego developing some important aspects of autonomy. This is but one of a number of examples of how tradition and culture shaped the direction that the reforms were to take.

No nation in the 1960s attempted reforms in so ambitious a manner as did France and therefore no nation fell so tragically short of its proposed goals. The reformers and, indeed, the nation set high standards for the new higher education reform law. The failure to meet some of these goals created a sense of frustration and disillusionment. As in other countries, however, various reforms in curriculum, governance, and even, to a limited extent, financial matters did produce some flexibility in a system that had previously had very little. Thus, the French university, like the American university, has emerged with positive changes which have remained as a result of the protest of the 1960s. A decade later, educational reform is once again being considered on both sides of the Atlantic. In the U.S., a quiet reform movement has begun and is spreading to all

4

major institutions. This movement is not a dramatic one, nor is it a student movement; rather it was begun by educators and desired by the society at large. Its focus in curriculum is a return to basic skills. In France, the movement is led by the ministry and by conservative or traditional educators and is designed to undo the reforms of 1968. The deeply ingrained tradition of centralization in France has been difficult to ignore and the old habits of authority have gradually returned. The 1968 reforms in France were all the more admirable because they had to look far beyond national traditions and because more than in any other country, they promised fundamental changes in the university. But, as in other countries, the reforms were specific to the demands and interests of the 1960s.

In the 1980s further changes will be demanded of the universities. In the 1970s in Germany and Italy students have been aggressively violent. In France, students protest from time to time but never with the same rage against the Establishment as their European neighbors. Depending on how they are allowed to develop in the coming years, French universities will either take the initiative and individually experiment and explore new avenues or else, as in times past, these changes will occur by fiat from Paris. The reforms of 1968 are gradually losing their meaning and, if the trend of the last few years is not reversed, it is likely that what was greeted as a radical new departure for the French universities will be judged to have been a mere illusion.

CHAPTER I

THE TRADITIONAL UNIVERSITY

En France, alors que tout a changé, . . . il y a cependant quelque chose qui reste rélativement immuable; ce sont les conceptions pédagogiques . . . les hommes de ma génération ont encore été élevés d'après un idéal qui ne différait pas sensiblement de celui dont s'inspiraient les collèges de jésuites au temps du grand roi.

—Emile Durkheim

The Pre-World War II University

Writing at the end of the nineteenth century, Emile Durkheim remarked that he and his generation had been schooled in a system little different from that existing under Louis XIV two centuries earlier.[1] In our century, Frenchmen might no longer look back to the Sun King, but they would at least recognize a strong continuity in the French educational system since Napoleon. One of the most enduring institutions that the Emperor bequeathed to France was the university, for which he created a centralized structure. No educational establishment could exist outside the university and the teaching corps was subject to militaristic discipline.[2]

The universities had declined during the eighteenth century. Corruption was rampant, diplomas were sold, and the curriculum was stagnating, "Their scientific education was deplorable, their reputation mediocre."[3] The twenty-two universities of the Ancien Regime were abolished by the Revolution of 1789. Their abolition reduced them to fragmented *facultés*. New institutions like the Ecole polytechnique, the Ecole normale supérieure, and a variety of *grandes écoles* were established to give professional training to the leaders of the Napoleonic state. Throughout "the nineteenth century, the traditional *facultés* dwelt in their shadow."[4] The state's concern with secondary education prevented any strengthening of the university. During the July monarchy (1830-1848), there was talk of reducing the number of small, isolated *facultés* and building up a few, larger, provincial centers of learning, but nothing came of this. In 1896 the *facultés* were finally united and the provincial universities were established. This amalgamation of the *facultés* into universities did not change the

7

essential nature of higher education. The *facultés* continued to be the main unit, and the new universities did not become independent institutions of higher learning. The best institutions, the *grandes écoles*, remained outside them. The rector represented the state at the regional level for all education, and the centralized structure remained.

After 1896, the new provincial universities received little support from the state. Only Paris and the *grandes écoles* were financially well off. Paris compared well with Berlin, but the French provincial universities could not match their counterparts in Germany, Britain or the United States. The war of 1914-1918 postponed reform: the universities were considered wasteful institutions during the financial austerity and depression that followed the war. On the eve of World War II, France's universities were institutions without direction. For the time being, the *grandes écoles* graduates satisfied the country's need for leaders in government, industry, business, and the liberal professions.[5]

The Grandes Ecoles

In the eighteenth century, a number of specialized schools outside the university system emerged to train the professional elite. The Ponts et Chaussées, the Ecoles des mines, and then others were established to train army and navy officers. The Ecole polytechnique was founded in 1794 to train public works engineers, as well as officers; and the Ecole normale supérieure first trained schoolteachers in 1795.[6]

Admission to these *grandes écoles* was regulated by rigorous competitive examination and the schools attracted the best students. The graduates of Ecole normale supérieure and Ecole polytechnique were the most sought after for leadership positions in public life and industry. Since both schools were residential, a "unique esprit de corps" developed among students, which lasted throughout their lives and which greatly influenced French society. These students became the ruling class in France. As Georges Pompidou dramatically put it, "One is a *normalien* as one is a prince of blood."[7]

Most of the *grandes écoles* were founded at the end of the eighteenth century or the beginning of the nineteenth. The secondary school system organized by Napoleon carried out the selection process, designating the very best pupils to enter the *grandes écoles*. Special preparatory classes were set up in the lycées to prepare aspirants to enter one of these prestigious institutions, and entry to the preparatory classes was itself

8

THE TRADITIONAL UNIVERSITY

highly selective.[8] Upon completion of the preparatory period (one or two years), the students took a competitive examination (concours). Those who successfully passed these concours entered a *grande école* and henceforth acquired a special aura. To be a graduate of one of these institutions assured one of a good position and the respect of society for life. By contrast, this was not necessarily the experience of the university graduate. The legacy of these two types of institutions remains to this day. In a 1971 study, the Organization of Economic Cooperation and Development (OECD), consisting of the major industrial countries in the West, compared the *grandes écoles* and the universities in France:

> The faculties are places of open access, the *Grandes écoles* of highly competitive access. The faculties give a general education for a range of posts, especially teaching, and also carry on high level research; the *Grandes écoles* give a closely geared training for specific professions and conduct little research. The faculties in general pay little attention to teaching; the *Grandes écoles* give it much and effective attention. The faculties have a high drop out rate en route and a high failure rate overall; the *Grandes écoles* have a low drop out rate and a low failure rate. . . . They have a better staff-student ratio than the faculties.[9]

In order to understand the present system of higher education in France, it is important to note that France has had a long tradition of intellectual institutions outside the university. While the universities were stagnant in the eighteenth century, cultural life flourished in France. Intellectual clubs and academic societies, "the world of the salons [all] continued more or less independent of the universities,"[10] and overshadowed them throughout the nineteenth century. And, in fact, until the 1940s, there was little public concern over the state of the universities.

The French University — Post-World War II

The existence of the *grandes écoles* made modernization of the universities unnecessary, since a small but well-qualified elite was always produced by these prestigious schools. This small, restricted elite was seen as sufficient to France's needs. But after World War II, new forces impinged on the universities demanding that they play a significant role

9

in higher education. Among these new developments were the growth in the French economy, the rising birthrate, and the changing class structure.

France's economy after World War II embarked on an era of unprecedented development. "It was an epoch of 'take off' for our economy" wrote professor Georges Dupeux.[11] The agricultural sector of the active population went from 36 percent in 1946 to 30 percent in 1954, to 16 percent in 1968. Modernization through new technology was the key to this change. Major structural modifications took place, especially in the largest and most powerful businesses and industries. This postwar growth in the economy created both the outlet and a need for a large, well-trained population, which had not existed before. The jobs were available, and people needed to acquire the necessary education to fill them.[12] Moreover, the number of births, which had been 600,000 in 1945, rose to 800,000 in 1946; the birthrate has remained approximately the same since then.[13] And further, the World War II experience had a generally leveling effect on the French social structure. The upper classes were discredited by the charge of collaboration with the Germans, while

GRAPH 1
PATTERN OF STUDENT ENROLLMENTS, 1900-1966 [14]

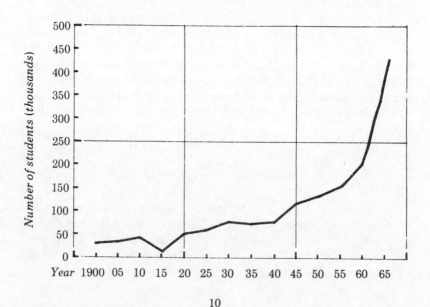

THE TRADITIONAL UNIVERSITY

the resistance movement spread egalitarian doctrines. To some extent, the hierarchical social structure was modified. It was now more conceivable for children of the lower-middle classes, or even working classes, to aspire to a university education. The public became aware of the importance of education as a means of social mobility.[15]

All these forces led to a dramatic increase in the number of students attending the universities (table 1).[16] While from 1945 to 1961, a period of fifteen years, the number of students doubled; their number more than doubled in the six years between 1961 and 1967. Graph 1 portrays the steep rise in numbers that occurred from 1960 to 1966.

Many other industrial countries experienced rapid growth in university enrollments, but France experienced an enrollment above the average of that of other industrial states. While the U.S. had a growth rate of 6.6 percent in student population in the 1960s, France experienced twice as much — 13.6 percent. The average growth rate for the industrial countries selected by the OECD was also lower than France — 11.3 percent (Graph 2, table 3).

GRAPH 2
UNIVERSITY STUDENT ENROLLMENTS
A COMPARATIVE GRAPH (1950-1970) [17]

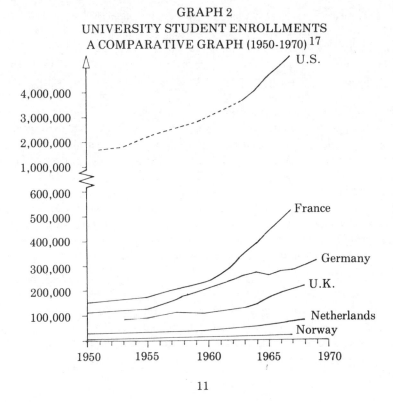

11

The French universities were ill-equipped to handle the influx. Being subject to a centralized administration, they had identical recruitment procedures for all students and common methods of recruiting professors and implementing the curriculum. The centralized educational system implied that change could come only from the ministry and had to apply to all universities equally. Because of these difficulties, change was embarked upon only with great hesitation, and educational reforms were often conducted haphazardly and piecemeal. The French university seemed unable to resolve the problems caused by the rise in numbers, to meet the need for a modern education in tune with industrial society, or to fulfill the expectations that large segments of society had of it — namely, that the university serve as a means of social promotion for them and their offspring.

The Baccalauréat and Secondary School

There were no selection procedures for admission to the university. The baccalauréat, a national examination administered at the end of secondary school, was the passport for entry to the university.

The lycée (secondary school) had been specifically founded by Napoleon to prepare youth for the *grandes écoles* and the university. The lycée had its own elementary classes. Because of its demanding curriculum, its concentration on preparation for higher education, and its fees, it attracted almost exclusively upper-class children. The less privileged attended the free primary schools, which incidentally did have upper grades to prepare pupils, not for higher education, but for either admission to primary teachers' training schools or apprenticeships. Attendance at a lycée, however, nearly automatically opened the road to later admission to the university and thereby to the liberal professions, while attendance at the primary school excluded one from such possibilities. The baccalauréat, taken at the end of lycée attendance, was a rigorous selection mechanism. As sociologist Emile Boutmy put it:

> . . . it divides the nation into two classes: the one which
> has parchments, the one which does not, the one which
> alone has entry into the liberal careers, the one which is
> rejected and confined within the old commoners' profes-
> sion, commerce and industry. The distinction is clear and
> decisive; either one belongs to the privileged class or one

12

THE TRADITIONAL UNIVERSITY

does not, and it is the baccalauréat which decides. The distinction is final and for life.[18]

The class nature of the secondary school system was well understood, and attempts at democratization occurred at various times. In 1932 tuition was abolished at the lycée. A more basic attack on the class structure was a proposal to create a single, unified primary school system. The idea was promoted by a group of university graduates who had served in World War I and who labeled themselves "Les Compagnons de l'Université." Partisans of a unified primary school met with resistance in the decades that followed. The only reform that could be introduced in the face of such opposition was to continue the double system of education, while allowing graduates of the primary schools to transfer into the lycée for their secondary education. The abolition of tuition in the lycée and this new mobility from one type of establishment to another most benefited the lower-middle classes, those who fell between the bourgeoisie and the working class, "the small grocer, the baker, the office clerk." Education for them was a means of upward mobility. For the working-class and peasant children, the lycée remained foreign ground. Families were too poor to forego the earnings of a child, and geographical location, especially for the peasantry, meant that lycée attendance would require additional expenses.[19]

Since 1959, there has been less structural separation between the pupil thought capable of later pursuing higher education and the pupil unable to do so. The school system, however, through various mechanisms, at several stages in the child's life, has tried to separate and place him into specific categories. In the classic book written in 1925 *La Barrière et le niveau* and still applicable in the 1970s, Edmond Goblot wrote:

> Education, above all, creates and maintains [social] classes, but the word "education" takes on a new and narrow meaning; education classsifies and sorts out rather than developing personal merit.[20]

Access to Education

It was only after World War II that serious inquiry into the relations between social class and education began. Studies showed that upper and middle-class children had an edge over other social groups from earliest

13

childhood and not merely from the beginning of formal instruction. (Graph 3 shows the social class recruitment of university students in the 1960s). These differences were due to the cultural backgrounds that each child possessed. Curiously enough, in spite of the forces of democratization after World War II, there was a new emphasis on aesthetic values in French schools, so that history, the arts, languages, and philosophy were paramount. In these subjects, upper-class children tended to do especially well.[21] It is also known that school success depends on aptitude (real or apparent) to manipulate ideas and that success in this domain is linked to those who have studied the classics. The opportunity for classical studies is class-related. In a group of students in the faculty of letters, statistics showed that the proportion of students who studied Latin in secondary school varied from 41 percent for the sons of workers and farmers, to 83 percent for the sons of senior executives and members of the liberal professions.[22]

In recent decades, a group of French sociologists have been presenting empirical proof of the inequality of opportunity in the French educational system. Thus Bourdieu, Passeron, Boudon, Bisseret, Saint-Martin, among others, have shown that school success is closely related to the cultural values of the home and that these in turn are class-bound. Success in the secondary school and admission to the university were also class-bound.[23] The chances of reaching the university varied according to the father's profession. In 1961-1962, the son of a senior executive was eighty times more likely to enter the university than was the son of a worker; the former's chances were double those of the son of a middle-level executive. Most of the determinants of one's social class at the university were already decided at earlier stages of education. This is not to say, however, that the university did not also play an important role in further selection, which, in fact, led to what has been called the "reproduction" of elites. This process has been described by Bourdieu and Passeron:

> The culture of the elite is so close to that of the school
> that the child who comes from a disadvantaged home can
> only through hard work acquire the style, the taste, the
> mentality — in short the *savoir-faire* and *savoir-vivre*
> which comes naturally to the privileged class. [24]

While the discussion has so far dealt with the universities, it should be noted that recruitment for the *grandes écoles*, which provides access to the most prestigious positions in France, is even more exclusive. In

14

THE TRADITIONAL UNIVERSITY

GRAPH 3
SOCIO-OCCUPATIONAL ORIGINS OF
STUDENTS IN HIGHER EDUCATION, 1961-1966 [25]

(in percent)

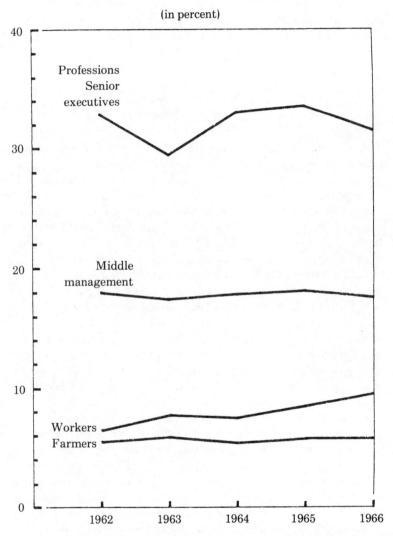

1961-1962, for example, only 2 percent of the student population at the Ecole polytechnique and Ecole centrale were working-class sons, compared with 9 percent at the universities.[26]

15

The students from the *grandes écoles* represented about 9 percent of the students in the universities, yet they constituted a large number of those wielding authority at the highest level of the private and public sectors of the economy. This contrast was sharpest in the 1960s: while very large numbers were attending the university, enrollments in the *grandes écoles* remained restrictive, 30,000 in 1958-1959, and 46,000 in 1966-1967.[27]

The French University on the Eve of May 1968
Admission Policies

While the class basis of higher education became one of the battle cries of May 1968, what seems to have been a fundamental cause of student dissatisfaction was the inability of the university to adjust to the growing enrollments (Graph 1). The universities were aware of their inadequacies but found themselves helpless. They could not control the numbers, since possession of the baccalauréat gave every student the right to enter the university in the *faculté* of his choice. It was unpopular to talk of stringent admission requirements (*sélection*, as the French call it), and the authorities rightly feared the political fallout of such a policy. The minister of education, Christian Fouchet, vacillated between instituting rigorous procedures and delaying such a policy.

In 1967, the universities found themselves crushed by the influx of students and without adequate facilities and personnel to receive them. This led many to talk about the necessity of selection procedures beyond the baccalauréat. While some thought that the baccalauréat should be made more stringent to limit admission to the university, others thought it unfair to have the degree serve as both an examination ending secondary school and a means of admission to the university. Rather they urged that the baccalauréat be retained as a degree or certificate marking an end of secondary education and that a separate examination giving entry to the university be instituted. That was suggested, for instance, by Raymond Aron, noted sociologist at the Sorbonne and later professor at the Collège de France. But there was considerable resistance to selection policies for admission to the university.

Admission policies were especially important for the French university since it had a unique problem: approximately three-quarters of the students entering university dropped out before completing a diploma. France enrolled twice as many students as Great Britain, yet produced

16

THE TRADITIONAL UNIVERSITY

half the graduates (France had 600,000 students in 1968, while Great Britain had approximately 300,000.)[28]

In Europe as in the United States, conferences on education from 1966 on, whether sponsored by universities, UNESCO, or OECD, all upheld the idea that in the future the majority, if not the whole population, had a right to some form of higher education.[29] In Great Britain and the United States, this demand could be met in part by continuing education, diversification of programs, and flexibility in the curriculum, but in France this was not possible. The system of higher education was tightly structured, inflexible and narrow, but a parallel system of higher education significantly different from the traditional one would have met with disfavor. The centralized system had produced a general consensus that any divergence from the existing one would denote a drop in quality education. Therefore, those demanding access to higher education could be accommodated only with institutions similar to those already existing.

In the face of large numbers of students, it was thought that something had to be done. The results of a questionnaire sent to the professors of the *facultés* of letters in December 1967 revealed that the majority opposed instituting rigorous admission procedures to the universities; rather they favored selection at the end of the first year of university study.[30]

During this same period, the teaching unions, as well as the Communist and Socialist parties, all came out against any form of selection in admission to the university.[31] In the debate on admission examinations after the baccalauréat, or eliminatory examinations at the end of the first year of university study, the baccalauréat itself was not questioned.

Since education was the most common means of social advancement, decisions about access to the university were potentially political problems, because the responsibility for implementing them lay with the French ministry of education. De Gaulle favored restricted admissions. The prime minister, Georges Pompidou, and Fouchet, were able to convince de Gaulle several times to delay a plan for selective admission to the university.[32]

Yet, restricting admission to the university seemed imperative in face of the influx of students and their high dropout rate. But the adoption of such a policy raised concern among many young people, for it may have given them a feeling that the government was trying to obstruct their educational opportunities and their social ascension. More time and energy were spent debating how the influx could be stemmed, rather

17

THE TRADITIONAL UNIVERSITY

than how the university was to adjust to the post-World War II economic boom, the demographic revolution, and the increased democratic expectations characteristic of the 1960s. As a specialist in French education, Antoine Prost, put it: "The selection procedure attacks only the symptoms, but not the malady itself."[33]

Teaching and Curriculum

While the number of students in France more than doubled between 1960 and 1967, the number of professors nearly tripled, increasing mostly in the ranks of the *assistants*, or junior faculty. Until about 1962, there was a genuine effort to improve the faculty-student ratio (Table 8). France, however, was not able to keep up with the faculty-student ratio of other major countries. In the U.S., U.S.S.R., Germany, and Great Britain, the overall ratio was approximately 1 to 10, while in France in 1967, it was 1 to 21. In certain fields, such as letters, the ratio was 1 to 43, compared to 1 to 40 in Italy, 1 to 15 in Germany, 1 to 8.5 in Great Britain. In medicine and pharmacy, France had a ratio of 1 to 10, compared to 1 to 7 in Italy and 1 to 6 in Germany and Great Britain. Graph 4 illustrates the ratio in several countries, and indicates that France had approximately 45 teachers per 1,000 students (ratio of 1 to 22), and the U.S. had 95 teachers per 1,000 students (ratio of 1 to 11).[34]

While the French university made arduous efforts to increase its faculty to keep up with the enrollments, no significant change had occurred in the traditional method of recruiting faculty. The young graduate student had to clear many hurdles before gaining a position as a tenured professor. This meant that career preoccupations often superseded all other concerns; there was little time left for the important task of teaching. An influential sponsor was crucial to career advancement. A graduate student could be nominated to the rank of *assistant*, teach, and at the same time prepare a *doctorat d'état*. This degree entailed researching and writing a long, detailed, encyclopedic piece of work that was rarely under 500 pages long. It often took many years to complete such a work (five or more in the sciences, ten or more in letters). In the fields of law or medicine, a professor could teach only after taking a difficult competitive examination (*concours d'agrégation*). The number of positions open was usually so small that the concours was given only every two years. The influence of a sponsoring professor, or the patron as

18

GRAPH 4
A COMPARATIVE GRAPH, NUMBER OF
FACULTY PER 1,000 STUDENTS, 1950-1970[35]

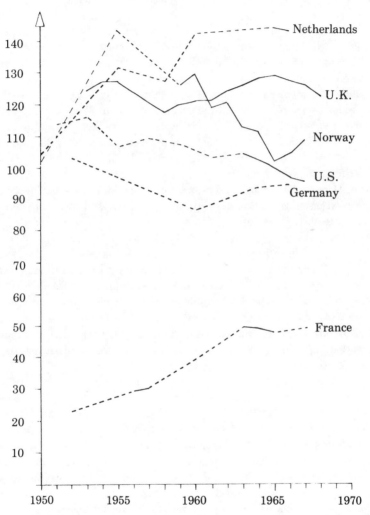

the French call him, was crucial, especially in the field of medicine.[36] Having reached the rank of *maître de conférences* (roughly equivalent to associate professor in the U.S.), a faculty member enjoyed many

19

THE TRADITIONAL UNIVERSITY

privileges: prestige, decent salary, and the prospect of eventually becoming an influential patron, even though that might be many years off.

At first, only full professors taught the *cours magistraux*, the large lecture classes, but as the numbers of students increased, the *maîtres de conférences* were also entrusted with this task. These lectures were given over and over again, and many criticized them for their impersonality. Some argued that it was impossible for students to have contact with their professors in such a setting. As one professor put it, "the whole thing becomes a spectacle."[37]

Full professors enjoyed the largest degree of independence, teaching three hours a week in a seven-month academic year. While the university itself was constricted by centralized structures and regulations, the university professors operated fairly independently. They taught what they pleased, even when a specific curriculum existed. Thus, one author ventured to say that "the French professor was the freest of all professors in the world," and he went on to explain that what prevented the system from falling into total anarchy was a firm hierarchical structure of the professorate. The senior professors were mandarins. The system, however, did not create a mentality of cooperation or of community, but rather nurtured rivalries for funds, chairs, and influence in the academic world. Professors did not concern themselves much with teaching; they taught one or two days a week and spent the rest of the time at home or in libraries and laboratories. Relations among professors were weak; this was perhaps more true of Paris than in the provinces.

The influx of students in the 1960s meant that new professorial positions opened up but not enough to take care of all the students. Hence, a new corps of university teachers was introduced to aid the professors, namely, the *assistants* and the *maîtres-assistants*, created in 1960-1961 (equivalent to teaching assistants and assistant-professors in the U.S.). In 1960-1961 there were 4,316 *assistants* and *maîtres-assistants* together, out of a total of 7,901 teaching faculty of all ranks. This corps of junior faculty increased rapidly in the decade of the 1960s.[38] The recruitment of the *assistants* was not done in any defined manner nor were their functions clearly spelled out. In some cases, they were secondary school teachers who had succeeded in the *concours d'agrégation*, but who now preferred to teach at the university level. Sometimes the *assistant* was a recent university graduate who, thanks to a "patron," was appointed as an *assistant*, or, in other cases, a graduate student in the process of preparing a thesis.

20

THE TRADITIONAL UNIVERSITY

As a rule, the *assistants* were not supposed to teach the *cours magistraux*, but they did sometimes teach the advanced students. This was especially true in the provincial universities. They were generally supposed to teach first year students, but in the sciences, they often had heavy responsibilities in research laboratories. The *assistants* aspired to become professors in higher education. To gain access to teaching positions they prepared ponderous theses in letters and sciences, while in medicine and law, they prepared for the *agrégation*. They were appointed for five or six years and were supposed to teach five hours a week while preparing for a degree, and there was no guarantee of a permanent teaching position. At the end of six years, those who had not completed their research or taken the *concours d'agrégation* could try to find some means of support. They might find a research position at an independent institute such as the Centre National de la Recherche Scientifique (CNRS) or, if they are lucky, they could be appointed to the rank of *maître-assistant*, thereby having a "slot position" in the university, although their functions remained much like those of the *assistant*. The strong desire to enter the teaching staff in a university and the uncertainty of reaching that goal made the *assistants*, according to one author, prone to assimilate the values of the professorial corps and thus their appearance in the university did not profoundly transform the system. Moreover, the *assistant* and *maître-assistant* did not participate in the governance of their *faculté*, for this responsibility was entirely in the hands of the full professors and the *maîtres de conférences*.[39]

The professors who were in charge of the curriculum had been able to maintain a system of education that in many ways was impervious to the modern world. There was little eagerness to institute practical courses; for instance, the university refused to institute new types of training for the expanding business world. While the U.S. prepared 50,000-60,000 graduates in business administration each year, France turned out 3,500, at the very most, and that included all higher education institutions.[40]

Traditionally, the university deliberately kept outside its walls new programs of higher education that prepared for technical careers. Such a policy deprived technical education of the prestige that it would have needed to attract students who, since the 1960s, have flocked into the studies of the humanities and law. Until 1968, the law *faculté* also taught political science, economics, and public administration. The universities have traditionally upheld the value of literary culture, and, in fact, even men of science have become famous because they were also men of letters. A famous mathematician, who was on the admission board of the

THE TRADITIONAL UNIVERSITY

Ecole polytechnique, told an applicant's father: "If you wish your son to specialize in science, have him study the humanities."[41] At the university level, while one out of every three students ought to have majored in the sciences, in order to help fulfill the national economic plan, only one out of every five did so in 1968-1969.[42]

GRAPH 5
NUMBER OF STUDENTS
Thousands   BY FIELD OF STUDY, 1900-1967[43]

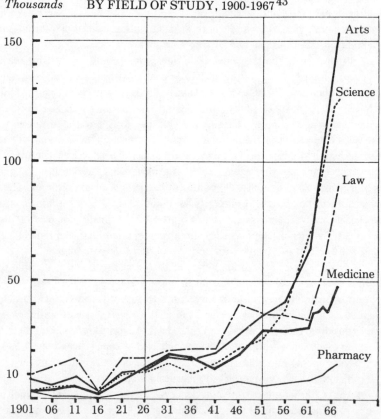

The low regard for science and especially for technological studies was also in part a result of the manner in which the educational system was structured in the secondary school curriculum, where studies of the humanities and mathematics were separated into two different tracks, the former being more prestigious.[44]

In 1966, University Technical Institutes (IUT) were founded to help

THE TRADITIONAL UNIVERSITY

deflect students from the university and to train them specifically in technical skills. These institutes suffered from their lack of contact with the universities. The two-year diploma they issued was not recognized as a national diploma, thus again robbing them of prestige. Since the IUT diploma was not transferable to the university, young people were further discouraged from entering the technical institutes. While the Fifth Economic Plan had intended that there be 35,000 students in the IUTs by 1970, there were in fact only half that many.[45]

Student Life

Unlike American universities, French universities had not taken responsibility for providing student services. Although an institution named Oeuvres Universitaires was established in 1955, its resources and responsibilities were very limited. For the most part students had to find their own housing. They could eat in student restaurants, but there were not enough of them. Only students at the *grandes écoles* lived in material conditions that were acceptable.[46] In the 1960s, the government extended services to students by increasing space in restaurants and dormitories, but in spite of this tremendous effort made by government, facilities were still insufficient.

RESTAURANT AND DORMITORY SPACES 1960-69[47]

	1960	1966-67	1968-69
No. of places in restaurants	16,500	54,000	88,000
No. of dormitory rooms	11,000	43,000	89,000

The Financing of the French Universities

The number of professors at the university, the facilities at their disposal, and the supplementary personnel were, of course, limited by budgetary considerations, but the French state made large expenditures on behalf of higher education. The budget for the ministry of education, for all levels of education, jumped from 1.84 percent of the GNP in 1958, to 3.4 percent in 1967. Its share in the total state budget also grew impressively from 9.62 percent in 1958 to 16.32 percent in 1967. It was

23

the largest single budget in the state. An increasingly large proportion of the ministry of education budget went to higher education: 6.6 percent in 1952, 7.1 percent in 1957, 9.2 percent in 1962, and 11.4 percent in 1967.[48] (Table 12).

An example of the improvement that occurred between 1951 and 1967 was, as mentioned earlier, that the faculty-student ratio improved by more than 100 percent during these years.[49] The libraries, however, received little support and continued to have a very small portion of the total education budget. In 1952, expenditures for the libraries cost 8 million francs; in 1957, 11 million francs; in 1962, 27 million francs; and in 1967, 55 million francs. These figures represented only 0.4 percent of the total education budget for the period 1952-1967.

The budget for research received a boost during this same period. Research was allotted 32 million francs in 1952 (1.6 percent of the total educational budget), 80 million francs in 1957 (2.4 percent), 300 million francs in 1962 (4.0 percent), and 732 million francs in 1967 (4.8 percent).[50]

While a growing proportion of the national income was spent on higher education in the 1960s, it was nevertheless difficult to meet the need, because the original efforts on behalf of higher education after World War II had been so modest. In the face of problems considered more important, the government had neglected higher education in the five years after the war. It never quite caught up with the lag, thereby putting French higher education at a disadvantage, compared with many other European countries. Moreover, at the very time that the French were spending more in the 1960s, they were still not matching, in proportion of the GNP, the effort of most industrial countries. While comparative figures on per student expenditures are difficult to calculate, those published reveal that France was seriously behind most industrial states. Thus, per student yearly expenditure on an average was $1,725 for Australia, $1,700 for public universities in Japan, $3,013 for the United Kingdom, and $4,000 in the U.S. for major, research, public universities; it was $860 for France.[51] Graph 6 illustrates the unit cost per university student in six major countries.

The growing expenditures were necessary, given the large growth in enrollments in the 1960s. Some of this increase was undoubtedly due to a change in the manner in which Frenchmen viewed education. But most of the increase in enrollment was the result of the baby boom during and after the war. From then on, it had been known that by the 1960s there would be an unusually large cohort of university age. Government

THE TRADITIONAL UNIVERSITY

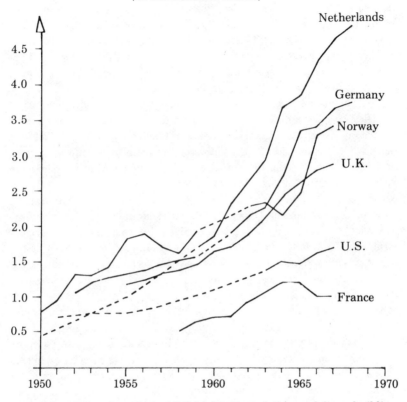

reports in 1948 and again in 1951 had indicated the need for a building program to accommodate the expected onslaught. Yet little was done to prepare in advance. Only when the baby boom generation started to enter the university were funds poured in, but they did not suffice and had little impact.[53]

Summary

The French universities were neglected institutions until World War II. Immediately thereafter, France was involved in the wars in Indochina

25

THE TRADITIONAL UNIVERSITY

and Algeria, which received priority. By the time the government poured resources into higher education, it was already too late to make up for the lag that had occurred.

In the 1960s, the universities were not prepared for the large influx of students. The rate of enrollment increase was between 10 and 14%. While the number of teaching faculty also increased (mostly at the junior faculty level) and the faculty-student ratio much improved over previous years, France nevertheless continued to lag behind other major countries in unit cost per university student, as well as in expenditure on higher education and education's percentage of the GNP.

Modernization of the university was obstructed, not only because of insufficient financial means, but also as a result of archaic structures of decision making and the pervasiveness of traditional attitudes. When a reform was instituted by the ministry, it usually encountered such opposition that the result was a reform of the reform. Hence, there were piecemeal "reforms" in the curriculum every few years, which exasperated students, professors, and university administrators. However, no fundamental change in the curriculum occurred before 1968.

Student recruitment was predetermined by the whole educational structure, so that the best students and the ones from families of the upper classes and liberal professions had the best chances of continuing their studies to the baccalauréat, and from there were guaranteed automatic admission to the university.

The influx of students to the universities in the 1960s and the strain that it put on the country caused many to question the validity of the secondary school national diploma — the baccalauréat — as a passport to the university. Hence, the issue of *sélection* was much debated in this period. The students opposed *sélection* and wanted the guarantee of "open admission" with the baccalauréat (while some clamored for "open admission" even without the possession of that diploma). The faculty was torn on this issue, because it was unpopular to speak of *sélection* when the whole world was talking about democratizing higher education.

Students found themselves in a situation where material conditions were deplorable, contact with professors impossible, and enrollment opportunities available only in programs of studies that offered little chance of employment. The university seemed to lack direction. Frustrations among students, professors, and administrators had seemed to reach a high point. It was an electric atmosphere in which grievances, real or imagined, could easily become a conflagration. And this was to occur in May 1968.

26

THE TRADITIONAL UNIVERSITY

CHAPTER II

MAY 1968

*Qui n'a pas connu mai 1968 à Paris n'a pas connu
l'ardeur de vivre.*

—Alfred Fabre-Luce

*En vérité il n'est pas de révolution que ne soit politique,
économique et culturelle à la fois.*

—Claude Lefort

"N'ALLEZ PAS EN GRECE CET ETE! RESTEZ A
LA SORBONNE."

Graffiti on wall — Paris, May 1968[1]

The Youth Crisis

The French educational structure established by Napoleon was by
1968 in need of change, but the forces of tradition still predominated.
Change is difficult in all societies, but in France it is particularly so, as
French sociologist, Michel Crozier has noted in an influential book, *The
Bureaucratic Phenomenon* (1964). France was a traditional and rigid
society in both its institutions and outlook, Crozier wrote. This very
rigidity created deep antagonisms among those desiring change. Finding
it impossible to transform society peacefully, the forces of change would
precipitate a political crisis. Faced by a profound challenge, the forces of
tradition would then bow to the inevitable and adapt quickly, thus
resolving the crisis.[2] And this is what happened in the universities as a
result of the political challenge to the Gaullist regime posed by simultaneous revolt of students and workers in May 1968.

That such a crisis would occur had not been foreseen by the highest
authorities in the land. Charles de Gaulle, in a New Year's address to the
nation on December 31, 1967, declared:

> It is truly with confidence that I envisage, for the next
> twelve months, the existence of our country . . . in the
> midst of so many lands shaken by so many jolts, ours will
> continue to give the example of efficiency in the conduct of
> its affairs.[3]

27

Within four months of this confidence-inspiring declaration, the entire nation was rocked by an upheaval that threatened to topple the Fifth Republic. This upheaval of French society has been called an "explosion," a "crisis," a "revolution," an "elusive revolution," a "faceless revolution," and a "hidden revolution." It has been described as a "crisis of civilization," a psychodrama rather than a drama, a comedy rather than a tragedy.[4] It is hard to know what it was. Jean-Paul Sartre found it convenient to borrow a quotation from Che Guevara, who had said: "When extraordinary events occur on the streets, that is Revolution."[5] Some, like Claude Fohlen, nonetheless felt in the short run, the events of May 1968 were not a revolution, but they may have constituted one in the long run. Whatever view one holds, one fact remains: the events of May 1968 brought the whole nation to a standstill for an entire month, and the social and economic fabric of the country was threatened. By the end of May, some 10 million workers were on strike.

What distinguished this uprising from previous ones in French history was the fact that it was precipitated by student unrest. Once the crisis was triggered, others joined the ranks of demonstrators, and the situation expanded into a major uprising.

A number of general factors aggravated the inflammatory situation, namely the pervasive youth culture of the 1960s, the Vietnam War, and the press coverage of student unrest in all parts of the world. A London newspaper, *The Observer*, declared: "From Warsaw to Cambridge, it is the same thing: students are revolting."[6] *Time* magazine described student unrest as a world phenomenon. Students existed in greater numbers than ever before; their numbers rose from the mid-1950s to 1968 from: 380,000 to 880,000 in Latin America, 2,600,000 to 7,000,000 in the United States, 739,000 to 1,700,000 in Western Europe.[7] In relation to the rest of the world population, the young formed a larger percentage than ever before or since, and there was a general empathy among them that Kenneth Keniston has called "the internationalization of identity."[8] Thanks to the media and air travel, an international youth culture developed; young people were conscious of themselves as a group. They shared common interests, including politics, which had as a focus a common opposition to the Vietnam War.

Other issues also led to youth protest. Since the fall of 1967, most Italian universities had been witnessing student demonstrations and the partial or total occupation of buildings. In February 1968, students demanded large-scale reform of the universities. In Spain, incidents were

28

occurring at the University of Madrid. "Free assemblies" were established and the students attacked the secret police, shouting "Down with the university gestapo."[9] In the U.S., the issue of Vietnam rallied youth, as did demands for curriculum innovation and student rights.

While the causes for student unrest in France were many, the immediate reason for student dissatisfaction was demographic. There were some 600,000 students involved in higher education in France in 1968 and about 11 million young people in school. The rise in the birthrate, discussed in chapter one, caused serious problems for the ministry of education. In spite of a large effort to adapt to the situation, the government began too late to adjust to the tide in 1968. The French universities were not prepared to receive the students born twenty years earlier: "hence the drama of the lecture halls bursting at the seams."[10] Moreover, new demands placed on the university were not simply physical. The social make-up of the student body had been slowly changing since World War II. In the immediate post-war years, only 2 percent of the age group from twenty to twenty-five went on to higher education; in 1968, 25 percent did so. Of this group a larger proportion came from humble backgrounds than before the War, but they were still heavily underrepresented.

The rise in numbers and the changing social make-up of those pursuing higher education put new demands on the university, but the curriculum was rigid and lacking in diversity. A university degree in letters prepared for teaching in secondary schools, but by 1968, those teaching positions were over-supplied with candidates. Those who passed the *concours d'agrégation* could have access to teaching positions in either a secondary school or the university; those who passed the *concours de CAPES* (certificat d'aptitude au professorat de l'enseignement du second degré) had access to secondary school positions. The number of teaching positions was controlled by the central administration.[11] The *facultés* of law, which included the discipline of economics, prepared students for administrative and judicial careers, but jobs in those fields were scarce. About 50 percent of the students in the university were enrolled in the *facultés* of letters, law, and economics.[12] University students faced poor employment prospects with or without a university diploma.

The rate of unemployment in France on the eve of May 1968 remained at the stable rate of 3 to 4 percent, as it had been since 1900. But the number of young people under twenty-five seeking employment increased from 29 percent in 1962 to 39 percent in 1968.[13] The bleak prospects of employment for university graduates helped increase their

29

general malaise. They experienced a high level of frustration, feeling that their education had, in a sense, entitled them to a job. The rigidity of the university program and the abstract nature of the French educational system elicited the outcry against its lack of utility and adaptability to modern life.

The Centralizing Role of the Ministry of Education on the Eve of May 1968

The ministry of education, as was described in chapter one, handled all the affairs of the university. Dogan put it best when he wrote "all decisions came from the Ministry, all petitions for further decisions went to the Ministry, and until the Ministry spoke there was little to do but continue petitioning."[14] The rigid centralization was to have serious effects. When trouble began in 1967, university authorities could not negotiate with the extremist students without consulting the ministry: "Thus the centralization of the system encouraged the students and the faculty to focus their dissatisfaction on the government."[15]

University officials were ultimately neither responsible for nor able to institute change. Thus, demands for university reform bore on the government. Those wanting change found themselves confronted by the resistance of a strong, centralized, educational bureaucracy located in Paris. Change could not come on each campus based on its particular needs or on the ability of local students to organize and cogently present their point of view to university authorities, nor was change dependent on particular personalities of individual administators on the campus. Change had to come from the top, from Paris, from the ministry, and it had to apply uniformly to all universities. While changes certainly had been made in the structure of higher education before 1968, they were done slowly and without any kind of coherent philosophy or plan.[16] The escalation of confrontation which led to May 1968 was probably necessary to accomplish needed change.

In many countries, including the U.S., the university was seen as an institution of the "Establishment" and was therefore attacked. In France, given the class nature of the university and its ties to the government, such a view was even more justified and thus, with some legitimacy, student revolutionaries could feel that in assaulting the university, they were also challenging "the system."[17]

30

Paris as a Revolutionary Setting

Paris, the center of the revolt had an unusually large student concentration. Out of a total student population of over half a million in the country, 160,000 students were in the capital. Dogan has typified France as a "macrocephalic" country, in which the capital dominates the whole country and where a disproportionate number of students are located. The impact of a demonstration in the capital, he argued, has greater importance and repercussions on the rest of the country than does a large demonstration on an American campus. Student demonstrations in a capital like Paris inevitably alarm the police. A student demonstration of mass dimensions differ from a mass worker demonstration. Workers obey the instructions of union leaders, while students tend to be less predictable and more defiant of the police. They also use surprise tactics that are disconcerting and frightening in a capital city. Dogan argued, moreover, that while student militants were as numerous in America as in France and other European countries, their action was more spectacular in Europe because of the concentration of European students in the major cities.

Paris had been the center of previous revolutions in which students, particularly in.the Latin Quarter, have been at the center of the action. The Sorbonne is in the heart of this area, where nonconformist and revolutionary ideas find support in intellectual circles. "This Parisian intellectual ambiance considerably amplified the university crisis of May 1968," Dogan aptly wrote.[18]

Student Unions and Politics on the Eve of May 1968

The institutional means by which French students could express their concerns were the student unions. By 1968, however, these unions had become far less representative of the students and there seemed to be no organization that could speak on their behalf.

The principal student organization, the Union nationale des étudiants de France (UNEF), officially founded in 1907, began to lose members rapidly after the Algerian War. In 1961, the union had more than 100,000 members in a student body of 200,000; in May 1968, the union had hardly 40,000 members out of a student population of over half a million, i.e., 8 percent (table 9).

The union's opposition to the Algerian War caused the government to

31

withhold its subsidies in 1961. The union had up until then been apolitical but this new political stance angered the government; in its place, another union, the Fédération nationale des étudiants de France (FNEF), was founded and funded by the government. Although it was supposed to be apolitical, the FNEF was for a "French Algeria" and attracted extreme right-wingers, while the UNEF, bereft of its subsidies and in debt, was driven totally into the opposition camp.

The UNEF offered only a limited number of services (travel, housing, xeroxing), but these were not enough to attract a mass student following. It had no control over the university curriculum and no impact on educational reform. It seemed to be divorced from the real and basic problems confronting the university. The UNEF could not boast of large membership, nor could it be considered to speak for the students. Nevertheless, it was the oldest union and still must have had some prestige, at least, enough to attract extremists who fought among themselves for control of the organization.

UNEF came to play an important role in May 1968. Students who had hitherto been indifferent or politically apathetic followed the extremist leader, Jacques Sauvageot, the vice-president of the UNEF. They now recognized it as a means by which they could make themselves heard and, thus, the UNEF became an institutional participant in the student revolt.[19]

Outside the unions, in the universities themselves, small extremist groups developed and began to disrupt the university even before May 1968. The most important were the Jeunesse communiste révolutionnaire (JCR), the Comité de liaison des étudiants révolutionnaires (CLER), the Union des jeunesses communistes-marxistes-léninistes (UJC-ML), and the Mouvement du 22 Mars (Movement of March 22).

JCR was a Trotskyite group, founded in April 1966 and headed by Alain Krivine, which included Trotskyites, anarchists, Catroists, and followers of Che Guevara. It was hostile to the orthodox Communist Party and its "bourgeoisification." JCR kept in close touch with foreign groups, especially the German SDS. It also created the Comité d'action des lycéens (CAL) to work within the French secondary schools.

CLER was founded in 1963 and joined with the Féderation des étudiants révolutionnaires (FER) in April 1968. CLER was another Trotskyite movement whose members, to quote Jean-Raymond Tournoux, "vegetated" around the Latin Quarter for several years and numbered at most one hundred. The group was noted for its violence. Unlike JCR, it infiltrated the UNEF organizations in Paris and in the

32

provinces.

The Union des jeunesses communistes (UJC) was founded by a splinter group of the Union des étudiants communistes (UEC). This group had been expelled from the Communist party for "deviationism." It was noted for its pro-Chinese ideas, which it tried to take to the factory workers. The movement was one of the first groups to advocate that students join workers in a common struggle. During the May events, this group insisted on the establishment of joint committees of workers and students.

There were other student groups belonging to the revolutionary socialists, the Parti socialiste unifié, and the Communists, who were divided into many factions, such as anarchists and situationists.

The Movement of March 22, was founded on that date in 1968 during demonstrations at Nanterre by a group of students who called themselves the enragés (the enraged ones), led by Daniel Cohn-Bendit. The group was a mixture of anarchists and JCR militants. They made their presence felt in Paris on May 3 when they went to the Sorbonne. From then on, their leader, Danny-the-Red (Cohn-Bendit was red-headed), became the principal figure in the student revolt.

The membership of these mini-groups (*groupuscules* is the French term used to describe the various extremist groups) could not have numbered more than a few thousand in all of France.

On the eve of the crisis, the large majority of students were neither unionized nor members of extremist movements. The extremist groups took advantage of UNEF and used it as a means for rallying the students. These groups argued among themselves. Each had its dogma, whether Maoist, Trotskyite, Communist, anarchist, situationist, revolutionary socialist, ultra-gauchistes, or ultra-right (known as the "white terror"). None had a well-defined program for the university.[20]

In spite of the fact that the majority of students was not affiliated with a movement, however, there had been a definite politicization of the student body rarely encountered in the U.S. but more typical of Latin American countries. Since World War II, the French political parties had been at odds with the youth movement. During the Algerian conflict, all parties, at one point or another, supported the war. Many students opposed the war and found themselves alienated from the political system and parties. They moved to the left and took on radical stands.[21]

In the months preceding May 1968, continued student unrest and agitation occurred at a number of French universities over a whole series of issues. These gave the students experience in demonstration tactics

33

and organization and led to ever-increasing tensions between students and the authorities. Students were angered over issues in every imaginable area. These issues included: visitation hours in the dormitories; anarchic conditions in university restaurants (long waiting lines, lack of seats, poor food); freedom of expression (in January 1968 a Vietnam rally had been forbidden by the ministry of interior); teaching and the curriculum; delays in payment of scholarship money; material conditions — especially the need for more classrooms; the Fouchet reforms of 1966, which imposed a reorganization of the curriculum that many considered too hasty; and, finally, the rights of young assistants and research assistants.[22]

Day after day in the winter of 1967 and spring of 1968, students gathered in collective protest, sometimes peacefully, sometimes resorting to the occupation of buildings and acts of vandalism against university property.

Nanterre on the Eve of May 1968

Of all the outbreaks of protest relating directly to May 1968, none was more important than those which centered around the campus of Nanterre. This institution has been described as the symbol of the new university. It was constructed in 1964 in a suburban slum in Paris near the railways and highrises, and its large glass windows were a contrast to the closed atmosphere of the Sorbonne. It was meant to be the "campus of the twenty-first century," but it turned out to be much like the Sorbonne, "a nineteenth-century place," wrote Frédéric Gaussen in *Le Monde*.[23]

In many ways, Nanterre was actually worse than the Sorbonne, because students in the latter could find cultural distractions, while at Nanterre the students could not. The suburban campus had no library, no cultural center, no sports facilities, no park benches, no trees or landscaping, no cafés or student hangouts.[24] Nanterre was neither a traditional French campus nor a self-contained, American style campus. One specialist on French students has stated that they are generally happier in an urban atmosphere; otherwise (as was the case in Nanterre), the students feel isolated and divorced from real life. As one student said, "The campus [idea] might be fine for American students, but it simply does not conform to the French spirit."[25]

Not providing many outlets for its students, the campus at Nanterre

34

became a hotbed of agitation. Activist students found support from the teaching faculty, whose members often had leftist political leanings. In late January 1968, anarchist students organized protests agains several policies: the presence of policemen in civilian clothes in the university; the existence of a "black list" of students whom the authorities wanted to expel; and the expulsion of a certain German student, Daniel Cohn-Bendit, guilty of having attacked a government official who had come to inaugurate the new swimming pool at Nanterre. Other curricular issues also caused protest at Nanterre.

On March 22, 1968, six militants of the Comité Vietnam National were arrested. Immediately afterwards, a protest was organized and a group voted to occupy administrative buildings. That evening, 150 students met in the professors' council room, debated a number of political issues till 2:00 A.M., drank, feasted, and left behind them greasy papers and wine stains on the green carpet.

This group of protesters, led by Cohn-Bendit, christened themselves the "Movement of March 22," or the *enragés*.[26] Fearing that immediate disciplinary action against the *enragés* might escalate the situation, the minister of education, Alain Peyrefitte, decided to hold disciplinary hearings on May 6.[27]

At the meeting of March 22, the students had decided to make Friday, March 29, a day for political debate. University authorities were alarmed over the preparations — tracts, leaflets, graffiti, posters, and the closing of the bookstore. In response, Dean Grappin, the highest responsible official at Nanterre, ordered the suspension of all classes until Monday, April 1. The students retaliated by putting off the date for the political debate till Tuesday, April 2. That day, the administration was unable to prevent 1,500 students from occupying the large amphitheater for political debate. The themes were: "no to police repression," "the critical university," and the "right to political expression and political action in the *faculté*." The movement at Nanterre was clearly politicized.

The movement of March 22 gained momentum in the weeks that followed. Meeting on the subjects of imperialism and Vietnam multiplied. Slogans at Nanterre read: "Professors, you are old," "Don't trust anyone over thirty." At the same time, general protest against university education became more and more aggressive.

Extremists outside Nanterre also became increasingly active. Presumably as a protest against the Vietnam war, a group attacked the American residence at the dormitory complex of the Cité Universitaire and another attacked the offices of American Express. These protests

35

were also aimed at the established political parties of the Left. When a Communist deputy came to Nanterre, the extremists, led by Cohn-Bendit, tried to prevent him from speaking and a confrontation ensued.

At Nanterre the administration was caught between extremist students disrupting normal life and pressure from professors calling for the restoration of law and order. Every decision or agreement had to be cleared with the ministry of education. In trying to grapple with the various protest movements, Dean Grappin alternately had to consider calling in the police, suspending classes, or closing down the *faculté* altogether. He often resorted to half measures to stall a crisis, hoping that it would blow over. Tournoux claimed that the tactics used by Grappin and the Rector of the Academy (the ministry's representative) followed the formula "let's put on a tough show till June. Then we will empty the Casbah."

On May 2, those responsible for the protest of March 22 were notified of a disciplinary hearing to be held on May 6. The Nanterre *faculté* was closed on a minor pretext, and the "enragés" went off to the courtyard of the Sorbonne on Friday, May 3.[28] From then on, the explosion was inevitable.

The Outbreak

On what was to become the crucial day, Friday, May 3, a few of the "enragés" from Nanterre gathered in the courtyard of the Sorbonne and met with student leaders of other political groups. The crowd was not causing any particular stir, but the authorities seemed to have acted precipitously and called in the police to disperse the meeting. The police surrounded the Sorbonne in large numbers and, by late afternoon, had entered the building, forcing the students out and herding them into "salad baskets," as the French call police vans. Other students began milling around and chanting "Free our comrades." From the few hundred students in the morning, there were now 2,000. Physical confrontation followed. Police indiscriminately arrested some students and physically assaulted others; students began throwing cobblestones and erected the first barricade. The crisis was underway. The government had needlessly provoked the students. Six hundred were arrested, but only four students were imprisoned; the rest were released. Immediately following their release, the student leaders met and called a nationwide university strike for Monday, May 6.

36

That Monday, 6,000 students and masses of police and security guards (known as the CRS) were in the Latin Quarter. On their way to the disciplinary hearing set for that date, the members of the Nanterre group entered the Sorbonne together, singing the International. The police remained around the Sorbonne, while the mass of students regrouped in other parts of the Latin Quarter, chanting "CRS-SS Down with police repression," and marched through the center of Paris carrying signs — "Profs not cops," "The Sorbonne to the students," "Down with repression." They unfurled the Vietcong flag at the Place de la Victoire and returned to the Sorbonne. Clashes with police ensued. The police charged and students retaliated by breaking up the street and throwing cobblestones. They built barricades with whatever they could find — branches, trees, billboards, railings, and cars. Most in the crowd were university students but highschool students, teachers, professors, and young workers were also present.

Bloody Monday, as May 6 was called, was followed by more demonstrations and marches. The numbers on the streets doubled to 12,000 according to some and tripled according to others. The Latin Quarter was declared forbidden territory and cordoned off by the police.

The students felt exhilarated by their show of force. Public opinion favored them, police brutality having helped to turn the tide. The Sorbonne became the symbol of the struggle, and Alain Geismar, one of the leaders, announced on May 8, "Whether the police frees it or not, tonight the Sorbonne shall be ours, it shall belong to students and teachers."

On May 9, the government ordered police reinforcements into the Latin Quarter, and the movement was underway again. *Le Monde* estimated that 60,000 students were demonstrating in Paris and the provinces. Cohn-Bendit declared the streets to be a lecture hall, and the Boulevard Saint-Michel, the heart of the Latin Quarter, became the arena of vast teach-ins. Speeches were made by the leaders of the student movements, as well as by eminent men like Louis Aragon, the Communist author. It was a spectacular scene.

On Friday, May 10, exactly a week after the beginning of the uprising, events reached a climax. Some 25,000 demonstrators were in the streets. The results were violent clashes with the police, more barricades, car burning, tear gas, and grenades. Students incessantly chanted, "CRS — SS."

As a result of the unrestrained activity of the police on May 3, the public had developed a generally favorable opinion towards the students. While the labor unions had been wary of the students, referring to them

37

as "fils à papa" (a pejorative term for pampered sons of the upper classes), they were nevertheless willing to take common action with the students and agreed to stage a general strike on Monday, May 13.[29] The largest strike in the history of France took place; half a million to a million people struck in Paris. The strike extended into the provinces. In Paris the march of strikers was led by students carrying red and black flags, wearing crash helmets, and carrying banners that read:

"Students, Teachers and Workers Together."

"13 May 1958 — 13 May 1968. Happy Anniversary General."

"Ten years, that's enough."

"De Gaulle to the archives."

"De Gaulle to the Old Age Home."

"De Gaulle to the Convent."

"Workers and Students Unite! The Regime is in Retreat. Let's make it fall."

The crowd marched to the Sorbonne and, for the first time since May 3, it was open. They took it over and, for the weeks that followed, the Sorbonne remained open to students and workers alike for teach-ins.[30]

The Rebels and the University

Although analysts of May 1968 are more or less agreed that the student extremists who precipitated the crisis had no program for university reform in mind, the issue is not quite so clear-cut. While extremists called for the destruction of the old order,[31] they also showed concern with fairly specific reforms. Cohn-Bendit, Geismar, and Sauvageot advocated "student power," meaning the granting to students of power to challenge and control the university. They argued for "university autonomy" and called for structural changes that would redefine relations between students and faculty, on the one hand, and between the universities and the government, on the other. They were concerned with the issue of "*sélection*" and examinations. Cohn-Bendit declared the need for a new university curriculum, even if temporary:

> In all the *facultés* we shall open seminars — not lecture courses . . . on the problems of the workers' movement, on the use of technology in the interests of man, on the possibilities opened up by automation. . . . Obviously this education will go in the opposite direction from the

38

education provided by the system and the experiment could not last long; the system would quickly react and the movement give way. But what matters is not working out a reform of capitalist society, but launching an experiment that completely breaks with that society, an experiment that will not last, but which allows a glimpse of a possibility; something which is revealed for a moment and then vanishes.

In a round table discussion on Radio Luxembourg, P. Castro (Movement of March 22) responded to a question about his definition of the ideal university:

We don't think it possible to define an ideal university. By criticizing what is, we shall finally define the themes of the ideal university. We know that the university is related to the society in which we live; it is part of it. The university cannot be changed without changing the society. We can have better adjusted universities but not ideal ones.[32]

Thus, the activist students engaged in rhetoric, much of it fashionably revolutionary, but they were also concerned about university reforms, such as better adaptability of the university to society. That meant curriculum innovation, as well as improved methods of teaching, such as the introduction of small seminars and the rejection of the large lecture system.

During May, the specific demands were sometimes lost in the fervor of the rhetoric. A Maoist philosophy student at the Sorbonne, declared, "Today it is Western society in its entirety which is rotting, including the proletariat. We are well aware that we will not save it by reflection and meditation. Our salvation rests elsewhere, in the Sin-Kiang." And again: "Tomorrow's philosophy will be a terrorist one. Not a philosophy of terrorism, but a terrorist philosophy tied to a policy of terrorist practice."[33] The extremists were largely sociology students and were supported mainly by others in the humanities. The rebellion was based on a hodgepodge of ideas: Marx and Marcuse, the anarchist philosophers of the nineteenth century, the communist psychoanalyst Wilhelm Reich, the thought of contemporary sociologists, Dada, and surrealism.[34]

Whenever one talks to Frenchmen about May 1968, they seem to light up as they recall those days when everyone was talking to one another. For the first, brief time, the hierarchical barriers came down on those days when the barricades went up. Raymond Aron called this phenomenon a "marathon of palabres," when Frenchmen talked and talked for five weeks. He added that all this confirmed what many sociologists have said, namely that "the French students, particularly those in Paris, constitute a lonely crowd"; they suffer from loneliness and lack of communal life. According to Aron, the crisis of May 1968 was an over-compensation for this lonely situation. During this month, they could all have the illusion of equality and fraternity.[35]

Once police repression brought public opinion to the side of the students, professors and schoolteachers joined the movement too. In large and small assemblies, they discussed the university and attempted to draw power away from the ministry. The quarrel for power occurred at two levels, between students and professors, and between the university and the ministry. For a time, the professorial hierarchies fell and all had an "egalitarian illusion."[36] Geismar saw something positive in the union of teachers and students:

> . . . the movement is irreversible; when teachers find
> themselves on the barricades with their students, relations
> can never be quite the same again; when universities opt
> for autonomy, so long as this autonomy has a real content,
> a breach has been made in the nature of the central author-
> ity, its uniformity and rigidity . . .[37]

Many faculty members, even the more conservative ones, were taking on some of the views of the protesting students.

A dean of the *faculté* of science in Paris, who in the past had spoken of *sélection*, and was considered a conservative, called a meeting of 950 professors to prepare a text for reform of the university. The first reform was university autonomy, which was to be defined by elected representatives of professors and students. "The French system of Rector-Prefect is dead. It must be replaced by a president elected from each university. . . ."[38] At the *faculté* of law in Paris, an assembly of the professors called for a commission of professors and students to examine problems of university life. And the deans of the letters *facultés* from all over France met in order to end the "absurd centralization" of the university. Commissions, which had sprung up spontaneously within the universities, worked day and night and discussed the draft of a reform plan for the universities that included autonomy, faculty and student participation in governance, the establishment of a democratic university, and the institution of a creative and open university.[39]

40

The crisis suddenly converted everyone into an instant critic and reformer. One author maliciously noted that Jean-Paul Sartre "suddenly discovered 'éducation nationale' and perceived that it was not functioning well." It was a revelation to many who had never questioned the system before. The journals of unions such as the leftist Syndicat national de l'enseignement supérieur (SNE-Sup) had not been demanding any radical changes, nor criticizing the bourgeois culture, nor proposing the subversion of society. On the contrary, they had confined themselves to the usual requests for more teachers and more funds and lamented the overcrowded conditions of classrooms and libraries, hardly denouncing the sclerotic methods or structures of higher education.[40] The Communists had also been unaware of the crisis brewing. In a 1964 document, for instance, which reveals the positions that they were essentially holding four years later, they did not oppose the existing structure of higher education, not even the elitist *grandes écoles*.[41] But now, suddenly, everyone was sounding as if for years they had wanted to see profound changes in the system of higher education.

Institutional changes seemed imminent. Committees sprang up to discuss educational reform and, although their legitimacy was in question, they fervently put forward proposals for reform. In the provinces, several *facultés* created new administrative structures with the participation of teachers and students. The new structures were to function in a democratic manner, and commissions were created in some instances by the new representative assemblies in the *facultés* to study various aspects of reform.[42]

Much play-acting went on during those feverish days of delirious speechmaking. In the midst of the crisis one Rector wrote:

> There is much talk of *cours magistral* and of wishes for its abolition. Why? Because it is a monologue. Who forbade
> . . . any teacher from having dialogue with his students?
> No one.[43]

Yet with the demagoguery that was plentiful during those exciting days of May came something new and fresh in French life: namely, the cooperation of groups in a democratic though often anarchical manner, probing the extent and limits of change in the university.[44] While constructive university reform was attempted in the communes of the Sorbonne, the *facultés*, and at the research center (the CNRS), activists were making overtures to the workers. In an interview with Sartre, Cohn-Bendit was asked how far the student movement could go. His

41

reply was:

> It has grown much larger than we could have foreseen at the start. The aim is now the overthrow of the regime. But it is not up to us whether or not this is achieved. If the Communist party, the CGT, and the other union headquarters shared [this aim] there would be no problem; the regime would fall within a fortnight . . .[45]

A banner carried by students read:

> The workers will take from the fragile hands of the students the flag of the struggle against the antipopular regime.[46]

This is what did happen and also what made the people of the universities feel that they were living in revolutionary times. From May 14 to May 27 the student rebellion spread to workers and then to all groups, so that the country was paralyzed. One factory after another struck. Students and workers briefly joined forces.

There were many reasons for this coalition. The majority of French workers were unorganized and not unionized; less than 20 percent paid union dues. French workers were and still are not as integrated into the society as the majority of workers in Great Britain, Germany, or the U.S.[47] Another interpretation of why the workers joined the student revolt (and a more fashionable one) was that since World War II a "new class of workers" emerged. With improved conditions and other gains, thanks to union bargaining (workers in the more modernized factories are often unionized in France), a highly organized group with a proletarian consciousness has evolved demanding an even greater share of the consumer society, as well as more of a voice in the management of the means of production. Alain Touraine, a prominent sociologist active in May 1968, has suggested that those employed in relatively independent positions in big organizations, technicians, teachers, and students have a new consciousness.[48] Whatever the level of worker dissatisfaction may have been, the condition of French workers was crucial in leading them to take part in the mass strike. In comparison to the standards of modern industrial societies, French workers were notoriously underpaid. At the beginning of 1968, 40 percent of the wage earners received less than $1,800 a year. The condition of the workers made them open to protest movements; their lack of organization meant that a small minority could easily take the lead. The established union leadership was against the

42

general strike, but, for fear of losing its followers, it reluctantly sanctioned it. Eventually, the leadership tried to negotiate with the government on behalf of all workers and thereby terminated the crisis.[49]

"The Spirit of May" — "Crisis of Authority"

There was, of course, "the spirit of May" and everyone got into the fray. The students wanted to break the "authority" structure, the hierarchy, and the rules that were stifling them. What the students wanted made sense to the workers. Their consciousness was raised and they too wanted a say in their own affairs. This "spirit" went beyond students and workers; it was infectious and groups in all walks of life struck. Architects, doctors, painters, actors, and writers all occupied their respective offices or associations, protesting their conditions and proclaiming change. Several city halls were occupied, as well as banks, insurance companies, and the press, including the government-owned and controlled radio and television station, ORTF. There was no mail service or transportation, .Orly airport was closed, the ecclesiastical hierarchy was unsure of itself, and even the police force was uneasy.[50]

The May crisis was a crisis of authority, a revolt against the old established order and against paternalism. It was an explosion against years of bureaucratic authoritarianism such as Jesse Pitts and Michel Crozier had respectively described in "Continuity and Change in Bourgeois France," and *The Bureaucratic Phenomenon*.[51] Lycée students were ranged against school principals, university students against professors, young medical doctors against patrons, authors against publishing houses, even "Jewish boy scouts against rabbis." It was every group against every old established system. The crisis was thus described as a "faceless revolution" aimed against power. The extremists led by Cohn-Bendit wanted "to open a breach," to use that leader's expression. In this traditional society, once the gap was open, all groups would be involved, the hierarchy overthrown, and self-government instituted.[52] Tracts and graffiti proclaimed:

"It is forbidden to forbid."
"The more I make revolution, the more I feel like making love."
"Don't change employers, change the employment of life."
"We are marching ahead."
"Reform the university."
"Reform teaching."

43

"Reform society."
"Be realistic. Demand the impossible."[53]

The Denouement

The students' protest developed into a national crisis because the workers joined them in declaring a general strike. But the labor unions probably never overcame their basic mistrust of the students and could not see where the crisis would lead them. The Communist Party, which controlled the largest union, the CGT, began to think that a deepening of the crisis would only bring to power the pro-American Pierre Mendès-France and the Socialists. De Gaulle at least was preferable, since he ran a pro-Soviet foreign policy, and the Communists feared a possible anti-Communist backlash (ironically, this did occur, even though the Communist Party on the whole supported law and order in May). By May 22, the CGT declared its willingness to enter negotiations with the government and with management, anxious to salvage what it could for the workers.[54] It demanded:

> Full payment for strike days; forty hour week, and a fairer
> distribution of work to reduce unemployment.
> Minimum salary of 1,000 francs ($200).
> Salary scale pegged to the cost of living.[55]

The Grenelle Accord was reached on May 27, was rejected by the workers, but was ratified in the first week of June when the government, wishing to put an end to the political turmoil, made further concessions.[56]

The general public seemed to have tired of the situation, and, while until May 30 there was relatively little support for the government, from then on, public opinion turned — especially when de Gaulle promised general elections for the end of June. Except to the ultra-radical students, that seemed like a fair way of deciding the issues that had been raised. The crisis that had suddenly erupted now subsided.

With problems of the workers out of the way, the government could now begin to address itself to some of the student demands. The requests for change in the university came from student and teacher unions and from different communes and commissions that had formed themselves during the month of May.[57] Prime Minister Pompidou made a firm declaration that no reform would take place without the concurrence and

44

decision of the government. He declared that to read some of the proposals, one would think that the universities "were organizing themselves outside public authority, outside the government; that would be an illusion and nothing more."[58] Declaring that he would not be precipitously hurried into any reform measures, Pompidou nevertheless now favored change. The general sense of crisis unleashed by student agitation had produced the basic willingness to transform the educational system.

The revolution had shown everyone, particularly the government, that it must not underestimate forces within the society. The workers showed that they could be strong as a bargaining force and could paralyze the country, the students that they could be an organized group that could ignite a rebellion. Those forces could not be disregarded. Once the Grenelle Accord settled the bill with the workers, the government was faced with educational reform. It had to wait till the general elections of June 24, and once de Gaulle was confirmed in power by an unprecedented majority for his party, his primary objective was to select a minister of education to undertake the difficult task of educational reform and, more specifically, reform of higher education.

CHAPTER III

THE ORIENTATION ACT
OF HIGHER EDUCATION

"La conception napoléonienne de l'université centralisée et autoritaire est périmée."

—Edgar Faure

"Les vraies réformes sont celles qui sont, inconsciement, déjà dans l'esprit des Français. On les met ensuite au crédit d'un homme, d'un parti ou d'un régime. Peu importe."

—Olivier Guichard[1]

A New Minister

On July 2, 1968, the elections promised by Charles de Gaulle returned him to office with the greatest majority, that his regime ever received. He had campaigned on the platform that a victory for him would be a mandate for establishing "participation" in all aspects of French society.[2] De Gaulle called on Couve de Murville to form a new cabinet. Given the importance that educational questions had had in the turbulence of May, it was clear that the new minister of education would have to be chosen with the utmost care. Edgar Faure was appointed to replace the interim minister, François-Xavier Ortoli, (the successor of Alain Peyrefitte, forced to resign on May 28). Faure was the former minister of agriculture and an independent not belonging to the Gaullist Union pour la Defense de la République (UDR) party. He was his own man, very much a political animal, yet not connected to an established party. He was a moderate, and de Gaulle felt sure that the reforms he would institute would not be a capitulation to the demands of extremists.

Faure had a dynamic, winning personality; he was articulate, giving speeches full of puns and learned quotations. Having demonstrated self-assurance and a little flattery in an interview with de Gaulle, Faure was entrusted with the "poisoned ministry."[3] At the time, there was some talk of separating higher education from the other levels of education and forming a separate ministry of higher education and research, but this did not materialize until June 1974. As an old colleague of Faure's said,

47

"One does not cut up a ministry when one offers it to Edgar Faure."[4]

Faure had been offered the ministry of education before, in 1962, by Georges Pompidou, but he had turned the offer down. By 1968, satisfied that he had completed a major task in negotiations with the Common Market, he hoped to be given the coveted position of the ministry of finance. Since he and the new prime minister did not see eye to eye on monetary affairs, that was out of the question. Faure has claimed that his aides advised him against taking the position as minister of education, because it would be a tough task. But his wife, Lucie Faure, advised that if de Gaulle called on him, he should take up the challenge. This he did.[5]

Once appointed, Faure recruited the ablest and most knowledgeable men on university affairs to aid him in the task of reforming the universities. He accepted the resignation of M. Laurent, former secretary general of the ministry of education, its highest permanent official. Faure's own predecessor, Ortoli, had upheld the merits of Laurent, saying that he was irreplaceable; Faure had then replied, "The man is definitely irreplaceable and that is why I have decided not to replace him." The firing of Laurent caused euphoria among high officials in the ministry who had resented his autocratic administrative methods. The action instantly raised Faure's prestige within the ministry. Among his chief aides, Faure chose Gérald Antoine, rector of the academy of Orléans, known to Faure by his renown as an educator and humanist and by a television series he had conducted on the American universitites; he had also been a technical adviser in two ministry of education cabinets (those of Joxe and Paye) and so was familiar with the ministry. Faure entrusted Antoine with the responsibility of coordination. He chose Michel Alliot, a law professor with a background in science, former paratroop commander, waterskiing champion, and former rector of Madagascar, as his cabinet director. Others appointed to posts of responsibility included university professors like François Furet and Jacques de Chalendar. Faure described his team with enthusiasm: "It was a team without limits. We used all preceding work, as well as any outside contributions made to us."[6] To gather information, he sent aides around the country to collect proposals for reform of the university. This had already been done by his predecessor, Ortoli. The aides:

> were thus in a position to gather, centralize and organize
> the bewildering number of reform proposals that have
> been drafted in May and June. . . . They classified most of

48

ORIENTATION ACT

the important projects prepared by high ranking civil servants, individual teachers and organized groups as well as those elaborated in the *facultés*. . . . They synthesized them, thereby making political decision makers fully cognizant of the universities' demands.

These men had met weekly for nine months after May 1968 in Paris with high officials of the ministry and played an important intermediary role between the government, on the one hand, and the rectors, faculty, and students, on the other. This procedure proved so useful that, upon coming to office, Faure continued it, and it was maintained during the time that the Orientation Act of Higher Education was being implemented.[7]

Background to Reform

Before a discussion of the working out of the initial plans of the reform, something should be said about the groundwork laid by earlier conferences, specifically during the feverish days of May and June. The ideas that were the basis of the French university reforms and that were incorporated in the Orientation Act of Higher Education were formed over a long period of time. As early as 1900, the historian Gabriel Monod had proposed restructuring the *facultés*. Later, in the 1920s, the Companions of the New University, a zealous reform group, had proposed even vaster changes in the structure and purpose of the universities.[8] In 1966, the prestigious Association de l'Expansion de la Recherche Scientifique sponsored a second colloquium at Caen (the first colloquium had met in 1957), which came to have widespread influence in French circles on the subject of educational reform. The colloquium specifically focused on decentralization, autonomy, and participation. Professors, mostly in the sciences, met to discuss the urgent problems facing higher education. Their report was to have important repercussions and eventually influenced the content of the Orientation Act. This colloquium was followed by another, sponsored by the same association, and attended by about 500 educators at Amiens in March 1968. The participants were concerned about teacher training, innovative teaching techniques, and psychological training in adolescent behavior for all personnel who came in contact with students; like the Caen conference, it reinforced the concept of university autonomy. The ideas engendered by both colloquia were often used by protesters in the days of May and June.[9]

Two weeks after the Colloque d'Amiens, a European conference was held at Pont-à-Mousson in France to discuss problems of higher education. It included representatives from Eastern and Western Europe. Although the two groups represented very different systems of education, participants from all countries discussed issues common to them: namely, admission procedures (*sélection*), teacher training, and university structures, particularly those of France and Germany.[10]

Thus, prior to May 1968, ideas about decentralization, university autonomy, curriculum changes in the direction of inter/multidisciplinary studies, and democratic participation in the decision-making process had all been in the air. When May came, it was not surprising that there was talk of "participation," "co-management," "the new university," "autonomy," "democratization," and restructuring of all higher education to include integration of the *grandes écoles.*

The programs of university reform were rich in suggestions and provided a convenient source of ideas. For purposes of convenience, the ideas of reform can be delineated under three headings: (1) the restructuring and governance of the university, (2) curriculum, and (3) finance. Each field will be examined in the light of the proposals for change prior to May 1968, the demands during the student revolt, and, finally, the actual reform provisions adopted in the autumn of 1968 by the French parliament.

The Emergence of the New University

I. Structures

At various times, the structure of the university, its division into autonomous *facultés*, had been criticized. Gabriel Monod in 1900 and the Companions of the New University in the 1920s, had proposed a transformation of the *facultés* into more flexible institutions. In 1922, the minister of education also considered similar plans. These are only examples to show that reforms of the structure of the university had already been considered long before 1968.[11] More recently, the general principles of reform of the universities had been announced at the Caen and Amiens colloquia (1966, 1968). The members attending these colloquia were prestigious academic figures in France. They called for the

50

abolition of the *facultés* and proposed their replacement by departmental units to be administered democratically. The departments would be interconnected so as to allow interdisciplinary research and teaching. These new institutions were to be modeled after the British and American universities. Each was to have a maximum of 20,000 students and should have an elected president.[12] The conferences criticized the university for its structures, administration, and curriculum, and proposed as alternatives universities that would be "interdisciplinary, autonomous, diversified, competitive," and that would have the freedom to be privately financed. The discussants lamented the existing double system of higher education, which reserved the elitist *grandes écoles* side by side with the universities. Research suffered in the former, teaching in the latter.[13] Thanks to these two influential university colloquia, "autonomy" became a key word, used with regard to governance, curriculum, and financing of the universities.

Other key concepts adopted were "participation," meaning representative elections and involvement in the decision-making process at all levels (by professors, students, university personnel, and lay persons). This "participation" would bring "co-management" to the university at all levels of the administration. Moreover, the advantages of multidisciplinary and interdisciplinary studies were proclaimed: their introduction would lead to vast changes in the structure and the curriculum of the universities. These concepts were familiar in the United States but not in France, where the pattern of decision making was based on authority and hierarchy, rather than on group cooperation and consensus.

The whole idea of autonomy, as it developed in May 1968, was directed against the centralized educational system. The renewal of the university structures was to be based on the two principles of autonomy and participation. Not everyone was clear about how much of the ministry's authority was to be replaced. Some thought that an organization, such as an annual conference of all rectors, could oversee the universities, while the main responsibilities of finance and coordination could be relegated to regional assemblies, with certain powers given to the university councils.[14] The influential Caen and Amiens conferences had called for competitive, autonomous universities; they had indicated that the universities should henceforth solicit private support. This meant that the national university, supported totally by the state and ruled by the ministry, would be abolished. But the revolutionary groups of May 1968, as well as the student and faculty unions, UNEF and SNE-Sup, did not share this view of autonomy. They wanted uniformity of quality among

51

all universities, opposed the idea of competitive universities, and thought that financial arrangements by which universities receive backing from private and business sources would lead to politically biased institutions. While fighting centralization, these groups still clung to a national system of education. To a large degree their program was an attempt to redistribute political power in their favor.[15]

University councils and commissions, acting outside the authority of the ministry of education, took upon themselves the task of drafting reform suggestions. On May 11, the first student council of the university of Strasbourg declared the autonomy of the university. On May 13, the general asssembly of the university of Paris likewise declared the university to be popular and autonomous, and open day and night to everyone. The university of Paris would henceforth be administered by "Occupation and administration committees," made up of workers, students, and professors.[16] Plans for reform were drafted, the most notable being those promulgated by the *faculté* of letters of the Sorbonne, the *facultés* of medicine, law, and economics of Paris. All proposals stressed the need for decentralization and university autonomy. Michel Alliot, who was to become Faure's cabinet director and was instrumental in drafting early plans of the Orientation Act, had already begun work in that direction as member of the law *faculté* of the university of Paris. The Alliot plan declared:

> The structure of the educational system will no longer descend from the ministry to the establishments below; on the contrary, it will be a federated structure of autonomous institutions which will regroup themselves from the bottom to the top.[17]

The basic operational unit, according to the Alliot plan, would not be the university, nor the *faculté*, but the group of faculty and students united in a department or laboratory of the same discipline. Each basic unit would be administered by an elected council. Delegates elected from these departmental councils would form a university council. Delegates elected from the university and other levels of education would form the Regional Council (Conseil régional de l'enseignement supérieur et de la recherche, CRESER) and delegates elected from CRESER would form the National Council (Conseil national de l'enseignement supérieur et de la recherche, CNESER). Besides this vertical structure, there would be a horizontal one, so that professors and students could belong to one or more departmental units. The system could also include representative

52

commissions entrusted with the responsibility of overseeing and receiving suggestions and complaints. These commissions would not have any decision-making powers, but would be responsible for circulating the information they received to councils at all levels.

In order to make clear what it meant by "autonomy," the Alliot proposal indicated that whereas in the past all decisions had come from above, henceforth the principle of autonomy implied the reverse; all decisions would be made from the lowest unit, from the department to the university and then to the national level. While the national council (CNESER) would be responsible for dividing up the budget for education, it was up to the regional councils (CRESER) to decide how much went to the different levels of education in their respective regions. None of the moneys allotted should be earmarked, thus enabling the universities to decide how to use their budgets. Each council at the departmental and university level should prepare a several-year plan, to be presented to the regional and then the national council.[18] This proposal closely anticipated the structures that came about in the Orientation Act of Higher Education. Although the proposal for autonomy did not specifically state that the *faculté* would be abolished, it seemed to point in that direction, since the discussion pertained only to departmental and university councils, and there was no discussion of councils at the *faculté* level.

Units of Teaching and Research

The debates in May and June in the *facultés* went on within departments or sections, and professors and students met to discuss changes mostly at that level. They wanted operational independence with regard to curriculum and examinations. Everyone thought in those terms in the early days of the drafting of the law. Faure was quick to recognize, however, that each "department," as in most foreign universities, encompassed only one discipline; this was also the case with the research institutes. What was needed was the combination of several disciplines within one administrative unit in a multidisciplinary manner; hence, the new entity could not be called a department. After considerable debate, it was decided to use the term "units of teaching and research (Unités d'enseignement et de recherche, UER).

Questions arose as to how these new units were to be instituted and organized, and how their members were to be elected. It was decided that

53

the minister of education would establish a preliminary list of UERs. The minister could modify or add to the list, and the new university councils, once they met, could question its composition in the process of drafting their university statutes. The aim of the plan was to avoid freezing the structures and to ensure sufficient fluidity so that a university could move the units around to fit its own needs. From the time the reform laws passed parliament on November 12, Faure had six weeks to draft the list of UERs by December 31, 1968. The main problem was making the new structures, which called for a real overhaul of the present universities, embody substantive change and not simply a change in nomenclature. The *facultés* could no longer exist in their present form. Departments and sections within each *faculté* had to combine with others from other *facultés* in a coherent, multidisciplinary structure. These new groupings, the UERs, would combine to form a university that could have a "major emphasis."

Early plans tried to determine the number of UERs needed. Approximately 600 and eventually, by 1969, 674 UERs were established. A UER could include 500 to 2,500 students. The traditional twenty-two universities would henceforth be increased to sixty-five.[19] The UER became the basic unit of the new university. It was governed by its own council; above it was the university council, then a regional council, and then a national council, which was to coordinate the activities of all the French universities.

The University Council

Prior to the drafting of the new reforms, each French university was governed by a university council that was presided over by the minister's representative, the rector of the academy. The council did not represent the university community, but rather consisted of the deans of each *faculté*, two senior professors elected by each *faculté*, and lay persons nominated by the council and appointed by the rector. The council, depending on the size of the university, had between twelve and twenty members. Decisions taken by the council could not be executed until they were approved by the minister. The university council gave its opinion on matters of university budgets, *faculté* budgets, and the creation of academic chairs. Within the university, each *faculté* had a *conseil de faculté*, made up of senior professors and presided over by the dean. This council had important powers in matters of funds and curriculum. Yet

54

another council, the *faculté assembly*, comprised of tenured faculty at all levels, had authority only in matters of curriculum.[20]

The structural reforms after 1968 abolished the *faculté* structure and introduced representative university councils at the apex of the structure. An elected president was invested with powers that had hitherto been assigned to the rector and the deans. Thus, in the area of governance, the new Orientation Act aimed at granting autonomy to the university and transferring some of the powers previously held by the central administration in Paris to the university councils and presidents. The new university council included faculty members, researchers, nonteaching personnel, students, and lay persons. There were to be at least as many faculty as students. Senior professors had to hold at least 60 percent of all positions allotted to the faculty, with lay persons occupying between one-third to one-sixth of the seats. If less than 60 percent of the students voted, their seats on the councils would be proportionately reduced. Thus, the law ensured that the faculty, and especially the senior faculty, would have a certain advantage. The size of the council was fixed at a maximum of eighty members (UER membership was fixed at a maximum of forty.)[21] It was the responsibility of the university council to divide the moneys among its UERs, according to priorities it established.

Regional Councils

Since the aim of the reform law was to decrease centralization in Paris and to give greater autonomy on the local level, regional councils were to be established. A regional council could administer one or several regions. The rectors of the academies (there are twenty-seven academies in France) would be responsible for coordinating higher education with other levels of education. They would be the chancellors of the university or universities in their academies, acting as the representatives of the minister of education on the councils and being present at their meetings. The rectors were to be the minister's representatives on the regional councils and were to preside over them.[22]

Many deputies of the majority UDR party, as well as many moderates, wanted to integrate the university more fully in the life of the region. It is a paradox that while the left wanted to open up the university and called for relevancy, it opposed the idea of integrating the university with the economic life of a region. It did so for fear that such an action would

55

mean the take-over by big business. By contrast, those who would have preferred to preserve the traditional universities were calling for more decentralization.

The plans for decentralization did not have much chance of success, because they were met by opposition from the left and from the teaching unions, which feared that autonomy would lead to business control of the university as was the case, it was alleged, in the United States. Regionalization went hand in hand with the idea of competitive universities; since that idea had been rejected, the intention of establishing a truly regional university suffered, and so did the *raison d'être* of the regional councils. In the final analysis, the regional councils were given a purely consultative role. They had no independent legal standing, no financial autonomy, and no role in the division of funds in their region.[23]

The National Council

Early projects for reform of the structures placed an elected National Council for Higher Education and Research over the Regional Councils. It was suggested that the council have an independence similar to that of the French Atomic Energy Commission, but such proposals were thrown out because they implied an independence that the government was unwilling to grant. Rather, the council was limited in its authority. Originally, reformers hoped that the council might have deliberative powers, participate in budgetary decisions with the ministry of finance, be allowed to justify its demands before parliamentary commissions, and have a say in the budgetary distribution of funds to all other public institutions under the authority of the minister (such as the Ecole normale supérieure, Collège de France, and others). When the law was passed in November 1968, the council was granted a purely consultative role, and no provisions were made allowing it to participate with the minister of finance or meet with parliamentary commissions to discuss the budget.[24] In a debate at the National Assembly, Faure indicated that the council would help to achieve decentralization and would be given enough responsibilities (planning, programs, diplomas) to make it an autonomous organ. But much of the law was so worded as to give the impression of greater autonomy for the national council than was actually the case.

ORIENTATION ACT

The Emergence of a New System of
Governance in the University

The new university structure, with its democratic councils at the unit, university, regional, and national levels, had as its chief aim, the decentralization from Paris and the granting of autonomy to all other levels. The new democratic structures called for elections. Measures defining the electorate, eligibility to the councils, and finally council membership had to be determined. In short, how was the new participatory democracy to function?

In May and June, one of the loudest cries was for "student power." This power took various forms. Since 1967 there were councils at the departmental level at Amiens, Lille, and Nanterre that included students and junior faculty.[25]

A document printed by a group of medical students and entitled "broad lines for reform born in the streets," stated:

> What we wish, is not to depend on an impersonal and ignorant administration to solve our real problems, but rather to depend on ourselves.
>
> We do not wish to isolate ourselves, however, but to work with our teachers, according to defined regulations . . .
>
> We wish not so much an inefficient reform of content, but of spirit and structures. A new spirit would give rise to supple structures and allow participation and thereby be open to demands of all students.
>
> We wish for student power as well as real student responsibility at all levels. . . .[26]

At Nanterre, participation had been on the basis of parity: an equal number of students and faculty. By May the idea of participation begun at Nanterre had spread to all French universities. Professors accepted the dissolution of the traditional system, some going so far as to accept student participation in discussing the nature and content of examinations, although to the majority this was tantamount to blasphemy.[27] In the midst of the May events at the *faculté* of law and economics in Paris, the principle of mixed commissions was adopted, whereby faculty and students participated. On May 20, the idea of co-management was also accepted; students and *assistants* would be equally represented after having been elected by universal suffrage and secret vote. In some cases,

ORIENTATION ACT

representation was done on the basis of one-third of the seats for professors and *maîtres de conférences*, one-third of the seats for students, and one-third of the seats for *maîtres-assistants*, *assistants*, researchers, and technical and administrative personnel. At Montpellier, two different systems were used. One system was based on parity, with an equal number of students and faculty; the other had tripartite representation of faculty, students, and personnel.

The various systems were tried while the methods of representation of the different university bodies were being discussed. A variety of plans was advanced. Some thought that students should be represented equally with the faculty, others that students should be elected to a separate body. Still other plans suggested 40 percent representation of the faculty, 40 percent of students, and 20 percent of university personnel. Giving students representation equal to the faculty was thought undemocratic by the radicals, who complained that students, after all, represented ten times the number of faculty. All these plans for mixed student-faculty organs created some hesitation. Some thought that mixed organizations might work during the initial period, but, once there was a return to normalcy, the professors would take control, leaving the students little or no voice on the committees or councils. Professors feared that any concessions to the students in matters of power would become a threat to their professional competence, while students argued that they needed equality of power to negate the authoritarian aspects of traditional faculty-student relations.[28]

The government opposed the new spontaneously elected commissions, fearing that their acceptance was tantamount to recognizing the rebellion. Therefore, the government decided to make co-management its own idea and baptized it "participation." "Participation" had belonged to the Gaullist vocabulary for some time, although it had a pejorative connotation of collaboration, complicity, connivance, or contribution of expenses. The term was not regarded favorably by leftists and extreme leftists, nor by employers, who saw the concept as a new kind of paternalism, smelling of the pro-German, collaborationist French regime of Vichy. Nevertheless, Pompidou and then de Gaulle began speaking in terms of "participation."[29]

When the reform law was drafted, the make-up of the governing bodies represented a thorny issue. In the first version of the law, Faure had retained considerable flexibility, giving to the universities the right to decide their own election system. He wanted the existing "provisional" committees to be legitimized, but to this there was enormous opposition.

58

ORIENTATION ACT

In his first draft, Faure attempted a compromise between the opposing parties. He proposed mixed councils at each level, that is, UER and university councils; but the faculty was given exclusive responsibility in voting on career decisions for their fellow faculty members (article 32), on examinations, rank, and diplomas (article 33), and on programs and funds for the scientific council of the university.[30]

In all other administrative and financial matters, students would participate with other members of the councils. The law allowed faculty and students to define for themselves their method of operation, thereby giving flexibility, which was praised as a real gain. Once the boundaries of authority between faculty and students were drawn, another problem was not so easily resolved: namely, what proportion of the councils should be faculty, students, and others. Senior faculty were leery of junior faculty and, in particular of the *assistants*, who, they feared, would align themselves with the students. On the whole, professors feared that the councils would be too politicized and would fall into the hands of extremist groups who were not representative of the students or the university. Students wanted a real share in the decision-making process, with those politically to the left in particular insisting on preserving the gains made in May.[31] Faure struck a compromise between the two groups. His strategy was to woo the moderates, the "reformist" element, by a reasonable compromise. In September, he let it be known that the law would require that "the representation of faculty, in the ranks of professors and *maîtres de conférences, maîtres-assistants* and *assistants* could not be inferior to those of the students in all mixed councils."[32]

A third group was also included on all councils — lay persons. The cry in May 1968 had been for relevance in education; including lay persons, argued Alain Peyrefitte, former minister of education and, in the autumn of 1968, president of the Cultural Affairs Commission in the National Assembly, would "increase the liaison with the region, with the century, we must open up the university toward the world. . . ." The issue of participation by lay persons elicited various reactions. The left feared that this action would give more power to business interests in university affairs. The union of teaching personnel, the Syndicat général de l'éducation nationale (SGEN) questioned whether lay persons would be qualified to make decisions on specialized problems in research and curriculum. Parliament considered whether it should make the presence of lay persons on university councils obligatory.[33] When the law was finally passed, it provided that no less than one-sixth and no more than

ORIENTATION ACT

one-third would be lay persons. The lay members would be chosen on the basis of their competence and their role in regional life (article 13).[34]

Method of Election

Conservative politicians and academics feared that the student representatives on the councils would be radical and represent only the extremist minority. They believed that if a means could be found to require the "silent majority" to express itself, then the radical minority could be negated. Some thought obligatory voting should be instituted, but that was difficult to enforce and oppressive. Faure elicited laughs from the Parliamentary benches when, with his usual humor, he suggested that one possible way of forcing students to vote would be to deprive them of the right to enter the university restaurants: "it would become a general joke, you haven't voted, you don't eat." But some were in deadly earnest in suggesting that students who had not voted should be deprived of their social security benefits.[35] The political right wanted obligatory voting, hoping that this would produce moderate student representation, but the left saw no harm in letting the vote be free of any constraints, or at least, in requiring a small quorum, 50 percent being suggested; Faure compromised and accepted a 60 percent quorum. Under this rule, if less than 60 percent of the students voted, the number of seats assigned to them on the councils would be proportionately reduced. The law stipulated that student representatives were to be elected by *scrutin de liste* (voting by slates), with proportional representation. This measure meant that competing slates of candidates would run, with each slate being represented in the council to the extent to which it had received votes; in other words, if the slate received 20 percent of the vote, it received 20 percent of the allotted student membership of the council.

None of the members could be elected in more than one university or UER council. Faculty at the rank of professor, *maître de conférences*, *maître-assistant*, and *assistant*, performing the function of teaching, must be equal at least to the number of students in the mixed councils. The representation of faculty of the two top ranks had to equal at least 60 percent of all the teaching faculty.

Student representation could not exceed 40 percent. Thus, in a council of sixteen members, for example, there might be six students (i.e., 37 percent), with ten faculty of whom six must be professors and *maîtres de*

60

ORIENTATION ACT

conférences. If lay persons were included with a one-third membership, the council would have twenty-four members. Student representation would thus be reduced to 25 percent even with a 60 percent quorum; that is, students would have six out of twenty-four seats. If the number of students voting did not attain the 60 percent quorum, but, as was more likely, only 20 percent, then students would have only two seats out of a total of eighteen, i.e. 11 percent. Thus, under the most favorable circumstances, students could have 25 percent representation, or, in the least favorable situation, they could have about one-tenth of the seats on the council.[36]

Presidents of University Councils and Directors of U.E.R. Councils

The president of the university council and of the university would be elected for five years and could not be immediately reeligible. Presidents had to be tenured professors of the university and members of their university council. If they were not tenured, they would have to have two-thirds of the vote in the council, and the appointment would have to be approved by the minister upon recommendation of CNESER (article 15).

Directors of the UERs were to be elected for three years. They had to be tenured professors of their institution and members of their UER council. If they did not have any of the desired rank qualifications, they had to be accepted by a two-thirds vote of their council and receive approval by the ministry upon recommendation of CNESER. Some feared that these democratic methods of electing heads of UERs and university councils, could lead to the take-over of the councils by the radicals. Therefore, special powers were given to the rector of the academy, allowing him to exercise full powers if the council were found to be malfunctioning.[37] As finally amended, article 18 of the law was less harsh, it provided that the minister could in the face of malfunctioning of a council upon consultation with CNESER, or at least after informing that organ endow the rector with full powers. But the rector was not given powers of dissolution, thus he still might have to face a hostile and intractible council. This procedure was to lead to problems later on.

61

The Orientation Act and Liberty of
Expression in the University

In democratizing the university, the reforms provided not only for participation, but also for the widening of the civil liberties of the university students *qua* members of the university. One of the strongest demands of students in May and June, and even in earlier months, had been the demand for liberty of expression. The students were determined to have the right to organize, meet, and discuss any subject of interest to them.

During the heated days of the debates in the *facultés* in June and July, many universities upheld the right of "liberty of expression," meaning that all current opinions could be expressed in the universities. The Provisional Assembly of the *faculté* of letters of Caen recognized the rights of everyone to information and to participation in political and union debates in the *facultés*, and it decided to specify a permanent locale for such meetings. It also granted the right to put up wall signs on reserved places in the buildings. If students reserved space in advance, kept order, and respected the rights of others, they were given the right to meet in amphitheaters.[38]

During the months of July and August, Faure explored the issue of student rights. In debate in the National Assembly, he took a bold stand on "liberty of information" in the university and the lycées. He said that it was a mistake to think that politization could be avoided if people were prevented from engaging in politics in the normal way. Murmurs were heard from the conservative benches when he added that he saw no reason why newspapers should be banned in the lycèes.[39]

In September, Faure demanded special buildings in the universities for political debate, but many UDR members were against this, as was de Gaulle. Faure decided to take out the word "debate" and substitute the more neutral term "information."

The teaching corps was divided on the subject of "liberty of expression," some wanting to construe the term "information" literally and others wanting to give it a wide interpretation. It was evident to many that the extreme right and extreme left threatened the traditional liberties of the university, but the reformers hoped that students and the teaching corps would practice self-discipline and agree to impose sanctions against violators of freedom of thought.[40]

The law enacted in October announced the following principles:

ORIENTATION ACT

Teaching and research imply objectivity of knowledge and tolerance of opinions. They are incompatible with all forms of propaganda and must remain outside the grasp of politics or economics (article 35).

Students have *liberty of information* with respect to politics, economics, and social problems, so long as they do not interfere with the activities of teaching and research, since those activities do not lend themselves to monopoly or propaganda, and do not disturb public order.

Buildings placed at the disposal of students should, whenever possible, be separate from those where research and teaching activities occur. . . . The conditions for their utilization will be defined after consultation with the council and controlled by the president of the establishment or by the director of the unit of teaching and research (article 36).

The presidents of the establishments and the directors of the units of teaching and research are responsible for the maintenance of order in their buildings.

All action or provocation to action which is aimed at threatening those liberties defined in article 36, or the public order inside the university, is subject to disciplinary sanction . . . (article 37).

This aspect of the law was received with mixed feelings. The left, as exemplified by the faculty union SNE-Sup, felt that the law did not go far enough in guaranteeing liberty of political expression, while the conservative Syndicat autonome was stupified by what it considered to be Faure's surrender to the radical forces.[41] Faure considered his use of the words "liberty of information" ambiguous enough to leave room for various interpretations, a compromise that would, he hoped, appeal to the moderate forces.

II. Curriculum Innovation

During the May-June debates in the *facultés*, manifestos were distributed with demands for curriculum changes, many of them closely tied to the need for democratization of education. Autonomy for the university meant that the university would have the power to define the method and content of teaching. The new university was to be the center of culture, open to all, and the universities would have to define for themselves the manner in which workers and wage-earners could participate in their activities. Student revolutionaries, swept up in the rhetoric of the day, wanted to give the working class and others access to higher education apart from the normal channels. This underscored the need for the further development of continuing education.

Continuing Education

In France continuing education had existed in a much more restricted form than in the U.S. or Great Britain. The Conservatoire national des arts et métiers, founded in Paris in 1819, opened branches in the provinces and thereby offered some hope of further education, but it was not at the university level. As for the university, an individual without a baccalauréat could not enter without passing a difficult entrance examination. Hence, most adults were deprived of continuing education at the university level.[42]

In March 1968, one French parliamentary deputy called for the development of a national plan of continuing education and observed: "Continuing education is the utopia of the years 1965-1970, just as free and compulsory education was the utopia for the years 1880-1885." In the May days, these ideas developed further. Not only student revolutionaries but also many in positions of responsibility came out in favor of continuing education. Capelle, reporter of the commission of education in the National Assembly, stated that those who worked should be able to reenter the higher education system after leaving school. There was much discussion regarding the fact that the work force needed to retrain from time to time. Continuing education or training could help people adapt themselves to change. An OECD study stated that the difference in the levels of production between countries, "is now a function of on-the-job training." The unions too had long demanded that the university be opened up to include the workers.[43]

The first draft of the new law called for a "second chance" for those who had left school but wished to continue their education. The final version of the law deleted this phrase and instead called for access to the university for those "who have the vocation and the aptitude," the universities should be available "for use by all segments of the population and for all possible purposes" (article 1). The university should

64

ORIENTATION ACT

provide for continuing education in UERs and in establishments connected with them; there should be coordination between the UERs and regional groups (article 24).

It is important to recognize that, while democratization was a magic word, it covered many aspects of education, and continuing education was only one of them. When the unions spoke of "opening up the universities" to workers, they did not mean only instituting continuing education programs, but they also thought there should be no admission requirements.

Admission

To make admission to the university more flexible, some envisioned that the existing uniform national standard be replaced by individual criteria. The Caen and Amiens colloquia upheld the concept of competitive universities, and during May, groups and commissions expressed the same views. Sometimes they did not come right out and say that they wanted a competitive university structure, but one important plan said "each autonomous organ can set admission conditions," and in the very next sentence added that "at the same time, higher education was to be open to all according to methods destined to erase social inequalities." It went on to say that anyone who had completed secondary education could enter an institution of higher education and transfer from one to another.[44]

During the debate in the National Assembly in July 1968, Peyrefitte announced that the universities could not be autonomous unless they were free to choose not only their faculty, but also their students. The present system of allowing the secondary school to select who went to the university had to be discontinued. Much of the support for autonomy of the university in fact came from those who wanted more rigorous selection. As Faure later noted, the plan of the political right had been to set up competitive universities, "thereby disengaging the superior universities by 'selective' limitation and throwing into the lesser universities . . . the rising number of student plebians."[45]

To the political left, the measures in the law granting autonomy to the university were attractive, but they worried that this autonomy could lead to some universities' exercising rigorous *sélection*.

Having to contend with a vocal political left, Faure found he could not institute a system of selection demanded by some of the educational

65

establishments. Faure compromised again. He upheld the baccalauréat as a means of entrance to the university (although he was willing to see the baccalauréat become more rigorous), while orally conceding to certain disciplines, notably medicine, the right to restrict admissions.

The political right was concerned with the large number of students who would continue to enter the university, the left with the failure rate, especially among underprivileged students. A solution that appeased both groups was the promise of a new "orientation," or counseling system, at the secondary school as well as the university level.

Counseling System

In the months prior to the May crisis, Peyrefitte, as minister of education, was aware that something had to be done to stem the flow of students into the already overburdened universities. He was also aware that while the secondary school sent only a small group of its graduates to the university, their dropout rate was between 50 and 60 percent of those entering. Aware of the lack of options for students and the narrow job and career opportunities awaiting university graduates, Peyrefitte drew up reform plans that were adopted in closed council at the Elysée on April 4, 1968, approved by the Cabinet on April 24, and scheduled for presentation at the National Assembly on May 14-16, 1968. The reform package included measures providing more guidance and counseling at the secondary school level. The type of system proposed did not resemble the voluntary system in the United States; it was, as many have called it, "authoritarian guidance." The advice of the counselor in the secondary school would have to be accepted by the advisees; if they refused to follow it, they had to appeal to higher educational authorities.[46] While Peyrefitte's plans were short of their declared goals and were duly denounced, they at least had the merit of bringing attention to the need for a counseling and guidance system. To give advice, the universities needed to have information.

It must be remembered that French universities, although administered in uniform fashion by the Paris administration, did not have a uniform system of information. The Bureau universitaire des statistiques (BUS) was supposed to provide information, but it fell short of offering a truly comprehensive system of data for universities and students. Students could get little information about possible programs, let alone anything about job and career opportunities. Due to centralization in the

ORIENTATION ACT

capital, students in Paris had better access to information than did students in the provincial universities.

Faure declared that he did not expect the university to be a "placement office," since one could not possibly know how many jobs were available at any given time, but he did propose to do something about improving the situation. He declared his intention of replacing BUS with a new institution, to be called the Office national d'information sur les enseignements et les professions (ONISEP). The theory behind improving the information system and organizing counseling procedures was to enable students and their families as well as teachers to have accurate information regarding the most suitable areas of study and employment. Many felt that if students were properly advised at the secondary school level, the *facultés* of law and letters would not be swamped with students who could not later find employment.[47]

The Orientation Act promulgated on November 12, 1968 made some provisions for a guidance and counseling system in the universities. Articles 21, 22, and 23 stipulated that the universities should make provisions for their UERs to organize orientation and advising sessions for new students when they deemed it necessary. In 1971, this was further elaborated, making the sessions obligatory. At the end of the session, recommendations might be made to the student, for instance, to enter another university or remain in the same one, to enter another program, or to enter a short term program of a professional nature. Students who did not follow the advice would be required to take another session, at the end of which the recommendation would be obligatory (article 21). Thus, the advising system was weakened, becoming rather a system of direction.

Grandes Ecoles

Traditionally, innovation and quality in French higher education were concentrated in the *grandes écoles*. This allowed for the training of a small, sophisticated elite, but deprived the universities of much of the attention that they would have needed in order to stay up-to-date. Some university reformers therefore suggested the abolition of the *grandes écoles* as separate institutions and their assimilation into the university system. Among the proponents of such reforms were the UNEF and the SNE-Sup unions, which argued that if all higher education could be streamlined to be part and parcel of the university system, it would allow greater flexibility and mobility of students within the same structures. Such proposals were vigorously resisted by the alumni associations of the *grandes écoles* and the Société des agrégés. Discussing the *grandes écoles*, an orator in the senate argued that "one must not destroy that which functions with excellent results, and which still exists and functions well. . . ."[48]

A draft of the law (September 2 version) declared an intention to legislate on all institutions of higher education, not just the universities. Opposition was quickly voiced by the other ministries which were responsible for the administration of certain *grandes écoles*, such as the ministry of war and the ministry of interior. Faure withdrew his proposals and the law henceforth was to be concerned with the universities only. The *grandes écoles* that came under the jurisdiction of his ministry were to receive special treatment and could continue to recruit selectively through competitive examinations;[49] they would not be integrated into the university system.

The failure to integrate the *grandes écoles* into the university system implied that some of the pressure for vast curriculum reform was removed. Quality education could continue unhindered in these prestigious schools, and the universities could be relegated to a secondary position. Nevertheless, an effort was made at the university to revamp the curriculum. The attempt to transform the teaching corps resulted from the need to adapt it to curricular needs, and was also a function of the agitation by younger faculty for a more flexible system.

Faculty Recruitment and Promotion

Until 1939, a section of the ministry's national council was responsible for matters of promotion to professorships and to university chairs. This system was considered inadequate in view of the fact that those responsible were not sufficiently competent to judge the appointments; a more specialized organ was needed. After 1945, the faculty was recruited from a national list, known as the *liste d'aptitude* drawn up by a national commission under the minister of education, the Comité consultatif d'université (CCU). Candidates had to fulfill certain diploma and research requirements to be recruited and then promoted. The CCU was organized along the same lines as the university structures, that is, by five groups corresponding to the five *facultés*: letters, law, medicine, sciences, and pharmacy. These subcommittees were reluctant to judge

68

candidates involved in research that fell outside their competence, and therefore sometimes neglected to promote them.

This structure was an obstacle to the development of some of the new sciences and new fields of study, such as pedagogical studies. Half the members of the CCU were elected by the faculty, the other half appointed from among university professors by the minister. This system was criticized because it led to the election of members who were either "oddballs," or "super-mandarins," with a clientele all over France. The members of the committee were eligible for more than one term and, since many had a network of supporters who owed their jobs to them, they were often reelected. The appointed members of the committees were often chosen by the minister from among those whom it deemed should have been elected; thus many members of the CCU were men and women who might have been specifically rejected by their peers.[50] In spite of the criticisms and shortcomings noted in the CCU, its existence was not seriously questioned in 1968 and it was retained. It was to continue declaring candidates apt for appointment or promotion, although the final decision was theoretically transferred to the local university and its subordinate bodies (article 31).

The Doctorat d'Etat

The sequence of degrees included the undergraduate diploma, the *licence* (three years, of which the first two years were called the *premier cycle*); the *maîtrise* (one year, combined with the third year of the *licence* are called the *deuxième cycle*); and the *doctorat de troisième cycle* (two years). After this, one could qualify for a teaching post as an *assistant*, or even *maître-assistant*, if one had taken the competitive national examination, the *agrégation*. Following that, the appointee would work for a *doctorat d'état*, an advanced doctorate degree, a task rarely completed before one's late thirties or forties, or even later. The young professor would struggle for years to teach, assist the patron, and continue his research piecemeal during vacations. Particularly disadvantaged were those who were not residents of Paris, for all the important laboratories and libraries were in the capital. The *doctorat d'état* was required of all academics who wished to enter the upper ranks of the teaching corps.

The financing of the *doctorat d'état* was onerous. Since May 1965, the ministry of education had given financial aid of up to 10,000 francs for a thesis of 500 pages. The printing of any additional pages had to be paid

69

for by the candidate, who also had to furnish his *faculté* with 160 copies. The cost of printing 500 pages for up to 200 copies was 27,000 francs. Added to that was the cost of typing (3,000-4,000 francs). Thus, even the candidate who received financial aid still had to pay 20,000 francs ($4,000).

A candidate for a *doctorat d'état* had to defend not one, but two theses. The first was known as the principal one, the masterwork, the other as the *thèse complémentaire*, which had to be an additional contribution proving the versatility of the scholar. All this had to be accomplished while the individual was teaching, assisting, and possibly preparing for a competitive examination. "The system holds back the progress and the completion of the work, wastes a man's energies and enthusiasm when it is most valuable — when he is young," wrote one professor.[51]

In June 1968, proposals for reform of the *doctorat d'état* included the suggestion that the candidate should appear before a national examination committee at which time he would present his publications and file.[52] Some suggestions were included in the 1968 law, which stated that "the title of doctor will be conferred after the defense of *a thesis*, or the presentation for defense of a group of original works. The thesis and works could be authored by an individual or, if the discipline justified it, by a group; and the works could be already published or unpublished" (article 20, my italics). The Faure law specified "a thesis" without any further definition as to content or length, leaving it to the universities to decide the standards.

The Clan System

The rigorous demands of the academic system rewarded those able and willing to fulfill its norms. Having climbed the ladder to the top and been appointed to a chair the chaired professors had unique privileges. They enjoyed power in matters of appointment and dispensation of research funds, and they ruled over the rest of the professors in their field. They were the mandarins of the university, raised in the French tradition of education and upholding the system with its labyrinths of examinations and *concours*. They were the elite and demanded quality. They taught three hours a week, spending the rest of the time in research or adminis-tration. But for the majority of the faculty, the *maîtres-assistants* and *assistants*, as well as for the many others who were employed without a

70

ORIENTATION ACT

contract the system offered fewer privileges. There was little hope of promotion. They were overworked and not only taught, but, in some cases, were also assistants to the senior professor. Up to World War II, nearly all the professors were of the rank of professor or *maître de conférences*; in 1960 the rank of *maître-assistant* was introduced. By 1968 the number of *maître-assistants* and *assistants* was three times the number of the two senior ranks. The wide base led to a bottleneck at the top.[53]

With the democratization of education and the influx of students to the university, the mandarinate neither changed its system nor adapted to the new needs and requirements. In 1966, the famous Caen colloquium called for the abolition of the *faculté* structure, and with it, the abolition of the system of chairs. Student commissions and faculty unions in May and June 1968 called for the abolition of faculty chairs.[54]

In the second week of June, a White Paper, published by a committee of students at the *faculté* of medicine in Paris, supported the abolition of the mandarinate system. It described the system thus:

> The present system forces the dependence of an entire service (department) on one person, or a chair which produces a stultified situation where everyone is waiting for the retirement of the patron. Moreover, the method of selecting these all-powerful persons has little to do with his organizational qualities, not to speak of human qualities . . .[55]

In his declaration to the National Assembly, Faure spoke of the need to do away with the Napoleonic concept of the authoritarian and centralized university and to abolish certain aspects of the administrative structures as quickly as possible. He added:

> The little empires, the little feudalities which have calmly constituted themselves over the years in certain sectors of higher education or research have shown their decay. It is not necessary to try to reconstitute them.[56]

In October 1968, Parliament abolished the chair system.

The new flexibility thus introduced into the *doctorat d'état* was intended to have an effect on the quality of teaching, for by making the degree potentially less demanding, the new law would free the faculty member better to fulfill one of his main obligations, teaching. The abolition of the chair system, the most formidable aspect of the hierarchy,

71

would presumably help make the professorate less formal and ease communications among faculty, and between faculty and students.

The demand in May was for more personal contact between students and teachers. This had been lacking. It was common for professors not to reside in the town in which they taught. Paris is the magnet that draws scholars because of its cosmopolitanism, its libraries, laboratories, and cultural life. If a professor could not have a position in the university of Paris, the next best thing would be to live in Paris, hop over to Poitiers or Bordeaux for a day or two, teach, and then come back to Paris. Often professors would leave the task of thesis-directing to their assistant; a graduate student would thus not benefit from contact with his professor except for a signature.[57] This situation was changed by the law: all professors henceforth were required to reside where they taught (article 33). Faure also came out in favor of reducing the large impersonal lecture courses, and of conducting classes in small groups whenever possible. He hoped to improve faculty-student relations by increasing the number of special assistants or monitors to 11,000.[58]

Multidisciplinary Studies

The method of teaching was to be different, and so was the content of what was taught. One way to do this was by institutionalizing inter/multidisciplinary studies, by abolishing the *facultés* and replacing them with multidisciplinary universities. Article 6 of the Orientation Act stipulated that:

> One or several universities can be founded in one academy [there used to be one university per academy]. The universities were to be multidisciplinary, associate as much as possible arts and letters with sciences and technology . . .

The law, however, permitted these universities to have a special emphasis. This provision insisted on the multidisciplinary, but not necessarily interdisciplinary, nature of the university; it did allow universities to escape the need to integrate science and humanities, for instance, and only necessitated the linking in the same university of science and medicine.

ORIENTATION ACT

Experimental Universities

The French university system was a national one, with national standards of admission, a national curriculum, a national standard of requirements for diplomas. Such a system allowed for little flexibility and experimentation. One of the innovations that Faure introduced was the establishment in the Paris region in 1968 of three separate, experimental centers of higher education: Dauphine, Vincennes, and Antony.

The first institution, Centre Dauphine, was founded by Faure at the old NATO headquarters, to provide training in modern business techniques. Such a program had not previously existed in the university. The curriculum allowed a student, even after one year of study, to receive a certificate and be eligible for continued study leading to a *licence* in economics. The curriculum included professional courses in such areas as business administration and computer studies.

The second experimental center, which was the most daring, was founded at Vincennes, located just outside of Paris. It admitted people without a baccalauréat and allowed its students to register for individual courses rather than full-year programs. The advantage of this system was that working people could receive their degrees piecemeal. To accomplish the same ends, evening classes as well as summer school were to be offered. The center at Vincennes was described enthusiastically as possessing attractive two-story buildings, and five amphitheaters seating between 200 and 500 students. It was to be a miniature town with a cafeteria, a bank, a post office, a bookstore, a well-stocked library, child care facilities, parking grounds, and a bus line connecting it with the rest of Paris. It sounded ideal. The promise of relevance held out by Vincennes made it particularly attractive to leftist faculty, many of whom left their teaching posts to join the new university. It is not unlikely that Faure deliberately hoped to concentrate the leftists at Vincennes in order to rid the other universities of their influence. The Vincennes diploma was to be given the same value as that of other universities.

A third experimental center was to be opened in another suburb at Antony; it was to have an interdisciplinary program combining human sciences and mathematics. Altogether, eight new centers were planned for the Paris region (Antony, Asnières, Clichy, Clignancourt, Vincennes, Montrouge, Sceaux, and Dauphine). It was hoped that there would be 35,000 new places ready to receive the incoming students by November 1968. In general, announcements regarding the new experimental centers elicited enthusiasm.[59]

Examinations

The French system of education had always emphasized the importance of examinations. Often these were long and grueling ordeals, testing knowledge acquired over a whole course of schooling, as the baccalauréat did at the end of secondary education; at least, they examined knowledge acquired over a one-year period, as was the case at the university. Critics of the examination system charged that too much depended on examinations. Suggestions were made to do away with the annual examinations and to introduce tests at periodic intervals (contrôle continu, as the French call it).[60] A student would theoretically learn better if he knew how he was progressing, and, presumably, the professor could give more personalized teaching, periodically readjusting his instruction to suit the apparent level of student learning. (These views were modeled after the U.S. system of midterms and finals.) This rather simple reform was the subject of controversy, and the compromise solution voted by Parliament affirmed that examinations would be "regular and continuous"; at the same time, it provided for final examinations.

III. The Institution of a New Finance System

The new transformations in the university required a change in the financing of higher education. Under the traditional system, the ministry was responsible for dividing funds among the universities; about 90 percent of all funds came from the state. The rector of the academy presiding over the university council played an important role in the budget of the university. After being prepared by the rector and discussed and voted by the council, the budget was then submitted to the minister who had to give his approval before it could be executed. The facultés had autonomy in financial affairs within the limits of the budget assigned to them by the state. They were allowed to administer their own funds under the control of the central administrations. The university budget consisted mostly of state funds for material equipment and laboratories. The university could also receive funds from student fees (which were miniscule, about $18 per student per year), legacies, publications, or

74

laboratory findings.

The protesters in May 1968 called for a change in this structure. If the demand for local democratic governance were to be meaningful, it would have to permit powers at the UER and university level. The universities did not want to ask permission for every decision. Proposals made in the discussions for autonomy called for *a posteriori* control, not *a priori*, as had traditionally been the case. The traditional system of financial control was *a priori*: the ministry's permission had to be received in advance, prior to an expenditure. The reformers demanded that it be *a posteriori*, meaning that the university be allowed to spend its funds, only later having to justify their expenditures to the ministry. The demand was thus also for financial autonomy.

Each institution was to have a budget to spend as it saw fit; each university should have its own treasury and the council of each university should determine how the budget was to be divided.[61] The first decision, the amount of funds to be expended for each university, should, some suggested, be voted by a national organ independent of the ministry. This new national office would receive a lump sum from the government and would be responsible for dividing funds among the universities. It would be composed of elected delegates from the universities and would resemble the University Grants Committee (UGC) of Great Britain, since it would be independent of the ministry of education.[62] This proposal was considerably emasculated; the law instead gave CNESER purely consultative financial powers. The government and Parliament, while preaching autonomy for the universities, were simply unwilling to allow an independent body to legislate university financing. It was suggested that the universities actively solicit funds from regional authorities and business groups, thus increasing the resources available to them. Such proposals perturbed the political left who feared that this system would lead to interference by capitalists in university affairs and maybe even capitalist control of the university, as was allegedly the case in the United States.

The ministry did not surrender its traditional financial control. The Orientation Act allowed universities to solicit funds, but Faure made clear they would purely complement state moneys.[63] It was the ministry, for instance, which decided the number of teaching positions each university would receive, and accordingly budgeted salaries for personnel. National criteria for budgeting other expenditure items were also established and carried out by the ministry.

The positive aspects of the financial sections of the law were: (1) that

75

the law foresaw the possibility of foundations giving funds as private gifts to the universities, (2) it permitted regional public bodies to contribute to the universities, (3) it established some intermediary body between the universities and the ministry — CNESER — which would help determine budgetary allocations, and (4) *a posteriori* control of the budget was established. On the negative side, ambiguities and contradictions remained in the law on financing. Was there any real financial autonomy if the university still received its budget and diplomas from the state?[64]

Conclusion

The Orientation Act of Higher Education was drafted between July 12 and October 25, when it was finally adopted by the senate and promulgated on November 12, 1968. Faced by a major political crisis, the government enacted university reforms in less than three months. Faure assured the government and the public that "necessary haste did not exclude serious preparation [of the law]."[65]

Faure diplomatically consulted all groups. The law was studied by three ministerial councils, by the Assembly Commission for Cultural Affairs, and the ministry's Council of Higher Education as well as the Higher Council of National Education. Other ministries, such as agriculture and the army, in view of the fact that they were responsible for some institutions of higher education, as well as the *grandes écoles*, were also consulted, as were groups representing the UNEF and SNE-Sup and the alumni association of the academic elite (the Société des agrégés). In addition, Faure had his own commission of educators who gathered information and gave advice. At the National Assembly, Faure indicated that he had touched all bases, adding that "some recommend that the law be more bold, others that it be more prudent — we have tried to hold ourselves in between the two."[66]

The law was affected by the pressure of time and political exigencies. Given the explosive political situation, university reforms were imperative. The forces of tradition, however, were also powerful; the educational bureaucracy and the majority political party were reluctant to accept too radical a transformation of the university. The law tried to appease both groups. It was the end result of a long line of compromises and thus did not completely satisfy any group. Among the critics were members of the government party. One deputy said:

ORIENTATION ACT

In France, centralization is a necessity . . . the university is no longer in the service of the state but in the service of herself . . . you have opened a breach which you are not closing. This is the reason why I do not accept autonomy of the university.[67]

On the other side, Christian Fouchet, former minister of education, accused Faure of not going far enough, saying:

Your reform is proclaimed to be liberal and audacious. I think it is quite the contrary. It is authoritarian. . . . I am a partisan of autonomy. . . . But where is the autonomy that you propose? The state pays, the professors have their statute, the universities do not compete, and the diplomas are uniform.[68]

Conservative professors accepted the law as a fait accompli but they remained nostalgic for the old Sorbonne. Whatever their point of view, all professors were aware that the adoption of the Orientation Act of Higher Education signaled the end of the old and familiar, and the beginning of a new, as yet unknown university.[69]

77

CHAPTER IV

STRUCTURE AND GOVERNANCE

Je n'ai jamais dit et je ne dirai pas aujourd'hui qu'il est certain que le type d'université que nous allons créer répondra parfaitement à tout ce que nous en attendons.

—Edgar Faure

Le rôle de l'administration est de faire faire, non de faire.

—Bloch-Lainé (1973)

Or, très souvent les réformes sont imposées par des raisons urgentes, qui sont d'ordre politique. . . . On adopte donc en général, des compromis, des demi-mesures, qui ne sont pas parfaitement satisfaisantes, et on les applique trop vite, donc mal.

—Jacques Bousquet (1969)[1]

I. Structure

The Ministers of Education, 1968-1978

Since 1944, France has had twenty-eight ministers of education.[2] After 1974, the ministry was divided so that higher education came under the responsibility of a secretary of state of university affairs, an office which was totally autonomous. In January 1978 the secretariat was elevated to the ministry of universities. If one adds the two secretaries of state who have been appointed since 1974, one may say that there have been thirty ministers in charge of higher education since 1944. Each minister drafted plans for reform. Usually these were piecemeal reforms, sometimes pertaining to other levels of education, sometimes to higher education, but no sooner were the plans presented than the minister was out of office.

This tradition of quick changes in ministers did not cease with the appointment of Edgar Faure. After a year in office, Faure made way for Olivier Guichard, a longtime associate of de Gaulle. While Faure was politically an independent, Guichard was very much a Gaullist party

79

man.[3] At the National Assembly, in his first speech on the budget for 1970, he described his role as he saw it: "My role . . . is to apply and make [others] apply the law, to the letter and in its spirit. It is to administer the autonomy, that is, to ensure public service as defined by the law."[4]

Guichard was asked to take on the ministry in the midst of a crisis. In 1969, "the national education system was an immense caldron which was still boiling . . . new universities were mushrooming out of the ground everyday," he noted. The situation was very confused. No one in the ministry or in the universities, he claimed, knew at which end to begin applying the new law. He attempted "to try and implant a sense of calmness" and to "dedramatize the situation," by requesting that whenever a crisis occurred, such as the occupation of buildings, a forty-eight-hour waiting period should follow. In the ministry of education, "as anywhere else, serenity is perhaps as contagious as exasperation." This type of person was probably needed to oversee the application of the Faure law. Guichard said that applying the law to the letter was the only way to "move along between those who thought it was not democratic enough and those who thought it too revolutionary." He was cautious.

> Strenghened by parliamentary unanimity, and thanks to Edgar Faure's talents, I have succeeded in putting into place from the bottom to the top all the pieces of this diabolical meccano.[5]

Olivier Guichard was replaced in July 1972 by Joseph Fontanet who had previously been minister of labor. He announced that his objective was to develop technical and professional education and that he was concerned about continuing education. Such proposals were, of course, in keeping with someone interested in labor affairs, but they were also concerns of the Faure law, which had called for more practical education and a development of continuing education. Fontanet entered the ministry quietly; his first public appearance on television in September 1972 gave a favorable impression of an ordinary provincial man, "a family man, courteous and somewhat shy, a good listener but not an orator." He gave the impression of being "open and liberal."[6] Fontanet remained minister for nearly two years. After Pompidou's death, in the spring of 1974 (Alain Poher was interim president), Valéry Giscard d'Estaing became the new president and, on May 30, 1974, René Haby was appointed as minister of education, replacing Fontanet.

80

STRUCTURE AND GOVERNANCE

Haby was the rector of the academy of Clermont-Ferrand. He was not a politician but "a simple pedagogue." It was observed that former ministers Fouchet, Faure, Guichard, and Fontanet had had a certain political standing that enabled them to have some independence from the Elysée. But a rector of an academy was someone who, because he was rector, would be familiar with educational matters, while at the same time being subservient to the government.[7] It was also argued that since Haby was not "from the university" himself, the higher education personnel would not object if an autonomous division of higher education, separate from the ministry of education, were established.

The large size of the educational enterprise had elicited suggestions that higher education should have a separate administration from other levels of education.[8] This was done in June 1974, when higher education was provided with its own secretariat of state of university affairs (autonomous, with its own budget, and independent of the minister of education). The powers of the secretaries of state were not dependent on the minister of education. Obviously the two administrations would have to coordinate their efforts in certain areas, such as the baccalauréat, teacher training, and matters regarding social affairs, and in the department of information and statistics. Otherwise, the students, faculty, and researchers would henceforth have a spokesman specifically for affairs of higher education. Jean-Pierre Soisson became the first secretary of state of university affairs in June 1974.[9] He gave the impression of being a good listener and met various educational representatives and unions when he first came to office. They hoped that universities now had a spokesman. But as he stayed in office, it became evident that his public relations style was no longer appreciated by the university community, which resented his arbitrary interference in its affairs. For instance, he developed curriculum reforms that in 1976 provoked student unrest.

In February 1976, after a government reshuffle, Soisson was replaced by Alice Saunier-Seité, a geography professor, a former rector of the academy of Reims, and the third woman in the Giscard d'Estaing-Chirac government. In January 1978, she was elevated to the rank of minister when the secretariat of state became a ministry of universities. Her role essentially was to try to carry through the Soisson curriculum reforms which became so unpopular. Unlike some of her predecessors, her style was not one of accommodation; she enjoyed jumping into the fray and polarizing a situation. When speaking in the National Assembly, she received loud ovations from the conservative benches.[10]

The efficacy of these different ministers and secretaries of state was

STRUCTURE AND GOVERNANCE

circumscribed by the bureaucracy in the central administration. The ministry of education was the largest government employer, yet it was tragically understaffed and its functionaries were ill-prepared for their tasks. They did not possess the necessary skills for modern management. The answer was not necessarily to recruit administrators from the professorial ranks, but to have administrators well trained in modern methods of administration.[11] Several years prior to 1968 one observer criticized them severely, noting that at all levels of the administration, reflection was absent. He illustrated the inadequacy of this ponderous bureaucracy by telling the story of a grant given by the Ford Foundation for construction; the grant remained unused for ten years before land could finally be found in Paris to build the Maison des Sciences de l'Homme at Sèvres-Babylone early in the 1970s.[12]

It was thought that the ministry should introduce more efficient, "business-like" means of management and administration. The ministry of education had officials with short terms of office and an overworked staff lacking in some of the tools of modern administration. These shortcomings meant that the ministry was often unable to do anything but react to the pressure of events.

Transitional Period

The Orientation Act of Higher Education was promulgated on November 12, 1968. Edgar Faure, the minister of education, was well aware that applying the law was a monumental task that would require "daily effort" and would take time. He was also aware that the burden of credibility lay on his shoulders, and he welcomed the challenge. He understood that application of the law would inevitably encounter obstacles from people who were sentimental about what they had been used to, and he cited the example of the mid-1950s when, at the moment of decolonization, Frenchmen felt sentimental about the empire. People were also bound to feel sentimental about the old university structure.[13]

The law itself included guidelines for the initial stages of implementation (articles 39-41). It stated that by December 31, 1968, the minister of education would establish, after consultation with interested groups, a provisional list of UERs which joined together would constitute the new universities. Elections would be held to choose delegates of the UERs.

The delegates would have two responsibilities: first, to draft statutes for the UERs, which would then need to be provisionally approved by the

82

STRUCTURE AND GOVERNANCE

rector of each academy; second, to appoint delegates from the UER constitutive councils to the provisional constitutive assemblies (i.e., future university councils). The UERs would have their statutes drafted by March 15, 1969. Those UERs which had not yet drafted a statute would have provisional statutes decreed for them by the ministry. Representatives to the provisional university councils would draft the university statutes which would then have to be approved by the minister; they would also appoint their delegates to the National Council of Higher Education and Research (CNESER) [article 41].[14]

Although these preliminary guidelines were necessary, they must have created a stir by calling for an "audacious reconstruction," as *Le Monde* called it, of the universities.[15] It was as if the new structures had to be built from the bottom up; only at the midpoint would the new university emerge as an entity. There would first be UERs, then universities, then councils for both, and finally a national council for the higher education system as a whole. The fact that the French university traditionally had not had the opportunity to experiment meant that this sudden change, as Faure put it, represented "a sort of leap into the unknown."[16]

No one could agree on how the new structures would be put into effect. The deans of the *facultés* of letters wanted provisionally to maintain the existing structures, and were concerned about the calendar of events set up by Faure, arguing that each *faculté* had its own ideas and needed time to enact them.[17] It became clear in November 1968 that there would indeed be a transitional period, but it could hardly be called one of experimentation; rather it was a period in which physical restructuring absorbed everyone's total energies. This transition period lasted three years, from November 1968 until the opening of the 1971-1972 academic year.[18]

As a result of the restructuring, by January 1971, twenty-six months after the law was passed, France had a total of sixty-five new institutions (fifty-six new universities, nine university centers), instead of the twenty-two universities that had existed under the old system.

The university constituent assemblies had the primary responsibility of working out the statutes for the new universities. When they could not agree, the ministry had the authority to intervene, as happened in Paris VI-Pierre-et-Marie Curie, and Paris X-Nanterre. Theirs were the last statutes to be approved by ministerial decrees in 1971. With the establishment of the sixty-five new institutions and the approval of their statutes, the transitional period came to an end in mid-1971. This was a relief to many. During the difficulties, notable academics, such as

STRUCTURE AND GOVERNANCE

political scientist Maurice Duverger, indicated concern about the time it was taking to restructure the university system. He argued that it was dangerous to maintain transitional regimes and that the students would not understand the long delays. Once the new structures were in place, it was believed that the law could be made a reality.[19]

The lengthy and difficult transition period resulted from a number of factors of varying magnitude. The issues included the problems of ministerial centralization, student disorders, multidisciplinary universities, and the interrelationships of the emerging centers of power: UERs, university councils, the national council, students, presidents, rectors, and most importantly, the minister of education. The law gave autonomy to the university, but no one knew quite the extent and limit of that autonomy. Some hoped the concept of autonomy would be generously construed while others preferred that it be narrowly interpreted. The issue was to be resolved by a tug of power that had to be worked out by all groups, now that the old structures and authorities were abolished.

The reforms of the Faure law had been wrung from the government during a major political crisis that had nearly spelled death to the Fifth Republic. Once these reforms were voted, however, their application was often timid. In many cases the natural caution of the ministry was redoubled in the face of continuing problems of law and order in the universities. May 1968 had shown students that disorder forced the government to listen; in the years 1968-1978, students applied the lesson they had learned time and time again, and the ministry could not disregard their activities. After the passage of the Faure law, student unrest continued and was especially sharp during the period from 1968 to 1972. According to one author, some 890 people were arrested between November 1969 and March 1970 for distributing leaflets and sticking up posters.[20] It subsided somewhat thereafter and revived during the Soisson administration in 1974. The unrest was triggered by many causes, some important, others less so. The deans of the *facultés* faced particular difficulties. Until the new structures were in place, the deans of the traditional *facultés* were still responsible for order in the universities.

Strikes were rampant. Students from different disciplines feared *sélection*. Medical students feared it most, knowing that only one-tenth of them would ever become doctors; students in languages knew that only one out of thirty would have a teaching job in secondary school, and those who failed to reach these prized jobs feared unemployment.

84

STRUCTURE AND GOVERNANCE

Students struck over fee increases, even though it was only a ten-dollar increase in 1969, and they struck over requirements and rules on transferring credits for obtaining national diplomas. Thus, many of the issues which had caused disorder before 1968 continued to do so thereafter.[21]

Nanterre was a hotbed of agitation, as it had been in pre-1968 days. In December 1969, students demanded the release of a female agitator, and for two days protesters held as hostages two lay persons who had come to sit on an examination jury. The police had to be called in. Students then cornered the interim Dean Beaujeu and asked him to explain his actions of the day before in calling in the police. They held him captive for two hours, threw tomatoes at him, and knocked him to the ground in a scuffle. When he later refused them the use of a hall for a meeting, they took the door and burned it. Police appeared on the scene again. At the Sorbonne other incidents occurred; at a thesis defense, agitators attacked Raymond Aron, renowned French sociologist and commentator on the French university. At the provincial universities, agitation was evident on some campuses. At Strasbourg, problems ensued after the arrest of three anarchists. At Aix-en-Provence, a demonstration occurred over the Russier affair, in which Leftists held members of the provisional university council for four hours, demanding that they "discuss the Gabrielle Russier affair," a question having no direct relation to higher education. In Caen, a professor who was a member of the ultra-conservative CDR (Comité de défense de la république), was locked in his office while students tried to force him to resign from the CDR. They tried to prevent him from teaching his class and wrote insulting graffiti on the walls outside his house, as well as sending many threats. At Grenoble, students struck because their scholarship funds were late in arriving. Tales of university atrocities continued throughout 1970. At Nanterre, two employees were held by extremists, dragged to a general assembly of students, and pushed around while one of them was totally covered with black paint. At Censier and at the *faculté* of science, extremists pulled off doors, floor boards, and telephones, and destroyed office equipment valued at about 400,000 francs ($80,000). At Nanterre alone facilities worth 430,000 francs (86,000 dollars) were destroyed in 1970.[22]

In January 1971, a ministerial decree spelled out the presidents' and UER directors' responsibility for the maintenance of order. The president had a right to forbid entry to anyone causing disorder for a period of thirty days, until disciplinary or judicial action could take place. He had to keep the rector of the academy informed of all actions taken with regard to the maintenance of order inside the university buildings.[23] In

85

March 1971, a ministerial decree spelled out the powers of the university councils in matters of discipline. Students were included on the disciplinary committee, but they were not included for disciplinary action involving faculty.[24] These decrees did not resolve the conflicts that the issue of law and order presented to the administration and to university authorities.

The problem of law and order preoccupied the university authorities and the government. The repeated acts of violence in the universities led the ministers and their bureaucracy instinctively to hesitate about making that "leap into the unknown" of which Faure had spoken. Even if they had been capable of an imaginative restructuring of the universities, the repeated acts of vandalism made the authorities feel that they could not allow the universities to drift. Indeed, the minister's control would have to be asserted and maintained. The desire for control often took priority over the essential thrust of the Orientation Act of Higher Education, which was intended to open the way for experimentation throughout the university system.

Restructuring

By December 1968, the ministry of education had put out a provisional list of 600 UERs, of which 368 were teaching units, 114 mostly research units, and 102 units for institutes or engineering schools which were partly allied to the system. The regrouping of the UERs into universities was a long and arduous project. The effort encountered hostility from many on the right and left and indifference from others. Bordeaux and Paris had the greatest problems, and their lists of universities were not established until March 1970.[25]

The UERs, established provisionally by the ministry, were to elaborate their own statutes and to select delegates to the university constituent councils, which in turn would elaborate the university statutes. The heart of the problem was which disciplines were to be grouped in UERs and which UERs were to be included in which university. The law had stated that the new universities had to be structured along multidisciplinary lines. It stipulated only that each UER should have between 500 to 2,500 students. The list of UERs for each academy was prepared by its rector after consultation with the different parties concerned. The rectors transmitted the desires of the majority of each *faculté* to the central administration in Paris. In some but not all cases, students were involved in this procedure.

In some small towns, each *faculté* approximated the size fixed for future UERs, that is, between 500 to 2,500 students. There the easiest solution was to rechristen the old *faculté* as a UER; that was done, for instance, at Amiens, Besançon, Limoges, Nice, Orléans, Pau, Reims, Rouen, Saint-Etienne, and Tours. In these *facultés*, no one proposed anything different. At Brest, however, the UER of letters and social sciences united several disciplines: letters, humanities, law, and economics.[26]

Once UERs were defined, they were regrouped into multidisciplinary universities. It took more than two years to complete this task. The law sought to abolish absurd divisions between disciplines such as geology (science *facultés*) and geography (letters *facultés*). It wished to bring closer together architecture and sociology, linguistics and mathematics and computer sciences. It wanted to bring together history, arts, and sciences, and to prevent narrow specialization.

To live up to the letter of the law required careful analysis of what multidisciplinary universities meant. No one was quite sure, and the result was either the maintenance of the *status quo* and a change in nomenclature, as was the case in small provincial universities, a haphazard uniting of disciplines for the sake of expediency, or forced "marriages" and "divorces," as some of the uniting and dividing were called. Some feared that the effort to replace the overlarge and impersonal structures of the traditional *facultés* by smaller UERs and universities risked introducing atomized structures that would be even narrower and more specialized than the old structures.[27]

The ministry provided vague guidelines for the regrouping of UERs into universities: a) The size of the new university had to be between 6,000 to 18,000 students, b) universities could constitute themselves into two types of groups, having either a scientific and medical emphasis or a social science one (this was surprising because the Faure law stipulated that letters and arts should be associated with science and technology as much as possible), and c) universities that were formed out of the existing groupings, i.e., essentially unchanged from the old structures, would be given consideration by the ministry.

The UERs themselves were criticized for having been constituted on the old basis (*faculté*, institute, engineering school), or being grouped by disciplines. A long debate ensued about vertical versus horizontal structuring. A vertical approach meant that a UER covered an area or discipline of study from first year through graduate and research studies,

87

STRUCTURE AND GOVERNANCE

while the horizontal meant that studies would be categorized by years, i.e., the first two years of undergraduate education, thereby combining several disciplines for the program of the first two years. To some, this kind of division of the UERs would have avoided too narrow specialization as had happened under the old system. Academics feared that if they opted for the horizontal division of studies, the government would save money by making the universities only teaching establishments and reducing their research funds. Hence, they opted for the vertical units, which included undergraduate and research in each unit.

It is difficult to judge which type of organization works best, for these problems are not peculiar to France. In the U.S., attempts to establish freshman programs, or area studies, were a response to some of the narrow specializations by departments. Students in France were opposed to the horizontal division for fear that the first two years of study would become an entity in themselves, restricting admission to other levels of university programs. They were afraid that this would lead to the introduction of *sélection* for the third year of the *licence* and the *maîtrise*. Faculty feared for their careers, since they might end up being a minority in their discipline in a horizontal multidisciplinary unit.[28]

Many feared that the new UERs were structured too much like the old system which would obstruct the multidisciplinary work which the law had desired. Charles Frankel stated that:

> The regrouping that has taken place suggests that this new reorganization of the disciplines may sometimes produce extremely narrow universities so far as the disciplines covered are concerned, and may actually represent simply a grouping together of people with common political outlook.[29]

Political considerations were indeed an important factor. Faculty of similar political leanings tended to stay together. In some cases where certain groupings might have been desirable, they ultimately did not join because of a "misalliance," since for one reason or another they were incompatible. For instance, the recruiting and administering of some sections of letters prevented the science *facultés* from joining with them. Some groups feared that by associating themselves with a powerful *faculté*, they themselves would be absorbed, and hence refused to join. Opposing interests or personality conflicts prevented others from grouping together. Calculations of self-interest also played a role in the

STRUCTURE AND GOVERNANCE

decisions of UERs grouping together into a university. During the constituent period, while some groups shied away from the medical establishment for fear of being engulfed by it, others were attracted to it, believing that where there is medicine there is also money.[30]

The multidisciplinary problem was in evidence both during the time that UERs were being formed, and later, during the grouping of UERs into universities. As mentioned above, in the smaller towns the small *facultés* dubbed themselves UERs, and in some larger towns, such as Lyon, UERs grouped themselves along traditional disciplinary lines. For example, in the sciences there were UERs in physics, one in biochemistry, one in natural sciences, and one in mathematics. At Toulouse, there was a UER in chemistry, one in mathematics, one in physics, and one in natural sciences. In the area of letters, the "cult of mono-discipline was pushed to its ultimate"; in Bordeaux, there was a unit only for philosophy, while at Nancy, philosophy, psychology, and sociology formed one UER. The most extreme form of restructuring was seen at Aix-en-Provence, where French studies were divided into three units: letters, language and expression, and literature. This occurred in other universities as well and resulted in maintaining the privileges of professorial chairs that had officially been abolished by the law. In the science *faculté* in Paris, even tinier units were proposed, based on "microdisciplines." For example, biology and physics were to be cut up into four units each.

Problems thus existed with unifying the different disciplines into UERs. Professors of science did not want to be linked with those in the humanities.[31] Those in literature denounced projects which separated them from other fields in the humanities, and which they feared would reduce their influence and budget. Bertrand Girod de l'Ain, reporter on the universities in *Le Monde* and a faculty member himself, wrote: "to all these family squabbles were added financial ones." The rich *facultés* (medicine and science), which owned important laboratories and had numerous researchers, feared that if they were regrouped with the "poor" ones (law and literature) in the same university, they would be forced to divide up the funds for research equally among all disciplines; as one researcher in physics said, "How do you make a professor of Greek understand, that we need millions to make a nuclear reactor function?"[32] This classic statement crystallized the antagonism, the self-interest, and the fears that had to be overcome in instituting change.

By May 1969, seventeen new universities had been founded (Amiens, Besançon, Pau, Caen, Clermont-Ferrand, Dijon, Limoges, Nantes, Nice,

STRUCTURE AND GOVERNANCE

Orléans, Tours, Poitiers, Reims, Brest, Saint-Etienne, Rouen, and Metz). All but Clermont-Ferrand, Nantes, and Nice had fewer than 10,000 students. In towns where there were large numbers of students, more than one university was founded (Lille, Lyon, Montpellier, Strasbourg, and Nancy). Paris and Bordeaux had the greatest difficulties reconstituting themselves.

Some of the universities were not at all multidisciplinary. The combinations resorted to were done either on political lines or in haphazard fashion. Law and medicine professors, who had more conservative leanings than those in letters, often joined forces. The following combinations, for instance, were to be found: letters-law (Lyon II); letters-science (Aix-Marseille I); science-medicine (Lyon I, Toulouse III, Grenoble I, Rennes I); science-law (Bordeaux I); law-medicine (Aix-Marseille II, Montpellier I, Lille II). Some *facultés* were merely transformed into universities, even though this ran counter to the stipulations of the law; for example, the *facultés* of letters were transformed into the following universities: Lille III, Toulouse II, and Rennes II. The *facultés* of law became Toulouse I, Paris II, and Strasbourg III.

Other institutions that became even less inter/multidisciplinary than before included the letters *facultés* that were transformed into Paris III, Paris IV, Grenoble III, and Strasbourg II. These divisions were made in order to comply with the provisions of the law requiring universities to have approximately 15,000 students. Such divisions created what seemed to be unnecessary duplication.[33]

In Paris, the struggles of creating the new universities led to the division of the University of Paris into thirteen universities. Some areas were split between different universities, and professors were allowed to opt for the university of their choice. Thus the *facultés* were divided in the following manner:

Paris I: Economics, public law, history, geography
Paris II: Law
Paris III: Modern languages, communications
Paris IV: Classical civilization and literature, computer sciences
Paris V: University Hospital Centers of Cochin, Necker, Gardes; UERs in psychology, social sciences, linguistics, applied mathematics, humanities (Sorbonne), pharmacy, and dentistry
Paris VI: Most of the science *faculté* at Halle-aux-Vins, department of geography from the Nanterre letters *faculté*, university hospital center of Pitié Salpetrière

90

STRUCTURE AND GOVERNANCE

Paris VII: Sciences from Halle-aux-Vins, mathematics, solid physics, genetics, biochemistry, UER Charles V (English from
the Sorbonne), clinical sciences from the Sorbonne, lower
level medical studies of Montrouge (1er cycle), part UER
of French and history of the Sorbonne

Paris VIII: Experimental university of Vincennes, multidisciplinary

Paris IX: Centre Dauphine, business administration

Paris X: Nanterre (Paris-Ouest), letters and law

Paris XI: Orsay (Paris-Sud), pharmacy and sciences

Paris XII: Créteil (Paris-Est), political science, humanities, university hospital center, ecology, urbanism, architecture

Paris XIII: Saint-Denis Villetaneuse (Paris-Nord), law, economics,
humanities, sciences

Thus Paris I, V, VII, and VIII were multidisciplinary, while the others
were essentially the old *facultés* dubbed universities or the new mono-
disciplinary university, Dauphine. The dean of the pharmacy *faculté*
resigned after protesting the division of the pharmacy *faculté* between
two universities, Paris V and XI. He argued that this break-up would
inevitably cause problems especially for team research.[34]

The Institut d'anglais of the Sorbonne, with 9,000 students, was
broken up into three UERs, and each of them joined a different
university. The break-up was along political lines. The leftist element
was incorporated in UER Charles V. This group, which deserved a multidisciplinary program, wanted to join with psychology, medicine,
computer sciences, and education, and therefore opted to join Paris VII,
which had the same political leanings. The professors were divided
among the three groups according "to affinities that were pedagogical,
scientific, and political, thus giving each group its particular
coloration."[35]

In the *faculté* of letters of the Sorbonne, there had been 40,000
students. The *faculté* was divided into several universities, Paris III, IV,
V, and VII. The problems of facilities, buildings, and materials, as well
as administrative deficiencies remained. Enormous problems still faced
the ministry and the new universities with regard to the distribution of
faculty members and researchers among the universities. Figures were
bandied about and contested by both the professors and the ministry.[36]
Faculty members had until April 10, 1970, to decide where they wanted
to teach in the Paris universities. After that date the situation would be
ripe for elections to take place for the UER and university councils; the
new university statutes could thus be worked out by the opening of the

STRUCTURE AND GOVERNANCE

1970 academic year. Although the painful restructuring of the Paris universities had taken until the spring of 1970 to be accomplished, the problems were by no means over. It was December 1970 when the last university statute was approved by the ministry, and not until the 1971 academic year did the new structures begin to function — three years after the Orientation Act had been passed in parliament.

The divisions made in 1970 did not freeze the situation, and further changes were made in the years to come. Thus, the dividing process that occurred in the two years after the passage of the law did not end there. The same antagonism between disciplines or *facultés* existed in 1976 just as it had in 1968. In February 1976, for example, a plan was considered to split Clermont-Ferrand into two universities. Eleven UERs were opposed, while the three UERs of medicine, pharmacy, and dentistry strongly favored the division. The rector of the academy tried to negotiate and to convince pharmacy and law to associate with the economics and the health professions. The letters people bitterly opposed the partition and insisted on keeping their ties with economics. Hence a deadlock ensued, until the secretariat approved the division of Clermont-Ferrand into two universities, one incorporating law and medicine, and the other, letters and sciences. Similar antagonisms have been witnessed in other universities; particularly dramatic were those at Aix-Marseille where one group ran off with the library of another.[37]

The restructuring of the universities raised the number of universities in France from twenty-two to sixty-five. By 1975, the number had increased to seventy-two (756 UERs). In 1977, there were twenty-one monodisciplinary universities, twenty-six bi-disciplinary, eleven tri-disciplinary and nineteen quadri-disciplinary universities[38] (appendix 2).

Regional Problems

The Paris region created special problems for setting up new universities. As always, the Paris universities were overcrowded and drew a disproportionate number of students. While Paris had 18 percent of the French population, the Paris region had about a third of all students in France.[39] The reasons for this are many. In Paris, students had access to better libraries and a greater variety of programs, particularly in languages and the arts; they could more easily find jobs on the side; and Paris offered them an escape from provincial life. Seven of the new universities were in the center of Paris and were called the universities of

STRUCTURE AND GOVERNANCE

Paris-Centre. The rest were in the suburbs and were known as universities of the periphery.

Governmental efforts to decongest the Paris region failed. In the 1960s, efforts were made to build a number of universities in the Paris basin. New academies were founded, each with a university, at Nantes and Orléans in 1962, Reims, Amiens, and Rouen two years later.[40] These came to be known as the universities of the Paris basin or the "crown universities."

The university of Orléans, only eleven kilometers from Paris, in wooded surroundings, was to become the "French Oxford." It was intended as a model campus for a group of universities outside Paris, in a move to help decongest the capital. But the plan was not very successful. For the most part, the students stayed faithful to the banks of the Seine, and only some 200 students from Paris attended Orléans in 1973. By 1978, the situation had not drastically changed from the mid-1960s. The universities of the Paris basin had not received the aid necessary to make them attractive to students, but the newly developed periphery universities in the Parisian suburbs, were attracting more students and thereby helping decongest the center of Paris. In 1970-1971, about 10 percent of the students in the Paris region were actually attending the universities of the periphery. By 1976-1977, with the development of those universities, 37 percent of the students in the Paris region attended them (107,097 out of 289,429 students).[41] To populate the peripheral universities, a rule was adopted in 1971-1972, which allocated university places along residential lines. Only if the university did not offer the particular program needed could a student petition to enter a university outside the area near his home. A student could state the order of preferences for universities to the rector's office in his academy of residence. In 1977 this rule was changed and students in the Paris region could choose their universities. However, universities could not admit more students than they had had the previous year.[42]

In the provinces themselves, attempts were made to create universities in tune with regional needs. In 1969, de Gaulle arranged for a referendum that would have established considerable regional political power; it would also have led to increasing collaboration between universities and local industries. But the defeat of the referendum prevented such an eventuality (the most serious result of the defeat, of course, was de Gaulle's resignation).

In 1974, Soisson, the new secretary of state of the universities, announced plans for the regionalization of the universities. His plan was

93

to found seven regions, each with a regional university assembly and a regional capital with a main university. This system would provide both more coordination and specialization for the needs of a particular region. Students could thus receive training at the regional universities, and, it was hoped, have better prospects when they entered the job market. This rather bold move on the part of Soisson caused bitter opposition, particularly from the Eastern region, where Strasbourg, Dijon, and Reims, already preeminent in their region, feared they might not retain that preeminence, since only one main university would be needed in the regional capital. The plan was conveniently shelved.[43]

While Soisson's plan did not succeed for all of France, he did make attempts in individual regions. He founded, for example, the university of Haut-Rhin at Mulhouse, which incorporated the former Centre Universitaire du Haut-Rhin with two private engineering institutions. The new university would specialize in chemistry, included the Ecole supérieure de chimie and the Ecole supérieure des industries textiles, as well as the IUT (800 students) and offered the adult education program already serving 10,000 of the population in the area. It was thought that the university of Haut-Rhin would answer some of the specific needs of the region, and the move pleased the business sector. When the university of Corsica was founded, its curriculum was tailored to meet the local needs; thus, special programs were instituted to help give training for the tourist industry. The founding of these universities, while answering one stipulation of the 1968 law, namely the establishment of closer ties with the business and industrial sector, failed to answer another, the respect for democratic participation in the decision-making process. The new universities were created by Soisson in a high-handed manner, often without regard for proper procedures.

II. Governance

UER and University Councils

While some aspects of the pre-1968 university remained, the Faure Law did mean a radical transformation in the participation of the academic community in university affairs. All groups were to participate: students were to have a say as were the younger faculty. The ancient authoritarian, hierarchical structures were to be submerged in favor of new, cooperative, democratic institutions. The system would

STRUCTURE AND GOVERNANCE

involve elections at all levels, from the UER to the university to the national council, a method that would play down the strong hand of the central administration and allow the universities more flexibility and autonomy.

Once the ministry approved the provisional UERs, professors, and students in these units were required to elect their representatives to the UER council. That council would elaborate the statute for its UER, and would elect from among its members delegates to the provisional constitutive assembly of the university. This latter would in turn define the statute for the university, and the provisional structures would give way to regular university councils after the first real elections based on the new university statutes. The outgoing national council for higher education (which in time gave way to the newly elected CNESER) approved a decree that defined the different constituencies or electoral colleges and the methods of voting. For the most part, there were six electoral colleges: (a) Professors and *maîtres de conférences*, (b) *maîtres-assistants* and *assistants*, (c) other teaching staff, (d) research staff, (e) students, and (f) administrators, technical and service personnel.[44] In establishing electoral colleges for their staff, most universities chose to adopt a simple formula of two electoral colleges, one for faculty and researchers of senior status (professors, *maîtres de conférences*, and directors and researchers of senior rank), and the other for all other faculty and researchers.[45]

The 1968 law stipulated that the number of faculty of all ranks had to be at least equal to the number of students on any council. Lay persons on the university council could constitute no more than one-third and no less than one-sixth of the members on the council. The number of lay persons on the UER councils was to be decided by the university council of the particular university (articles 12 and 13).

The composition of the councils was designed to give conservatives the upper hand. The council was to be equally divided between faculty and students, but its other members would tend to be conservative, such as lay persons, administrative, technical, and service personnel. Most importantly, the law provided that if less than 60 percent of the students voted in the UER elections, their seats on the UER council would be proportionately reduced; thus frequently the faculty would have most seats on the councils and among them the senior-rank faculty would have most influence. As one observer put it, "the elementary law of classic liberalism, 'one man one vote,' is abolished." According to him, the new system of participation made one professor worth four *assistants* and 350

95

students.[46] Thus the students were far from the parity of power they had asked for on university governing councils.

Lay persons were believed to have a definite political utility in the establishment of councils; if they had the "right political leanings," they could negate any particular tendency of the faculty or student members. As one deputy noted, the presence of lay persons should be carefully supervised for "their utility is unquestionable."[47]

Despite the small number of students seated on the UER councils (since in most elections the students did not attain the minimum of 60 percent, and their seats were reduced accordingly), these same students had the right to elect from among themselves their representatives to the university councils. This second election was not subject to a "quorum" rule. Student representation on the university councils was thus proportionately greater than the UER councils. Furthermore, students on the university councils had the right to elect from among themselves a total of seventeen representatives to CNESER, out of a total of ninety members. After 1975 the secretariat attempted a reduction in student representation, both on university and national councils. The minimum figure for students set in the 1968 law was amended by law in July 1975 from 60 percent to 50 percent, and a clause was added that future decrees would restrict the number of seats on university councils by applying the "quorum" rule, not only to UER, but also to university council elections.[48]

By lowering the minimum to 50 percent, the amended law of 1975 made student representation more advantageous at the UER level (provided that student participation in elections was high, which was usually not the case), but at the same time dealt a blow by restricting the number of seats they could have on the university councils based on the total received in the UER elections. While previously the lack of student participation at elections penalized representation only at the UER level, after 1975 representation was proportionately reduced at all levels. At one Parisian university, student representation on the university council was reduced from nineteen to two as a result of the application of the "quorum" for elections to that council, but it was not so drastic everywhere. Strasbourg III, a law university, had its student membership reduced from twenty-two to seventeen, while Strasbourg II, a humanities university, witnessed a reduction only from eleven to nine, which by 1977 was back to eleven again.[49] The amended 1975 law on quorum regulations was contrary to what Guichard, minister of education, had stated in 1971, when he declared, "It appears to us,

STRUCTURE AND GOVERNANCE

juridically, that the quorum instituted for the UER council could not be applied to the university council. This has been confirmed by the conseil d'état."[50] If Olivier Guichard thought such a step was illegal in 1971, Jean-Pierre Soisson, secretary of state for university affairs, did not, three years later. Concerned that elections were producing councils with which they were out of harmony, government officials tended to tamper with established election procedures. At Toulouse-le-Mirail, Soisson decreed a series of mixed election procedures in order to produce a conservative majority on the university council. As secretary, he was empowered by article 18 of the Faure law to assume power in cases where a university encountered difficulties in the functioning of its statutory organs, but only after consultation with the national council. He conveniently ignored this part of the law. His authoritarian manner led to a series of resignations among university administrators at Toulouse. In January 1975, seven out of twelve UER directors resigned, and there were three acting presidents.[51] The concept of participatory democracy in the university, as assured by the law of 1968, thus at times had been rather brutally mangled. This deliberate flaunting of the spirit, and even letter of the law appeared even more flagrant, since it was a law sponsored and adopted by a government which then chose to ignore it.

Faculty-Student Participation in Elections

For Edgar Faure as for the university community, "participation" was the magic word. The 1969 elections were to be the first test of whether in fact the new structures and the new participatory democracy were to function. All eyes were on the universities: the news media covered the elections and reported the results at all stages. As one observer noted, the "first meetings were in large amphitheaters, students milled around in the halls, and television cameras were there." Then the cameras disappeared, the amphitheaters emptied, and the number of participants diminished. This occurred both at the UER and the university level. During the first year or two of the new regimes, the picture was not totally negative. There was greater awareness on the part of the faculty and the students, and both hoped to find a new definition of their roles in university affairs.[52]

Student participation in later elections was weak compared to 1969, when 52 percent of the students participated. For that year, participation varied from one academy to another; at Poitiers 37 percent of the

97

students voted, while at Nancy 67.33 percent did so. Participation also varied by disciplines. It was weakest for letters and highest in the technical institutes. Participation among first-year students was weakest, presumably because they were less integrated in the community and therefore were generally less acquainted with university affairs, let alone elections.

Among the teaching, research, and other university personnel, the highest participation was among the senior professors, and the lowest among the *assistants* and other supplementary teaching staff: 83 percent of the professors and *maîtres de conférences* voted, 76.8 percent of the *maître-assistants*, 56.9 percent of the other teaching staff, 64 percent of the researchers and 67 percent of the other personnel. Overall, 70.1 percent of all groups together voted in the 1969 elections to the UER councils.

After 1969, student participation in elections lessened generally over the years from 52 percent in 1969 to 25 percent in 1975; 1975-1976 saw a

GRAPH 7

STUDENT PARTICIPATION IN UNIVERSITY ELECTIONS [53]
1969-1975

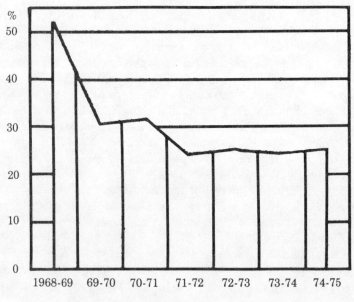

STRUCTURE AND GOVERNANCE

rise in the percentage to 28 percent, thanks to greater participation from more conservative groups.[54]

Elections to university councils did not involve all students as did elections to the UER councils. The students on the UER councils elected from among themselves their representatives to the university council. Even in those cases abstention occurred, but nevertheless involvement was higher than for the UER councils. In Paris the average participation in 1971-1972 was 77 percent, and in the provinces 71 percent for 1972-1973. But at Lyon I, it sank to 22.7 percent probably due to difficulties faced in the division of the university.

Under the indirect voting system representation in student elections to the university council was stronger in Paris than in the provinces. Extremists profited from the indirect voting system, especially in Paris. Although Parisian students participated less in UER elections than did students in the provinces, they were better organized and thus had greater influence at the university council level. The Soisson and Saunier-Seité administrations disregarded the provisions of the Faure law about student presence and participation on the university councils by insisting on reducing their number commensurate with their UER representation.

Many factors were involved in the poor participation of students at elections. Students on UER councils sometimes resigned because a director had the upper hand and they felt superfluous, or they turned away in disgust, feeling that there was no opportunity for change and that the system simply created student bureaucrats. There was, moreover, often a sense that decisions were short-circuited by the administration, and that the UER had no real financial powers. Many commented on the fatiguing "interminable palabres" that had to take place under the new system. One professor said that where there used to be two meetings, there were now a dozen. According to him, much of the discussion was a waste of time and discouraged students and faculty from participating.

The whole election procedure was so cumbersome that it exhausted the time and energies of everyone involved, especially the organizers. All the elections did not take place at one time. Most universities held elections annually, while some did so every two or more years, but even where they were held at two-year intervals, there were always partial elections that took place now and then. The work of control commissions in elections was enormous, but because of the vast extent of their responsibilities, they could not exercise the control they intended to have in election procedures.[55]

99

STRUCTURE AND GOVERNANCE

Politicization of the University-Student Unions
and Political Groups

The intricate system of seats, votes, slates, and candidacies in post-1968 elections was complicated by the number of political groups involved, all vying for the apportioned seats on a council. It was a known fact that law and medicine tended to fall into the hands of "moderates," while letters and sciences were in those of the "progressives." Councils were sometimes composed of just one political grouping, sometimes of two or more. The extremist elements tended to boycott elections.[56]

In chapter two, the role of unions and political groups in the university was discussed. In 1978 some of the same groups remained, but under different denominations. Early in 1971, UNEF (Union nationale d'étudiants français) split into two camps. From then on, there existed two organizations: UNEF-Renouveau (subsequently called UNEF-ex-Renouveau), consisting of mostly Communist students, and UNEF-Unité syndicale composed of Trotskyites of the AJS (Alliance des jeunes pour le socialisme). Both camps focused on issues of student life, such as financial aid, fees, housing and restaurants, but differed with regard to university elections. The UNEF-ex-Renouveau wanted to participate in elections, while the UNEF-Unité syndicale called for the boycott of elections. In 1976 as in 1968 membership was approximately 50,000 (table 9). By 1976 it attempted to restore its waning influence over students by rallying them against the curriculum reorganization proposed by Soisson a year earlier, and in 1978 continued its efforts to reunify the non-communist Left and the extreme Left within the same organization.

While there were a number of political groups, all of them differed in their policies regarding participation in university elections. In the late 1970s these groups were:[57]

UNEF-ex-Renouveau (Communist)

UNEF-Unité syndicale (AJS-Trotskyites)

Comité de liaison des étudiants de France (CLEF, conservative)

Le Comité de liaison étudiant pour la rénovation universitaire (CLERU, conservative formerly part of CLEF)

Le Comité pour un syndicat des étudiants de France (COSEF, socialists)

La Fédération nationale des étudiants de France (FNEF, moderates)

100

STRUCTURE AND GOVERNANCE

Le Mouvement d'action et de recherches critiques (MARC, close to CFDT, Leftist catholic worker's union)

L'Union nationale interuniversitaire (UNI, extreme right included many faculty members)

UNEF-ex-Renouveau's prime concern was to be represented on the UER and university councils. In 1972-1973, it had 28 percent of the student members on the UER councils and 39 percent on the university councils. On the CNESER or national council, it had seven out of seventeen student seats. Other groupings that had not boycotted elections had one or two seats on the CNESER and generally only a tiny percentage of all seats on all councils. In 1976, with 50,000 members, 50 percent of the elected students on UER councils represented UNEF-ex-Renouveau. That year, UNEF-ex-Renouveau launched a campaign to increase its membership and improve student services. It opposed the government when it limited the number of elected students to the university councils, curbed student participation on disciplinary councils, and introduced senseless curriculum reorganization.[58]

Under Soisson's administration (1974-1976) the secretariat showed its approval of other more conservative student groups. In the summer of 1976, Saunier-Seité, Soisson's successor, dealt a blow to the UNEF-ex-Renouveau by cutting its funds. Instead, money went to other groupings (the sums were not divulged for 1976, but in 1975, the UNI on the extreme right received 190,000 francs or $38,000; FNEF, a moderate group, received 70,000 francs or $14,000).

This of course was not the first time that the central administration interfered in student politics. As mentioned earlier, the Algerian war, which politicized UNEF, caused the government to cut aid to UNEF and to support the more conservative FNEF in 1961. In 1976, the government disapproved of the political role that UNEF-ex-Renouveau had played in the university and exercised its power by cutting off its funds. It appeared that the government wanted to see student participation in university affairs only so long as the more conservative elements were well-represented and did not hesitate to intervene to help them win control over the councils. In 1976, Guy Herzlich wrote in *Le Monde*: "The government is little by little draining the [Faure] law of its content, instead of seeing to it that it functions."[59]

101

STRUCTURE AND GOVERNANCE

Earlier in this chapter, the long, difficult, and laborious effort that went into the creation of the new structures as defined by the 1968 law was discussed. The real test was to come in the years following 1968. How would the university and UER councils interact with one another? How did they relate to their representative organs, the CRESER and CNESER, and what role did the new presidents play in the new universities? What was the relationship of the universities to the minister's representative, the rector, who was also the chancellor of the university in his academy? How did all groups relate to the central administration, and how much real autonomy did they experience?

Article 19 of the law gave the universities and the UERs within them the power to determine their own teaching, research, curriculum, and methods of examinations. This stipulation contained possible conflicts. The university and UER councils were at odds over many issues. Legalistic interpretations or deliberate misinterpretations were prevalent, with regard, for example, to who could be called a lay person or who could become president. In the latter case, the law specified that, he must be a senior professor, but the system had various ranks of senior professors — a *professeur sans chaire* was also a senior professor but not quite as high as a *professeur titularisé*. In such situations the secretariat played an arbitrary role; that is, if the individual were not of the preferred political coloration, then the secretariat opposed his nomination.[60]

Until 1972, the central administration was busy watching over the restructuring, after which its role was to supervise the functioning of the new universities within the realm of the new autonomy that the law had given them. What then was the ministry's power? Besides holding the purse strings (chapter VI), it was the watchdog over the universities. Thus, it was in charge of decreeing how much autonomy a university could have. Until the arrival of Saunier-Seité, the image that the central administration wanted to convey was that of the objective outsider who did not meddle in the internal affairs of the university, but who encouraged change. Yet in the face of perceived turbulence or opposition to government policies, the ministers and secretaries of state were quick to assert their powers, even when it went against the spirit of the law. In his eagerness to innovate, Guichard, for instance, conveniently ignored the CNESER's opposition to the founding of a university at Compiègne.[61]

STRUCTURE AND GOVERNANCE

The Role of Presidents

Jean Capelle, speaking at the National Assembly in 1970 said:

> We are struck by the fact that deliberative powers, in our
> new university structures, crush the executive powers . . .
> University democracy, as in any democracy, has to
> respect certain rules, as a condition of success, and that
> presupposes true executive power . . .[62]

The presidency was a new office. It was perhaps one of the most
important innovations of the Faure law. Qualified and dedicated individuals were vested with the important responsibility of guiding the university. Their powers have gradually been defined.

While the ministry tried to make certain that presidents were vested
with strong powers, the role of the president depended on his university,
for a president was elected by the university council for a five-year term
and was not reeligible. In some cases, presidents were elected because it
was understood that they planned to interfere as little as possible in the
autonomy of the UERs; in other cases, presidents were asked to present
a program before they were elected. Presidents were elected for their
negotiating abilities and their tactical skills in dealing with councils
which were often divided, because they stood outside the "clannish"
struggles that went on in the councils, because they made particular
efforts to give responsibilities to a group of notables, or because they
"democratized" life in the university at all levels and made a great effort
at disseminating information to all segments of the university community. Some saw their role as policy makers, others as administrators.

These descriptions of the role of the president do not differ much from
how American presidents, for example, are described (although very
often the American president is required to have most, if not all, of these
qualities, including being a public relations man in his efforts to acquire
funds for the university). But the American presidents have no central
administration to bolster their executive authority. While their powers
are circumscribed by boards of trustees and state legislatures, they have
considerable executive powers. They can choose their committees or have
them elected, as the case may be. In France, the central administration
sometimes tried to make these decisions for the presidents. For example,
presidents were to be assisted by a permanent committee whose members
were elected by the university council. But the ministry insisted that
these committees be appointed by the presidents. After a president chose

STRUCTURE AND GOVERNANCE

the committee members, the university council could then give its vote of confidence.

The ministers and secretaries of state favored the accretion of authority in the hands of the presidents within the individual universities, at the cost of UER and university councils. Such a development was thought essential in the face of repeated indecision by the councils, their unwillingness or inability to make unpopular decisions. One council member exclaimed in 1971, "the ministry absolutely wants the presidents to be dictators."[63]

The National Council and the Conference of Presidents

The law of 1968 made no mention of a national presidential council. But after long debates two national organs to represent the universities emerged. The first was a national council, the Conseil national de l'enseignement supérieur et de la recherche (CNESER), which was foreseen by the Faure law and was to replace the old national council for higher education. It was to be an elected, representative organ (article 43). The 1968 law did not spell out how the council was to be organized, and it was left to the ministry and the university representatives to decide. There were several debates over whether it would be an assembly with university representatives and students in one group and presidents of the universities in another, or whether they would all be represented together. If all sixty-five universities were represented, the council would end up with 600 members. The ministry wanted to limit the membership to eighty, which meant that not all universities would be represented. If all university presidents were on the council, the size would still be too large. Hence the idea developed of having two separate organs: (a) elected members from national and regional list of candidates, and (b) a council for all university presidents. Probably in the back of the experts' minds was the British system of the University Grants Committee (founded in 1918 when universities began needing state support), which had twenty members of whom two-thirds were university people and which was responsible for dividing up state funds among the universities, and the committee of vice-chancellors, which defended the interests of the universities before the ministry of education and the University Grants Committee. In France it was unclear which of the two organs was to be the upper and which the lower chamber. CNESER gradually emerged as the lower chamber, and the Conference of Presidents as the

104

STRUCTURE AND GOVERNANCE

upper chamber. CNESER was designed to have ninety members. Of the ninety, fifty-four were to be university members elected from a national list of candidates by the members of the university councils (there were to be eighteen senior professors and researchers, thirteen other teaching faculty and researchers, one for library personnel, five other university personnel, and seventeen students). Added to the fifty-four university members, would be six representatives from other institutions of higher education, and thirty lay persons appointed by the minister.[64]

The CNESER was established in April 1971, its elected members to serve for three years; by April 1974, a new council was to be chosen. This was not done and elections have continued to be delayed. The council was plagued by absenteeism. Elected students who could serve for three years at a time were rarely present; some of them had graduated, while others had become *assistants* but continued to serve as student members. Only about six out of the seventeen students attended a 1975 meeting.[65] The fact that the thirty lay persons could be appointed by the minister meant that serious restrictions could be placed on the functioning of the council and reduced the effectiveness of the council as a representative organ.

Since their founding in 1971, both the CNESER and the conference of presidents were consultative organs. The secretaries of state were supposed to consult them on all issues of importance in matters of policy, diplomas, and finance and they also presided over CNESER.[66] Although they were officially presidents of the Conference of Presidents, the meetings were usually presided by one of the vice-presidents (three university presidents were elected as vice-presidents of the Conference each year).

Exactly how powerful the CNESER or the Conference of Presidents had become was not clear. Some argued that the CNESER council had the responsibility of long-range planning and was a policy-making organ, while the Conference of Presidents, supposedly a better structured and more homogeneous group, was responsible for making the university function in difficult conditions; thus it was understandable if the latter were given more weight by the ministry, especially since the number of universities was increasing. CNESER was not regarded as an important organ nor did it appear to have the autonomy that the law promised all councils. When CNESER voiced opposition, the central administration ignored the council's objections. Saunier-Seité's authoritarian style further reduced the influence of the CNESER.

Since its inception, the Conference of Presidents has remained a

105

STRUCTURE AND GOVERNANCE

consultative organ, but it was taken more seriously by the ministry in Paris, which could not totally disregard the views of seventy-five heads of universities. When it chose to act authoritatively, it still could do so. According to René Rémond, one of its vice-presidents in 1975, most of the seventy-five presidents, came to the meetings. With regard to the role of the Conference, he said: "The precariousness of the Conference is due to its oddness in the French administrative system; there is hardly another organ where dialogue has taken place as openly and fruitfully as among these responsible executives."[67] The truth of this statement cannot be overemphasized. Out of the discussions regarding the Faure law emerged an organ not provided for by that law, but which has been truly significant in its contribution. Although as one president put it: "Saunier-Seité would like to abolish the Conference," it remains a "mediating organ" to be reckoned with.[68] The French educational enterprise will need more of these self-created organs where cooperation and dialogue can take place.

The Rectors

The final part of the discussion on the university balance of powers leads to the role of the rectors. When the new structures were being established, the new presidents were concerned about the powers that would be given to these officials and the repercussions that these powers would have on their own roles and powers as executives of the autonomous universities. The rectors were designated by the Faure law to be chancellors of the universities in their academy. They were the minister's representative for all levels of education, just as they had been under Napoleon. The Faure law was worded cautiously, so as to preserve the powers of the rectors, but at the same time to give the impression that universities were responsible for their own internal affairs. For example, the rectors no longer presided at the university council, but could attend as the minister's representatives. Moreover, they were empowered to suspend council meetings in situations of conflict or chaos until the minister reviewed the problems.[69] They were coordinators among the different levels of education in their academy, as well as coordinators for the universities in their academy. One American professor, inquiring about the possibility of setting up a faculty exchange program with the three universities in one town, was informed by the president of one to consult with the rector, since he said, "we have autonomy but the rector is the coordinator."[70]

106

STRUCTURE AND GOVERNANCE

The rectors received instructions from both the ministry of education and the ministry of universities on every possible issue, from using more apples in the diet of university restaurants to organizing classes in elementary and secondary schools, from providing financial aid to pupils to issuing directives to school principals on many issues of detail, including how to respond to the press.[71] In conflict situations, they had to play the role of arbitrator. In the struggles in UER or university councils, and where disruptions prevailed, the rectors were in the midst of the imbroglio. Sometimes, they sided with the president against the members of their university councils; other times, they sided with the bodies opposing the president. In any case, they had extensive powers and sometimes used them. The rectors, by the nature of their appointments, had the confidence of the minister. This cannot be said to be true of the university presidents, even though some of them carried some weight.

The rectors were to preside over the regional councils of higher education and research (CRESER) established by the Faure law.[72] The membership of those councils was to be similar to that of the CNESER. Although members for the regional councils were elected in 1972, the councils were never convened and the law establishing them remained a dead letter. As one observer noted, "no one really wanted them."[73]

Conclusion

After 1968, there was a vacuum of power in the university system. Although the ministry of education proclaimed autonomy, when it so chose, it could arbitrarily interfere in the internal workings of the universities. Ironically, in some cases the universities requested intervention. In the disorders between 1969-1971 at Vincennes, Nanterre, Assas, Dauphine, Clignancourt, Bordeaux, and Marseille, the ministry was directly involved and the university councils were often helpless. As a result, one professor said that "the autonomy is purely imaginary . . . the state is always and everywhere and at all levels present."[74]

Political opposition faced those who wished to see autonomy develop to its full extent, with universities setting their own admission standards and curriculum, abolishing national diplomas, and seeking financial support from sources other than the state. Leftists, supported by the faculty union, SNE-Sup, did not want to see competitive universities, since that would mean that some would be better than others; admission

107

standards would then vary, and the abhored *sélection* would follow. They feared that universities dependent on business and industry for income would become political captives of capitalism. Universities, it was claimed, should be funded equitably by the state, yet state interference was suspect.

Those favoring autonomy often cited the American model as typical of how a decentralized system should work.[75] But to follow the American model would mean the introduction of competitive universities and admission requirements. That, was the hitch. As Debbasch said, "The law has not pushed autonomy to its ultimate consequence: competition seemed like the natural partner of autonomy . . ."[76] University autonomy seemed illusive if there were still a national system of diplomas, national standards of curriculum, and national financing of universities, as well as state regulation of university elections and a policy of reducing representative national organs into consultative ones.

The French tradition of centralization was hard to uproot; ministers instinctively clung to their authority, and even the universities sometimes called for it. One commentator lamented the lack of dialogue and the fear of competition among Frenchmen, and said that leaders found themselves "in a prodigious labyrinth whose invisible walls were harder than concrete: that is, the French mentality, our mentality."[77]

The tradition of authority from above in the French administrative structure did not allow or encourage participation and dialogue from below. It was this type of system that led Paul Valéry to give a definition of politics as "the art of preventing people from being involved in what concerns them."[78] Undoubtedly, the knowledge that the central administration was present and could, if necessary, bail out the university sometimes discouraged the various councils from exercising their full responsibilities; still, the central administration did not consistently encourage autonomy within the university, but arbitrarily interfered when it wished to impose its authority. A centralized system is not necessarily disadvantageous; countries such as the U.S. and Britain, discovering the shortcomings of a totally decentralized system, are moving in that direction.[79] Clearly something more is involved: the cultural values of a people which are reflected in their institutions. The emphasis on cooperation and dialogue at all levels in Anglo-Saxon institutions reveals itself in their educational systems. Shortcomings occur in those systems too, but there are checks and balances because people do participate in the daily life of their institutions. In France, the authoritarian pattern reveals itself in all levels of society — in the family,

STRUCTURE AND GOVERNANCE

in the school, and in the government. To reverse certain traditions of a country by one educational reform law is not possible. As one notable observer wrote:

> What paralyzes the reform of education in France, is that it has to be applied from one end of its territory to another, and as a consequence has to be imposed from above. Hence it fails.[80]

STRUCTURE AND GOVERNANCE

CHAPTER V

CURRICULUM

L'imagination est nécessaire aux enseignants, aux enseignés et aux pouvoirs publics pour provoquer une profonde mutation des habitudes de pensées et d'action. Si ceux qui prétendaient détenir l'imagination n'ont pas pris le pouvoir, il reste au pouvoir à prendre l'imagination.
— Edgar Faure (1968)

Ce n'est pas en ajoutant un cours de biologie à la licence de psychologie, ou un cours de sociologie aux études économiques qu'on change les choses.
— Henri Claustre (1974)[1]

Pedagogical Autonomy and the Diploma

Reform proposals in 1968 called for sweeping changes in teaching and learning methods and for the improvement of faculty-student relations in the universities. In addition, the faculty wanted to change the graduate programs and establish more fluid career opportunities for themselves. There was a general quest for a more flexible system of education, and above all the cry for the democratization of higher education was loud and clear. Democratization was closely tied to the idea of open access to the university, meaning either that the baccalauréat at the end of secondary school would not be required, or that if it were, university entrance examinations would not be established to select students.

The dilemmas facing the new French universities were enormous. If they were to practice autonomy in the true sense, they should be able to select their students, and, within the limits of their budgets, provide quality education. But those who in any way considered themselves progressive could not favor *sélection*, which politically was thought to be a reactionary stand. The French universities were faced with having to renovate themselves and to provide simultaneously for quantity and quality education.

The UER and university councils were empowered by the Faure law to define their own programs and content of teaching (article 19). As in the past, university faculty members were free to do as they pleased; the

111

restraints were on the students, who were tied to a rigid curriculum for specific diplomas as defined by the central administration. The national diplomas still existed, and although more flexibility was introduced into the curriculum, the fact that the national diploma remained meant that experimentation was often left aside or discouraged. Olivier Guichard, while declaring that the time had come to abandon rigid uniformity and to introduce flexibility in the teaching and content of the curriculum, affirmed that "with regard to pedagogical autonomy, the law has placed some limits by retaining the national diplomas."[2]

The Faure law allowed universities to grant "university diplomas," but these did not necessarily have the sanction of the central administration, and thus would not be nationally recognized. To upgrade their "university diplomas," faculty and students agitated for the inclusion of as many diplomas as possible into the list of national diplomas. They seemed hesitant to exercise pedagogical autonomy and were convinced that a ministry of education label would be more prestigious than that of their own university — "an unthinkable situation in any Anglo-Saxon country," commented Jean Capelle.

When a university introduced a new program and wished to obtain the sanction of a national diploma for it, it could do so by negotiation with the ministry of education. Unless validation came from the ministry, diplomas emanating only from the universities suffered. Faure stated in the National Assembly:

> It must be understood that each university will have the right to organize its own diplomas as it sees fit, so long as it does not concern itself with the *national diplomas that lead to certain professions or which are subject to concours*.[3]

Universities insisted on the ministry's seal of approval in order to give their students the opportunity to obtain national diplomas and the chance to enter competitive examinations. The ministry, by contrast, wanted to encourage the development of university diplomas and made national diplomas more restrictive, thereby guaranteeing the quality of the diploma and simultaneously reducing the number of candidates entering the job market. Employers were likely to continue to hire first those with training from the *grandes écoles*, then those with a national diploma, and finally those with a university diploma. This would maintain the mechanism of selection.

What was the magic to obtaining a national diploma instead of a

CURRICULUM

university one? Frédéric Gaussen pointed out that "French society, as is well known, has a taste for diplomas and for equality. It considers that the first will be a guarantee for the second." Uniform programs and examinations were the only means of ensuring that the diplomas given out would be identical. The debate on diplomas and on who should be responsible for granting them was closely connected to the issue of university autonomy. Some argued that in order for true autonomy to evolve, diplomas had to lose their national identity, but that did not happen. The problem was complex. Many, who would have liked to see full autonomy granted to the university, in all aspects, at the same time wanted to ensure the value of the diploma.[4]

The political left, which had been against centralization and for the autonomy of the universities; opposed the idea of university diplomas, fearing that they might not be of equal value; for the same reason, they were totally against the notion of competitive universities. If national diplomas did not exist, then certain university diplomas would be more valued than others; hence, the system would be undemocratic. As Debbasch noted, those who wanted university autonomy did not seem prepared to take the consequences — namely, the disappearance of the national diploma. Others held the view that to establish competition between institutions would give rise to innovation and experimentation. But for the most part, the general public exerted pressure for the retention of national diplomas. Even the ministry worked in that direction by sending circulars to employers, warning them about certain university diplomas.[5]

Democratization

The emphasis on the retention of the national diploma created uniformity in curriculum, limited the opportunities for experimentation in individual universities, and led to less diversified student recruitment than otherwise might have been possible. The key issues of May 1968 had been democratization and modernization of higher education. Faure had stood for open access to all individuals with a baccalauréat and came out against selective recruitment. He wanted to improve the counseling system and to open up diverse educational programs so that dropout rates would decrease in the universities. Many of the same problems that had existed before 1968 — issues of democratization, sélection, and orientation (counseling) — persisted a decade later.

113

The granting of scholarships was important to those who wanted to see democratization of recruitment. In 1968-1969, there were 129,140 students in the universities receiving scholarships. In 1970-1971, the number increased to 144,036, but decreased thereafter (table 11). Of the scholarship holders in 1975-1976, 95.7 percent attended public institutions and 4.3 percent went to private ones. Scholarships for higher education were given out on the basis of confidential statements. After 1969, the method was changed to resemble that used in secondary schools, with a list of fourteen or more criteria based on a points system. The amount was calculated on the basis of family income, the number of children in the family, and other factors. The more points one had, the larger the scholarship.[6] In 1975-1976, scholarships ranged from 3,069 francs for the first (least needy) category, up to 6,417 francs for the seventh category, and from 6,417 francs for first-year graduate students, to 6,975 for those preparing for the *agrégation*. Those who served in the armed forces received an additional supplement; thus, for the first category, such an individual would receive no less than 4,603 francs, and for the seventh category no less than 8,653 francs. An attempt was made to keep up with inflation. While the first category received 1,386 francs in 1969, the amount almost tripled to 3,438 francs by 1977. For the seventh category, there was a 45 percent increase for that period, from 4,734 to 6,780 francs. Furthermore the percentage of students receiving the lowest sum, that is, those in the first category, declined from 20 percent of all students receiving scholarships in 1969 to 10.1 percent in 1976.[7]

Students holding scholarships received both direct and indirect aid. The latter came in the form of exemptions from fees of various sorts, and in the form of compensation for foregone income to their families. The total sum of direct aid, in 1974, for example, was 494 million francs ($100 million), but to that was added another 219 million francs in aid to families, thus totaling 713 million francs ($142 million). Table 11 shows only the sums allocated in direct aid to students. It should be noted that the table includes scholarships for all of higher education, of which approximately 90 percent were allocated to university students. Moreover, 84,500 scholarships out of 92,460 in 1977 were given to students on the basis of need, and the remainder on the basis of merit.

While there were 129,140 scholarship recipients in 1968, in 1977 there were 92,460. The number of recipients thus decreased by 29 percent, while the student population increased by about 33 percent during this period. Moreover, while about 20 percent of all students in higher education received scholarships in 1968, the percentage was reduced to

114

11 percent in 1977. The lower number of scholarship recipients does not necessarily indicate diminished response to student needs, for fewer scholarships went to less needy students while greater amounts went to those from lower income families. Thus, for example, in 1974-1975, 25 percent of the students receiving scholarships fell into the sixth category, but they received over 40 percent of the total money allocated for direct scholarships (200 million francs out of 494 million francs). In 1975-1976, 36.4 percent, and in 1977-1978, 47 percent of the students receiving scholarships fell into the sixth category.

In 1969, the Mallet Commission on student life criticized the scholarship system. The main criticisms were that the sums were often not large enough, that students still had to find work on the side, and that those given aid in the form of work-study often had to put in thirty hours a week as monitors in schools. Also, the scholarships did not take into account the need for repeating courses (in case of failure) and vacations. Students had to apply for their scholarships each year. Various groups made different proposals for payments of financial aid, but the commission recognized that the government was already extending itself to the best of its abilities. The Aigrin commission found the sums allotted to be too low, claiming that students needed about 6,000 francs a year to live on, instead of the average of 3,000 francs a year which was being given. On the basis of the 1975-1976 statistics, the median figure for the seven categories came to 4,743 francs ($948).[8] Whatever the shortcomings of the scholarship system, it seems that the French government was making efforts to increase the amount of aid given and to take into account the complex needs of families burdened with large responsibilities and small incomes. It was unable to serve those whose incomes were slightly above the category of "needy," and for whom it was still an immense sacrifice to attend an institution of higher education.

As was repeatedly pointed out by sociologists and politicians, scholarships were not the only remedy to the problem of democratization. So long as the university was a culture bound institution, some students would continue to be culturally disadvantaged. While more people from working and agricultural backgrounds attended a university in 1976 than in 1962, nevertheless they were still underrepresented in terms of their distribution in the national population[9] (table 6). The most recent analysis made by the bureau of statistics of the ministry of education revealed that there had been very little change in the social make-up of students at the university. There was a slight decrease in the number of sons of employers of industry and commerce, professionals, and senior and middle executives, and a modest increase of sons of workers and those in "other categories." But the shift was small; if one added up the numbers of those attending the university from the middle and upper social strata (sons of employers, professionals, and senior and middle executives), the result would be that in 1974-1975, 61 percent of the university population came from these categories, although they represented only 30.5 percent of the active population. While farmers and workers together represented at most 19.3 percent of the university population in 1974-1975, those categories represented a minimum of 49 percent of the active population.

In 1974-1975 statistics indicated that sons of workers and farmers tended to enter short-term study programs, such as the technological institutes, and were more represented in science and technological studies than in letters, while the sons of those in the upper social strata had about an equal proportion entering into both the sciences and the humanities. This latter group, moreover, was better represented in the professions of medicine, pharmacy, and dentistry (46.8 percent, 42.7 percent, and 46.7 percent respectively), compared to a very tiny group from the farm and working class, or, for that matter, from the middle management category.

The fact that the sons of the upper classes tended to enter these disciplines in much larger proportions was closely tied to the length of studies. The attrition rate was extremely high among the lower classes. For example, while workers' sons represented 14.9 percent of those in the first two years of university studies, they represented only 8 percent in graduate studies. While sons of the upper classes represented 28.9 percent of all those attending university in the first two years of university studies, they represented 39.3 percent of those in graduate studies.

While there was a slight increase in the numbers of working-class sons attending the university, the increase was not a result of the May 1968 crisis or of the reforms of higher education. The trend for greater democratization began in the 1960s. The proportion of workers' sons attending the university was 8.3 percent in 1964-1965, 11.1 in 1967-1968, and 12.6 in 1974-1975; thus, there was less of an increase in the five years after 1968 than there had been in the two years before. The increase in the proportion of workers' sons attending the university was complemented by a decrease in the proportion of the sons of employers (from 15.2 percent in 1964-1965 to 11.7 percent in 1974-1975), and a slight decrease in the proportion of the sons of the upper classes (from 34.5 percent in

116

CURRICULUM

1967-1968 to 32.9 percent in 1974-1975). In view of the large increase in numbers of students between 1964-1975, the small changes in percentages of the different classes attending do not appear to be significant.

There are discrepancies in the figures given for the student population from working-class backgrounds, but the proportion stood somewhere between 11 and 12 percent. Edgar Faure, in February 1969, said that he wanted to see the working-class recruitment average of 10 percent increased to 25 percent. In 1976, eight years after that wish was expressed, the recruitment had increased by 2 percent, and France was still only halfway toward the goal spelled out by the former minister of education.[10]

In 1968, the idea of open access was also supposed to mean unhindered admission to the university without any examination or requirements beyond the baccalauréat. But in 1971, an examination was instituted at the end of first-year medical studies; only those who passed could enter the medical school program. There was a huge uproar by medical students, but selection into this field remained a reality. The government also decided to restrict other professional studies, such as pharmacy.[11]

What seemed to make selection into the universities imperative was the increasing student enrollment, which severely stretched available resources (table 1). To compound the problem, a very large proportion of the students who entered the university did not finish. A ministry of education report in 1974 showed that the student success rate varied from 30 to 40 percent, depending on the discipline. Only that proportion was able to graduate within the time allotted in fields such as medicine (seven years) and pharmacy (five years), or for degrees such as the *licence* (three years), and the masters (four years). Measured by those criteria, success in the different disciplines varied as follows:

Letters	-40 percent
Law/economics	-30-35 percent
Medicine	-33 percent
Dentistry	-39 percent
Pharmacy	-40 percent
Sciences	-40 percent

The dropout rate in the first year of studies was anywhere from 50 to 60 percent. There were many reasons for dropping out, but the main ones were financial. Studies in 1974 and again in 1978, not surprisingly, also found that most of those who left the university came from economically modest backgrounds.[12]

117

One remedy for the enormous waste due to the large dropout rate was to change the baccalauréat so that it would no longer guarantee automatic entry into the university. Ministers of education Joseph Fontanet, and, after him, René Haby, attempted to draft plans for reforming the function of the baccalauréat. The Haby reforms recommended that the baccalauréat be granted at the end of the next to the last year of secondary studies, leaving those who wished to attend the university the chance to pass examinations for each area of specialty at the end of the last year of secondary studies (similar to the British system of advanced level examinations). Success on those examinations would then open the door to the university. Although the Haby reforms became law in 1975, they were not made applicable with regard to the most important aspect: the changing of the baccalauréat from its double role of marking the end of secondary studies and giving automatic entry into a university.

Those favoring a more rigorous selection procedure into the universities presented several arguments: that the students were ill-prepared for university studies, that *sélection* would at least ensure university graduates employment, that Britain had half as many students as France but graduated the same number. If France could select its students, it could also have the same rate of "success." Others argued that the U.S. practiced selection through the SAT tests and that 85 percent of the universities practiced a combination of selection methods, while 20 percent of them made entrance very difficult. Japan also had entrance examinations into the universities, and in 1970 only 17 percent of those who applied were admitted, compared to 25 percent in 1968. Germany too introduced a "numerus clausus" and stringent regulations regarding the length of studies in order to curb the growing number of students. Sweden had rigorous entrance requirements, and in 1970 only 25 percent of the applicants were admitted, compared to 40 percent in 1960. One French deputy in the national assembly declared in 1971: "We are the only country in the world which does not utilize control for entry into the university. The U.S., Russia and China utilize methods of control."[13] Table 4 indicates the average length of university studies in seventeen countries and shows that France had a lower success rate than most.

The resistance to selection led to a continuous growth in the number of students attending French universities. While the rate of increase slowed considerably in the 1970s, the number of students continued to grow, thereby making heavy demands on the state's resources (table 14). Many saw no other solution for the French university problem than the

118

institution of some selection criteria. These people recognized very well that while other countries practiced selection methods, they offered other alternatives for their young people. The British system had alternative short-term programs and technical institutes; the U.S. system had different types of universities, and particularly the community colleges, as well as "open universities" and continuing education programs. In France, IUTs, founded in 1966, were seen as possible alternatives to long university study, but they had limited success.

Technological Institutes

Students attending the French technological institutes (Instituts universitaires de technologie, IUTs) represented 5.3 percent of all students attending universities and IUTs. They represented about 16.2 percent of all first-year students. Attendance for 1976-1977 was 44,243 out of a total of 821,591 students.[14] Students were not attracted to the IUTs for several reasons. First, technical studies in France had always been given an inferior place in the values of the society, and it was difficult, in a period of ten years, to overturn those values. Second, the two-year diploma given by these institutions was not favored by employers, even though students had vociferously demanded that the government take measures to give the diploma greater recognition in the job market. Third, those who obtained the diploma, called a DUT (diplôme universitaire de technologie) could not automatically continue university studies if they so decided. The law that founded the IUTs in 1966 had specified that only 15 percent of IUT graduates could enter upper division studies at the university. The transfer from the IUT to other institutions was not as easy as it was from an American community college to a four-year college. Fourth, the upper classes were satisfied with the system as it stood, since they themselves had a vested interest in keeping the present selective mechanism in operation, thereby ensuring their sons and daughters of entrance into the elite institutions.[15] The leaders of France were graduates of the grandes écoles, not the universities, and they were not about to abolish a system which they claimed worked well.

Countries that used selection procedures to maintain the high quality of an education at Ox-bridge, Tokyo-Kyoto, or the Ivy League schools still provided alternatives to those who did not enter these institutions. In France, alternatives were much more restricted by class at earlier

119

stages than was the case in the U.S., so that while selection took place in the U.S., it was done within a context of alternatives. Universities had varying admission standards. A student made his choice of an institution on the basis of geographic location, financial resources, and on the basis of a university's, or even a department's area of specialization. The student who entered a junior or community college was not prevented from excelling there and entering a university. But in France, if selection to the universities were instituted in the form of an entrance examination, these alternatives would not be present, nor could they be made available without loud objections from many sectors. If an institution established its own selection methods, it would lead to some universities having higher admission standards than others. This would be against the French concept of *égalité* and against the tradition that education was a public service. Moreover, it would go against the French educational tradition of relative geographical immobility for undergraduate students, who usually attended the nearest university.

Undergraduate Curriculum Reform

The large number of students at the universities and the lack of job outlets for them were of concern to the government in the early 1970s. In 1973, Joseph Fontanet, the minister of education, developed plans for a two-year diploma known as the DEUG (*diplôme d'études universitaires générales*). The introduction of a new two-year diploma in major areas was opposed by the students, who feared that it spelled *sélection* for further university studies. Fontanet promised, however, that the new diploma would not mean restriction into further upper-level studies. Its purpose was, first, to give students more of an opportunity to discover their aptitudes before going on for further study; second, it was designed to introduce more multidisciplinary programs; and third, it gave a certain amount of autonomy to the universities with regard to curriculum planning.[16]

The ministry of education emphasized the DEUG as a degree preparing for practical employment, but it was little more than an interim degree in the middle of university studies, which enabled some upper-level programs to put restrictions on the number of students they admitted. The new diploma spelled out the distribution requirements in the fields of law-economics, economic and social administration, humanities, applied mathematics, social sciences, and sciences. In most

CURRICULUM

cases, the central administration set requirements for approximately 45 to 60 percent of the curriculum, the universities set requirements for about 20 percent, and the students could choose from 10 to 15 percent as electives.[17] The reorganization of the first two years of university study was considered a step toward fulfilling the 1968 call for an overhaul of the curriculum. Fontanet had accomplished that, and it was left to Jean-Pierre Soisson to reform the rest of the university program.

Soisson introduced a plan in 1975, whose thrust was to "professionalize" the upper division curriculum. This suggestion immediately produced a loud outcry that this would "fasten the hold of big business" on the universities. Students feared that the new professionally oriented programs, which they had incessantly demanded since May 1968, would in fact mean restricted admissions. Some of the new master's programs in science and technology, which were developed in 1975-1976, had a limited number of spaces. Slightly more advanced programs granting intermediary graduate degrees, such as the DEA, *diplôme d'études approfondi* emphasizing research and the DESS, *diplôme d'études supérieures specialisées*, stressing professional training, also restricted the number of applicants. In January 1976, a group of students went on strike when told that there were not enough places for them to register.[18]

The strike spread on many campuses, in Nantes, Rennes, Tours, Toulouse, Paris, and several IUTs. Faculty and student unions helped organize the strikes. By April 1976, 20,000 students were demonstrating in the streets of Paris, and 1,500 in Strasbourg; altogether it was estimated that 100,000 students demonstrated in mid-April. The helmeted police, the molotov cocktails, the tear gas, the police vans and the students in the streets conjured visions of another May 1968. The strikes lasted longer than they had in 1968; more students struck for more days than during any other university strike in French history. And it was the third time in a period of ten years that students had organized against the introduction of curriculum changes that they deemed senseless (1966, 1968, and 1976).

Giscard d'Estaing, the French president, said that students were concerned about job outlets, and that was why the reform of the university curriculum had to be put into effect. The purpose of the reform, he emphasized, was to prepare students at the university for jobs. His argument was not convincing. Professors as well as faculty and student unions opposed the changes on several grounds. The programs would be introduced without additional funds forthcoming for the universities. This meant that the universities would have to abandon traditional

121

programs for the new professionally oriented ones. Many professors felt that their academic liberties were threatened, while university presidents worried about implementing such an immense overhaul without any additional funds. Students worried about access to these programs.[19]

Alice Saunier-Seité, the secretary for university affairs, inherited from Soisson the reform of the curriculum and had to ensure its application. Upon arrival on the job early in 1976, she was immediately faced with student unrest. She stood firmly by the curriculum reorganization plan of her predecessor and stated that its application was a commitment to the law of 1968. She announced, however, that she would not proceed with its application until she had studied the matter further. This was a face-saving gesture and an attempt to get the students off the streets and back to the classroom. Ministerial decrees followed in 1977, calling for implementation of the curriculum reorganization. But, as one president said, "the reform of 1976 has been put into effect by ministerial decrees, but remains a dead letter as far as the universities are concerned."[20]

Although it was clear from conversations with university staff and students that no one quite understood what the curriculum reorganization plan for upper division studies was all about, the plan did attempt to indicate to the universities that they must change their programs to include more professional training. The plan also included more restrictions regarding student transfers from one university to another, by giving the universities the right to decide their own requirements. Universities could establish their own regulations for granting credit for work done in other institutions. The ministry further antagonized the university community by stating that the new programs to be devised by the individual universities would have to be approved, not only by CNESER, but also by specialized commissions whose members would be appointed by the secretariat.

The new curricular reform plan made the university community nervous, because it left matters undefined. The principle of university autonomy was forgotten in the face of potentially more stringent selection procedures. The cutoff was to occur not at entry to the university, but after the obtention of the DEUG. Moreover, the new plan seemed to be trying to restrict the mobility of students. The faculty was nervous because it might have to teach subjects for which it was unprepared. And all these transformations were to be carried out to provide training for jobs which might never exist. Most importantly the experts had failed to outline what jobs were needed in the employment market. The government shunted the responsibility to the universities,

CURRICULUM

stating that they would have to decide what training was needed. Yet the universities had no clearer idea than the government or the experts.

Relevance of the Curriculum

In France in May 1968, "relevance" was the key word for curriculum innovation, as it was in the U.S. and elsewhere. In the 1960s, an attempt was made to introduce Centres hospitaliers universitaires, to enable the medical schools to combine theory and practice in medical studies.[21] After May 1968, small attempts were made to introduce other such programs in the university curriculum. At Lille, twenty first-year students from each of the three Lille universities began a program whereby they worked for four months in a business firm in the region.[22]

The Lille program was the first experiment of this kind. A year earlier at Rennes, a colloquium discussed "alternate programs" that had developed in other countries. It was argued that such programs should be introduced into law, social sciences, economics, and teacher training. In 1969, the French paid close attention to the planning of the Open University in Britain, which began its broadcasts in January 1971. In France, an elaborate system of radio broadcasts developed in several regions, and correspondence courses were offered.[23]

In the university curriculum experimental programs flourished dealing with the history of the cinema, contemporary esthetic expression for theater and cinema, women studies, urban studies combining geography and computer science, and sex education. New programs developed in business administration and management. Several Instituts d'administration des entreprises were formed within universities to teach business administration; unfortunately, they drew hostility from the universities to which they were attached, because their teaching staffs saw themselves as pioneers in their efforts to make contact with the economic sector. Students seemed attracted to these programs wherever they were offered. Business administration was taught at the Centre Dauphine in Paris and at the University of Compiègne, founded in 1973. American business schools were much admired in France in the 1960s and the desire to emulate them was evident.

There were other innovations. Educational research was developed at Paris V and Paris VIII in particular. At Paris VII efforts were made to facilitate the transfer of students from one line of study to another without the obstacles that students usually encountered when they

123

wished to transfer. Attempts were made to combine programs, for instance, grouping linguistics with psychology, or physics with pathology of language and acoustics. Special efforts were made to make the first two years of study multidisciplinary, by bringing together medicine and psychology, medicine and biological sciences, mathematics and human sciences, and environmental studies and sociology.

Attempts to develop new programs at the master's degree level in technical and professional areas were made at other universities. At Dauphine, a two-year master's program was offered in applied economics; master's degrees in computer sciences were available in some of the Paris universities, Grenoble, and Toulouse. The number of places was limited, and, in 1970, 600 students applied for 250 places in Paris.[24]

New master's degrees were given in the area of communications for different professions: personnel services, adult education, group leadership, editing, public relations, and personnel relations for business. A new two-year program was organized for interpreters and translators; others were founded in leadership training for recreation and cultural centers. Paris I introduced a master's degree in the history of cinema. Paris V and Paris VII coordinated to provide a two-year undergraduate diploma (the DUEL, which was suppressed in favor of the DEUG in 1974) in human sciences and mathematics, with one language required. Paris VII offered a diploma in clinical psychology (a university diploma that gave the student great latitude in the choice of courses), a DUEL in environmental studies, and a graduate degree (DEA) in basic geochemistry. A DUEL and a master's degree in the plastic arts were also a new addition to the curriculum.

According to some reports, the new programs faced difficulties and encountered obstacles at various levels whenever they were introduced. On the whole the central administration denied funding to universities who wanted to establish ambitious programs, to become, in the words of one official in Paris, "another Sorbonne." "If we accept all the requests for music programs, France would produce 20,000 musicologists a year; what would we do with them?" he demanded.[25]

Continuing Education

Among the promising new developments was the attempt to expand continuing education. In the 1960s, the call for adult or continuing education was universal. In the U.S., there was an upsurge in the devel-

124

opment of these programs, particularly in the state universities and community colleges. In Britain the Open University was established in 1971, and the French were very much aware of both these developments. In early 1968, at the Colloque d'Amiens, Pierre Mendès-France had said, "the renovation of our eductional system can be realized only in the development of continuing education." Later that year, Edgar Faure, in his early draft of the reform law, described the program as "a second chance" for people to continue their education (the phrase was deleted from the final draft of the law).[26]

Financing these programs was often a problem. A law was introduced in 1971, which required all employers who employed more than ten people to pay the equivalent of 1 percent of all salaries for the training of their employees. The government also encouraged the founding of special centers by giving 150,000-250,000 francs to each university to study local needs for a continuing education program. Such programs faced difficulties in organizing classes outside the regular class hours, finding competent personnel, developing programs, acquiring materials and lodging, and developing courses of a professional nature as well as courses by correspondence, radio, and television. Expenditures on continuing education programs at the university level was 98.7 million francs in 1976 ($20 million) out of a total higher education budget of 8,375.7 million francs ($1,700 million).[27]

Development of continuing education took place in certain universities, such as Paris X (Nanterre), Paris VII (Jussieu), Paris VIII (Vincennes), Paris IX (Dauphine), and Toulouse. The program at Nanterre began with 300 students in 1968, but grew by 1974 to more than 2,000 participants. The financing of the program came from many sources, including the university budget, employers, and contracts with business and industry. The programs varied in their thrust, depending on the clientele; some were designed to help those already in executive positions to improve their situation, while others were specifically designed for workers, senior citizens, housewives, young people, and auditors.[28]

After 1968, those universities definitely committed to the development of adult education struggled to maintain their programs. At Nanterre, where it was not always clear whether the program could continue from one year to the next, it did so in the face of many obstacles. The struggle for sufficient space was constant, as was the problem of interesting teaching faculty from different UERs to participate. Apparently, only pressure from the unions made some UERs (history, English, and sociology) participate. There were problems with the teaching staff since

125

CURRICULUM

not all belonged to the official teaching corps. Some were employed from the business world and did not have the qualifications to teach. The program at the Centre Dauphine in 1974 had a total teaching staff of seven, of whom three were part-time and only one was from the regular faculty (a faculty member released from other teaching duties).[29]

For the most part, all sources agreed that adult, or continuing education, had been far less developed in France than in the U.S., or Great Britain, and that the effort on the university level had been modest. The largest effort was made in institutions outside the university and by private business, and most of the funding was done by private sources, not by the state. The latter, at times, even placed financial restrictions on universities wishing to cooperate with a municipality in offering courses.

Once out of office, Edgar Faure voiced concern in his memoirs over the limited access that working people had to education. This theme was reiterated in October 1974, by a colloquium at Rennes attended by the directors of continuing education programs in the universities. Any success continuing education had had was mostly outside university structures, while in the U.S. and Great Britain it was taking place within these establishments.[30]

The Experimental Universities
Vincennes

The ambitious plans for changing the French universities in 1968 involved the opening of experimental universities. Each new institution was to have a personality of its own. Many centers were planned in 1968 and opened during the 1970s — Antony, Luminy, and Villetaneuse — but the most important ones were Vincennes, which had about 80 percent of its students in letters, and Dauphine, which was oriented toward business administration. Vincennes was located in the woody suburbs east of Paris, and Dauphine in the abandoned North Atlantic Treaty Organization building west of the city. Vincennes was intended mostly for adults and working people who wished to improve their education and embark on a degree program; it welcomed students who did not possess the secondary school diploma. Dauphine, by contrast, restricted its admission policies. Each university was to introduce small classes, improve faculty-student relations, and work out a totally new method of teaching and examinations. While students with degrees in letters were

126

CURRICULUM

flooding the market, it was generally supposed that individuals with administrative skills for the developing industrial and commercial sectors were still in demand. Only the selective Ecoles de commerce supplied these administrators. Dauphine was also given that responsibility, followed by Paris I and Grenoble, which granted masters degrees in administration.[31]

Vincennes (Paris VIII) was to be the model of the multidisciplinary university. It was the place where freedom of expression would truly exist, and where flexibility in the curriculum would be unlike anything that had yet existed in the French universities. "Progressive" students and faculty flocked there in support of this ideal. When it opened its doors in January 1969, it already had 8,000 students registered; the buildings were designed to provide for 7,000 students. There were 240 faculty members (a ratio of 1 to 33).[32]

Vincennes gave people without a baccalauréat easier access than any other French university. In 1974, 34 percent, and in 1977 42 percent of the students did not have a baccalauréat. Of the 30,000 students at Vincennes in 1975-1976, 41 percent worked full time, and 27 percent part-time. Students who did not possess a baccalauréat could register on condition that they were twenty-one years old and had worked two years, or were twenty-four years old and had taken an oral examination for entry. An examination committee would determine the level and the program to be pursued. In other universities, students who did not have a baccalauréat had to take the traditional written examinations if they wished to pursue university studies. Students without a baccalauréat could, upon being admitted, take the equivalent of six U.S. credit hours as deficiency credit, and once they passed the courses, they could then dispense with the baccalauréat and continue their university studies. In France as a whole, 12 percent of the students (110,000) entered the university without the baccalauréat in 1977. Vincennes had hoped to be an example to other universities, but found that during the 1970s it had to educate a disproportionate number of students without a secondary school diploma. This was a heavy burden on its budget.[33]

Vincennes was authorized to work out its own curriculum requirements and its own examination structures. This led to conflicts with the ministry over the granting of national diplomas when the ministry felt it could not approve the departmental organization of teaching or examinations in certain programs. Hence, the famous case of the philosophy department where a *licence* from that department was not recognized by the ministry of education; the ministry was quick to send out circulars

CURRICULUM

warning employers of some diplomas. The ministry did not approve of the manner in which examinations were conducted in philosophy and felt that the list of courses did not cover the full area of knowledge that one would expect from a *licence*. Other conflicts with the ministry developed. Guichard had indicated that the *licence* from Vincennes ought to have the equivalent of sixty U.S. credit hours out of ninety in the major areas, whereas Vincennes had decided to reduce that to forty-eight credit hours. This governmental action greatly angered students, who argued that the ministry was trying to make Vincennes a traditional university.[34] In spite of the proclaimed autonomy of the universities, the ministry continued to meddle with Vincennes, imposing regulations on admissions, on diplomas, and on curriculum. Approval of programs for national diplomas at Vincennes was held up for bureaucratic reasons, leading to student and administrative frustration.[35]

While on the one hand, the government attempted to follow the advice of many educational conferences (the OECD, UNESCO and others), on opening education to the masses, on the other hand, it felt that it must protect the quality of the national diploma. The government and the Orientation Act of 1968 had made a commitment that individuals without a baccalauréat could accede to higher education, yet circulars and decrees gave with the one hand and tended to take away with the other.

Many of the regular programs were inter- and/or multidisciplinary, and led to specific professions, such as recreation and cultural leadership training, documentation, or cartography. The departments in education science and urbanism also attracted students. The departments of theater, cinema, music, and the plastic arts altogether drew 40 to 50 percent of all students. Psychology saw a large increase in enrollments. Various government agencies, such as the postal, telephone and telegraph administration, and the social security service, sent their personnel to acquire degrees in psychology. The number of students in the traditional disciplines decreased because students were more attracted to the new type of courses.

Vincennes' multidisciplinary programs were criticized and called "enseignement à la carte" (education from a menu). Without admission requirements, Vincennes seemed to have a disproportionate number of students with little motivation or sense of discipline. But Vincennes did have the merit of allowing access to higher education — for people who otherwise would not have had this opportunity. The university was also in the vanguard of innovative and multidisciplinary teaching of the type

128

CURRICULUM

Faure had discussed in 1968.[36]

Vincennes had financial problems; since its founding it has declared itself on the brink of bankruptcy every year. Michel Beaud, its young, energetic first president, resigned in 1971, accusing the ministry of putting a stranglehold on the experimental institution. The faculty-student ratio worsened with the influx of students. By 1975, President Frioux claimed that in more than ten departments, the ratio had climbed to 1 to 150, or even 1 to 200 students. Apparently the institute of urbanism had 450 students and thirteen faculty members in 1970, and in November 1975 had 3,500 students and twenty-four faculty.[37]

In the face of great obstacles — interference in its curriculum from the ministry and the lack of material and financial means necessary to teach and lodge 30,000 students — Vincennes continued to be a novelty in the French university system, and to appeal to young people and to many faculty members who fought hard to build a new type of university.

A study group was established by the ministry to investigate the situation in Vincennes. The group included professors from Paris III, Paris XII, Dijon, and Dauphine, and in January 1975, it gave a positive report, indicating that the university's mission was accomplished. It praised the great diversity in the curriculum, the flexibility in transferring from one line of study to another, and the introduction of innovative courses (although the commission frowned upon the teaching of sexology, which had been banned by Soisson). The commission declared that the manner in which examinations were handled did not indicate that Vincennes was more lax than other universities, nor was the dropout rate any different. The financial situation did not at first appear any more delicate than at other universities, but the committee voiced the hope that there would be a fairer way of dividing up the funds among the universities. For example, certain programs that were very important for Vincennes, such as urban studies, psychology, and the arts, were given the same funds as other disciplines in the humanities, whereas in fact these programs were much more expensive. The introduction of costly and sophisticated teaching materials required expensive maintenance and therefore strained the small budget usually allotted to the humanities. Moreover the school had to be open longer hours to accommodate the large number of evening class students, another circumstance that required additional funding.

The Commission expressed confidence in Vincennes, but its future was by no means assured. In 1977, the conservative Paris city council envisaged terminating the lease on the land on which Vincennes was

CURRICULUM

located. The government seemed to approve of this eviction and considered transferring the university to Marne-la-Vallée, even further outside of Paris. It stressed the importance of making the university "relevant" to the needs of this developing community.[38] Although the government has not carried out the dislodging process, this could potentially be an alibi for dismantling or discouraging the more experimental programs of the university and for making it more conformist in both its programs and political coloration.

Dauphine

Bertrand Girod de l'Ain, a faculty member at the new business administration university and a columnist on education in *Le Monde*, vividly described those first days in the autumn of 1968 at the old NATO building, which was being remodeled to become an educational institution. Where once foreign functionaries rode the elevators, Algerian workers carried blocks of cement for the remodeling of the offices into classrooms. Equipment for simultaneous translations was left by NATO, and the new university had thirty-three new language laboratories. In the place of the restaurant on the sixth floor, the new library was set up to seat 1,000: "for once, a university has the right number of library spaces in proportion to its student body," wrote Girod de l'Ain.

Dauphine was planned for 5,000 students; it was to be a thematic university devoted to business administration. The new university was to introduce a curriculum designed to equip the future executive with modern techniques of administration. The curriculum was intended to be multidisciplinary, but this approach "is not a simple problem and contacts are often very difficult to establish," as Girod de l'Ain said. While classes were to be small, with twenty-five instead of 1,000 students, problems remained. In 1968, for 4,000 students, there were twenty-one professors, twenty-two *maîtres de conférences*, 100 *assistants*, which was an overall ratio of 1 to 29. But according to Girod de l'Ain, faculty members did not revamp their courses to suit twenty-five students, and instead taught in the same way as they had for 1,000 students. The small study rooms provided for students were eventually turned into faculty offices, thus depriving students of a valuable meeting place. But Dauphine did introduce some innovations; for instance, field projects were instituted, which gave students practical experience and allowed contact with the outside world. Dauphine boasted a continuing

CURRICULUM

education division which offered teaching in English and economics. It established liaisons with the social service agencies to retrain hospital administrators, and with the Commission centrale des marchés de l'état (an interministerial organ attached to the ministry of finance) to conduct consumer studies on a number of projects.[39]

The development of experimental institutions such as Vincennes and Dauphine (and Compiègne, another thematic university founded in 1973 as a university of technology and labeled "the prototype of the universities of the third generation") indicates that after 1968 France made efforts to introduce new programs relevant to the economy and its needs. It sought to introduce new teaching methods based on small classes and on field assignments. While these efforts were not all totally successful and did not revolutionize the educational system, they injected a little diversity into it. These institutions involved only a small proportion of French students; in 1976, Vincennes had 31,996, Dauphine 5,550, Compiègne 743, and Mulhouse 1,752 students. Moreover, several factors vitiated the experimental nature of these universities: first, the efforts of the universities themselves to gain national diplomas for as many of their programs as possible, so that they might more closely resemble the other universities; second, the burden of open admissions was relegated to one institution; and thirdly, the negative attitude of the central government toward the largest of these institutions, Vincennes.[40]

Faculty-Student Relations

While the experimental universities sought to provide special settings for innovation and curriculum, the Orientation Act of 1968 aimed to renovate the learning process in all universities. The law attempted to improve teaching methods and faculty-student relations in general. The *cours magistral* was abolished, the examination system changed, and the credit hour concept introduced. Small classes and practical work were to be given priority, and teamwork was to be encouraged in the classroom. By abolishing the chair system, the lawmakers hoped that the hierarchical nature of faculty relations would be broken down; a more collegial community of students and scholars would then emerge, with both groups cooperating democratically in the various councils in which students, teachers of all ranks, and even lay persons served. The decade following passage of the law demonstrated that the *cours magistraux* system continued to exist alongside small classes. In Vincennes, where a

131

supreme effort was made to introduce small classes, the influx of students made the teaching of small classes nearly impossible, and there was a growing tendency to depend on the large lecture classes.

The largest proportional increase of students had occurred before 1968 and this made it difficult for the universities to improve the faculty-student ratio (see table 8 for faculty-student ratio 1951-1977). The average faculty-student ratio was reduced from a high of 1 to 46.3 in 1951 to 1 to 24.5 in 1960. In 1967, it was 1 to 22.5, and little change has occurred since then. The best it ever was thereafter was 1 to 18.2 in 1970-1971. These ratios represented an average, and many disciplines, such as letters, economics, and law, continued to suffer from poor faculty-student ratios, while the sciences and medical professions were better endowed.

Faculty-student ratios varied by universities. In 1969-1970, for example, Orléans had a notably better ratio than Reims. The reasons for these differences may lie in the number of students in particular disciplines. In 1969-1970, Orléans had an impressive faculty-student ratio, but one-third of its students were in medicine (2,400 out of 7,627) and an additional 1,700 students in sciences. Reims had 1,100 students in medicine and 1,700 in sciences out of 8,992 students.[41]

Quality education is judged partly on the basis of faculty-student ratio, but good teaching remains a quality that is difficult to measure. Abolishing the *cours magistraux* did not necessarily improve teaching. Some pointed out that faculty continued to give the same lectures that they gave to large classes to the small classes and did not adapt themselves to the small class concept. As in the U.S., teaching was relegated to second place, after research; the eminent faculty were the ones who had published. They were the ones later acclaimed and rewarded by an "invisible community" of scholars. As one critic said,

> The candidates for professorship are by definition individuals who have published. I have participated for fifteen years in dozens of elections in the Sorbonne: I can affirm that all [decisions] were made on the basis of the candidates' publications and the reports made on them.[42]

In 1974, a poll quoted students as being disgruntled about faculty-student relations:

> As before 1968, we never see him, said a student in history.
> As before '68, he does not know us. He continues to give

CURRICULUM

cours magistraux "en amphi" [in amphitheatres]. It is always their *assistants* who make us work.

Some of the fault rested with the students who remained reticent even when offered the opportunity to participate more actively in the classroom. Students, interviewed in 1972, 1975, and 1977, who participated in classes where the instructor tried to introduce discussion, found them dull and unrewarding. Manuals and xerox copies of the *cours magistraux* continued to be printed, so that theoretically students did not even have to attend class. Absenteeism was high. In the *cours magistraux*, student heckling was common and sometimes approached riotous behavior. Often this did not denote particular hostility toward the professor, but rather seemed part of a ritual.[43]

The law had intended the creation of a university community on a human scale, in order to improve interpersonal relations. This was far from the case in French universities, and was even less true of Paris than of the smaller provincial universities. To encourage better contacts between students and faculty, the law required faculty members to reside in the area of their university. This regulation was not enforced because it was nearly impossible to do so, although one faculty member pointed out that the practice of living away from one's university was not as rampant as believed. He said that a poll taken at a university close to Paris, reputed to have the highest number of nonresident faculty, showed that 350 professors (70 percent) were residents in the area. At any rate, it was difficult to define the area adjacent to a university. It took two hours to get to most of the universities on the outskirts of Paris. Was Paris to be the residential center for the outlying region? The law seemed arbitrary. One faculty member wrote that most teachers had two duties — teaching and research. Since there were no research facilities in many provincial towns (and especially for IUT faculty members), the faculty had to work out some arrangement whereby they could be in proximity to facilities in Paris. An historian at Clermont-Ferrand wrote that since he needed the libraries for his research, it was easier to take the train to the university and live where the documents were. The residency requirements, according to Fourrier, were "a timid return to the concept of the university for the student as it was in the Ancien Regime and as it is now in Anglo-Saxon countries." Under the regime of Alice Saunier-Seité, secretary and later minister of university affairs, there was a tightening of residency regulations. The town and its suburbs were listed, and faculty who did not live within those boundaries could not

133

expect to be covered by workmen's compensation in case of accident en route to and from their university.[44]

The patron system continued. Although the chair system had been abolished, it was reinstituted because of tradition and because the rights and privileges of those who had held chairs were not abolished. These professors moved to various universities based on political and philosophical grounds, where they had their own clan. In many cases they became directors of UERs and sometimes presidents of universities. Many of them sat on the national faculty recruitment committee, the CCU. After 1968, some grew discouraged by the situation, and resigned or became inactive in university affairs. But, as Capelle pointed out, the patron system was as feudal as before; the balkanization of departments in some cases gave the patrons even greater powers, making them even bigger fish in an even smaller pond.[45]

The malaise of the younger teaching faculty, the *assistants*, *maîtres-assistants*, and contractual staff, did not subside. Many of them were on the *liste d'aptitude* for higher posts, but in the meantime, they continued to do the work of a professor without the same privileges. They continued to feel that they were in vassalage to the professors. They wanted a new statute to define their position, since the responsibilities of *assistants* and *maîtres-assistants* varied from one discipline to another. The *maîtres-assistants* were also anxious because of a ministerial plan to unite *assistants* and *maîtres-assistants* into one rank. The latter naturally wanted a gurantee that they could at least preserve their function and their better prospects for access to the rank of *maître de conférences*.

In the academic year 1968-1969, a large proportion of new faculty were hired, 25 percent more than in 1967. Such a dramatic increase was not unprecedented, however, for even higher rates of increase had occurred in 1960 and 1962. Once the initial increase occurred in 1968, the rate of growth decelerated, which may in part have reflected the slowdown in the growth of the student population. While more faculty have been recruited in all ranks since 1968, the proportionate representation of each rank remained approximately the same until 1976 (table 7).

Critics charged that the bottom of the pyramid was growing larger. While in fact the bottom level widened in real numbers, the proportion of *assistants* was nevertheless reduced. They represented 49 percent in 1967-1968, but in 1975-1976 they were 47.7 percent; by 1976-1977 the percentage was down to 37 percent of the total faculty. Until 1976, the number of *maîtres-assistants* and *maîtres de conférences* grew at a rate

134

that preserved their relative proportions, but in 1976 upward mobility changed the balance of the ranks. As the secretary of university affairs said, describing what a graph of ranks might look like, it was not "a pyramid, but a pagoda."[46]

Several ministerial commissions reported on faculty conditions and made suggestions for improvement. The Grégoire report (1972) submitted to Guichard was considered so earthshaking that it was never published. It was followed by the Baecque report (1974), commissioned by Fontanet and not published until the arrival of Soisson to the ministry in June 1974. The report suggested improving the mobility of faculty and limiting local recruitment. It tried to abolish the secretiveness of the CCU decisions that placed faculty on the *liste d'aptitude*. For those appointed on a contractual basis and those not in tenured spots, the report suggested the possiblity of integrating them into the teaching corps. It recommended that *maîtres-assistants* teach only six hours a week, and that professors who taught only three hours should in addition take on a laboratory or discussion section. The Grégoire report had gone further in the direction of giving the universities total autonomy in deciding how many hours its faculty was expected to teach. The Baecque report also recommended that teaching positions be advertised to ensure real competition in the recruitment of faculty by the universities; it suggested that the role of the CCU was to guarantee high quality among the faculty, but that the university council would have the last word in deciding actual recruitment. The report recommended that faculty be allowed to take leaves of absence and still be guaranteed their positions. Finally, it recommended that the standing of faculty and researchers be equalized to enable interchange between the two groups. But, in 1978, the new statute for faculty called for by Edgar Faure in the National Assembly in 1968 still had not emerged.[47]

In 1977, promotions were conferred on an unprecedented number of *maîtres de conférences* who became professors and on *assistants* who became *maîtres-assistants*. Fewer *assistants* were hired, however, presumably to reduce the usual pressure from below for new faculty positions. But these kinds of promotions could not continue, and faculty feared that their careers would be blocked. In 1976-1977, only 200 professors retired, and the same situation was foreseen up through the mid-1980s. The number of new positions in all ranks had progressively diminished: there had been 1,467 in 1973; 1,055 in 1974; 203 in 1975; 275 in 1976; and 75 in 1977.[48]

The chances for promotion, or even initial appointment, lessened

135

CURRICULUM

towards the end of the 1970s but for those who had a faculty position, the remuneration was attractive. Monthly faculty salaries in 1976-1977 ranged as follows:[49]

Professor	:	7,500-12,158 francs	($1,500-$2,400)
Maître de conférences	:	5,811- 8,000	($1,200-$1,600)
Maître-assistant	:	3,713- 7,260	($ 750-$1,500)
Assistant	:	3,000- 4,200	($ 600-$ 850)

Faculty Recruitment and Promotion

Chapter three dealt with the importance of the CCU, a national recruitment and promotions committee for the appointment of university faculty. It was noted that the CCU was founded in 1945 in part to prevent haphazard recruitment of faculty by an incompetent organ in the ministry of education. The CCU, with a membership of university professors, was the regulatory organ at the national level, which certified candidates as eligible for consideration by universities for faculty appointments or promotions. The committee came under fire in 1968 for inbreeding and inadequacies in its structural system.

It was controlled by the mandarins or patrons of the universities. These members had a mandate for three to four years and could be reelected to the committee by people whom they had helped appoint. These shortcomings persisted in 1978. It had been suggested that members of the CCU should not be reeligible; in fact article 31 of the Orientation Act of 1968 stated that anyone who served on a national organ dealing with faculty careers could not be immediately reeligible. The law was disregarded.

The criteria for selecting faculty for the national list had to be reviewed, because the 1968 law, which gave autonomy to the universities, also gave the faculty administrative tasks which they had not performed earlier. The notion of "service" was at first not taken into account in career promotions; the CCU had judged a candidate purely on research qualifications.

After 1968, many dedicated faculty members worked hard in applying the law and participating on the new university committees, but they did not receive career rewards for their efforts. This was particularly discouraging to young faculty. While in American universities a *modus vivendi* had been worked out, whereby promotion and tenure were based on the three criteria of research, teaching, and service, in France, the

136

CURRICULUM

notion of service was an entirely new development after 1968 and was not officially recognized by the CCU. But, beginning in 1977, steps were taken to redress the situation. Thereafter, candidates for the national list had to submit three files, one each for research, teaching, and service; they were then to be judged separately for each function. But, as one president said in an interview, "whether the CCU will take note of the teaching and service is hard to tell."

The outdated organizational structures of the CCU, set up as five divisions corresponding to the *facultés* (law, letters, medicine, pharmacy, and science), were seriously in need of change, in order to be more in line with the new disciplines that had emerged since the 1960s. In 1969, the CCU was reorganized. Instead of the five disciplines, forty-seven sections emerged, which corresponded to disciplines and took into account some of the new fields such as sociology, education, thermodynamics, and electronics. In 1972, the number of sections was increased to forty-nine. Each section consisted of three colleges of elected, tenured members: 1) professors and *maîtres de conférences*, 2) *maîtres-assistants*, and 3) *assistants*. Besides the 1,200 elected members, the ministry appointed 400 more, making a total of 1,600 members. Also in 1972, the size of each subsection was reduced from twenty-four to twelve members, depending on the section. This move was criticized because it meant that those who served on a section also sat on the recruiting committees in the universities and thus would have too much power. They would serve at both the nominating and the controlling end. Moreover, candidates in new disciplines, such as computer science, biochemistry, urbanism, or technological or pedagogical research encountered serious difficulties. An individual who had done research in the pedagogy of mathematics had to win the approval of both the mathematics and literary sections, thus being subjected to double scrutiny. The CCU was accused of putting restraints on original research and encouraging traditional research that could be more easily evaluated. Sometimes it refused to consider work that belonged to two fields of study. An individual, who had completed a *doctorat de 3ème cycle* on the Austrian poet Trackl and German expressionism, was not placed on the national list even though the sociology section of the CCU said that his work was excellent, but it claimed that the topic fell in the area of aesthetics. The philosophy section of the CCU said it appeared to be a worthy piece of research, but felt itself not qualified to judge and recommended that it be reviewed by the German section.

The 1974 Baecque report on faculty recruitment specified that the role of the CCU was to judge candidates and place those qualified on a national list for a post. The government also saw this as the CCUs' role. Some felt that after 1972 the CCU had tried to take on more powers in the appointment of faculty. When it was not satisfied with an appointment, it sent the file back to the university council, requesting that it review the case. Usually, the recruiting committee in the university or the presidents themselves were able to reach an understanding, but some presidents saw the CCU as a threat to their independence and to the autonomy of the university. One of them, referring to the CCU announced: "The mandarins in the universities have been abolished, but a super-mandarinate has been constituted more powerful than the old."

The CCU claimed that it had a double role to play, both to judge the quality of faculty members and to approve their appointment to the university. It justified the latter by claiming that this was the only way to limit "inbreeding." This practice was so strong in the French universities that even the most ardent supporters of full university autonomy and adversaries of the CCU tended to agree that a national organ was necessary.[50]

The method of faculty recruitment witnessed little if any change after 1968. An article by a notable scholar who had taught at Columbia University for many years and then at l'Ecole internationale de Genève, opined that the system had not changed for the better; if anything it was more cloistered than ever.[51] The suggestion that the CCU be abolished in order to allow universities full responsibility in recruitment came to nothing. Professors wanted to safeguard the CCU for one reason or another, either to limit inbreeding by universities or to have a uniform system of judging the quality of their peers.

Counseling

It was recognized in 1968 that the learning environment could benefit from the establishment of a professional counseling service. Accordingly, the government attempted to reorganize the information dissemination agency, the BUS, and introduced a new organ called ONISEP in 1970. This publication service gathered and prepared information, coordinated research findings at the national level, and conducted research projects on educational topics and career opportunities. The office issued publications and had a computerized service.[52]

Information for students at the university, let alone counseling, was

138

CURRICULUM

totally lacking. In 1942, counseling centers were opened, but they served pupils only at the end of elementary school; in the last twenty years, counseling has been extended up until the equivalent of the American ninth grade, then through the lycée. Many counseling centers were opened for elementary and secondary schools after 1968, and all universities were given a *cellule d'orientation*. But whatever the numbers of these counseling services, interviews with officials indicated that staffing and funding were very limited, thereby restricting the services they could offer.[53]

The training of counselors was limited. They usually possessed a DEUG (the two-year undergraduate diploma) in any discipline, preferably in psychology; they then passed a concours allowing them to enter a Counseling Institute for two years. After taking another concours at the end of their studies, they were assured a position. Most university counseling centers had one administrator (often a professor who volunteered his services), one counselor or part-time counselor, and one documentalist. Sometimes the counselor was involved in counseling for the school system and was assigned by the rector to the university.

Although the Orientation Act of 1968 had been intended to provide universities with a more sophisticated system of counseling, what developed was very limited. The hopes voiced at the Vienna Conference on Higher Education in 1967 for a wide system of guidance and counseling for both academic and professional ends had not been realized in France, but the seed had been planted.[54] Other means of helping students were devised. In 1975, a guide to the university was published by a student association and was available in Paris, Strasbourg, and Toulouse; this practice has spread to other university towns. More common since 1968 had been the proliferation of information desks, orientation sessions by UERs, and more official bulletin boards with information and updates. And some universities published weekly bulletins about elections, faculty publications, meetings, job opportunities, campus lectures, scholarship opportunities, and a listing of theses being defended.

Examinations

Prior to the law of 1968, students took annual examinations. Succeeding at these examinations meant passing on to the next year's studies; failing meant either dropping out or, when possible, repeating an entire

139

year. The new reforms introduced some flexibility into the system, instituting examinations by *contrôle continu* (roughly the equivalent to the U.S. system of midterms and quizzes), *examens partiels*, which signified the examinations at the end of individual courses, and finally *examens terminaux*, which were final examinations at the end of a year.

There was much debate over the extent to which each type of examination should be used. At one point the ministry decided that at least two subjects ought to be tested by semester or by final annual examinations. Moreover, written examinations ought to be followed by oral ones, and practical work ought also to be examined. Some opposed the system of midterms, arguing that it would lead to the devaluation of the diploma. Others favored it, claiming the opposite — that it was annual examinations that encouraged cramming and obstructed real learning. Still others wanted to see "objective" testing instituted, since presumably that would guarantee efficiency and objectivity. In some instances, students themselves clamored for the traditional annual examinations held in June and October. There was a strong feeling among government deputies that there should be a return to annual testing. As one individual wrote, "the religion of examinations remains strong."

Reports of abuse of the new system of examinations made professors and deputies nervous. It was reported from time to time that some professors promised students at the beginning of the course that they would all pass. Full professors, reportedly, were sometimes absent from examination juries. In 1969, at the end of the first two years of medical studies, the percentages of success varied from 20 to 80 percent, depending on the institution, but the proportion of those passing examinations altogether was little different from 1967. Guichard, as minister of education, tried to clarify the examination policy by ministerial decrees. On the one hand, he reinforced the universities' power by stating that students and faculty had to follow the method of examinations decided upon by their institution; on the other hand, he added certain stipulations, such as that examinations could not be given more than twice a year, and that when work was done by a group, a method had to be found to test members individually. It was agreed that in some disciplines an annual examination might be necessary to determine whether students could pass into the next year or not. Since 1968, all observers agreed that different methods of testing have been carried out. While the "progressives" used a variety of methods, the traditionalists continued to use the old method of annual examinations, for as one of them pointed out, "Traditional examinations look better after one tastes

140

CURRICULUM

the ideas of innovation."[55]

The new system of credit hours (*unités de valeur*) also increased flexibility in the curriculum. At Vincennes, a student who failed a course was not obligated to take it over again, but could choose another and pass it. The credit hour system was used in some UERs and in some universities, but not all universities adopted it. Sometimes, a mixture of crediting systems existed within the same institution. This added to the flexibility of the curriculum, but increased the burden on understaffed university administrations and caused difficulties for students wishing to transfer between either UERs or universities.[56]

Facilities

1968 was seen as a turning point, after which university education was to be personalized by small classes, team work, and practical as well as theoretical training. Faculty-student relations were to be radically changed, as were relations among faculty members themselves. The rigid, hierarchical structures were to be torn down and replaced by the introduction of democracy and parliamentarism. Students were to receive recognition in the university, not just in the classroom, but in all aspects of student life — in residence halls, restaurants, libraries, and cultural and sports facilities. Material conditions in the classrooms were also to be improved. These were the hopes of those who participated in the events of May 1968.

In July 1968, Edgar Faure quoted a statement made in 1928 by a dean to Prime Minister Edouard Herriot of France:

> We will have 7,000 students this year, and we do not have sufficient means to care for them, neither in personnel [nor] in buildings. . . . Higher education, whose purpose is the initiation toward personal research, is failing in its goals . . .[57]

The same problems plagued higher education forty years later. The government made a concerted effort to construct new buildings, recruit new faculty, improve libraries, and provide more space in restaurants, housing, and library and classroom facilities. But nothing seemed enough. The reports during the decade after 1968 were similar to those of the pre-1968 days. While the rate of growth of the student population slowed after 1968, their numbers were still rising.

141

In Paris, the restructuring of the universities into thirteen institutions created new problems in housing the faculty and students. Some buildings were shared by two or even four universities. Space allocation was often based on student enrollment, a system which did not always meet the immediate needs of each university. The science disciplines, which had always been well endowed, often had unused space; in 1976, there were 100,000 spaces in science buildings that were not in use. Some universities experienced space shortages that would not have existed had classrooms been more rationally organized. In 1976, some universities began to employ computers for classroom allocation.[58]

Some of the new campuses had been built without cultural, sports, or entertainment facilities and were cut off from daily life, giving students a great sense of isolation. A student poll at Grenoble in 1973 indicated dissatisfaction with the isolated and stark "campus" life devoid of cultural diversions.[59] Students often experienced fatigue from the dispersal of facilities; classrooms, laboratories, and libraries were spread out, not only over the campus, but often over the town or city. Since the number of spaces was limited, universities shared facilities often with ill grace.

Resources were strained; universities continuously threatened to close down if they did not receive more aid. Yet they somehow managed to survive, in spite of the problems that remained.[60] Some improvements in library services were in evidence, however. For example, the Bibliothèque nationale witnessed a remarkable change after 1968. It was carpeted, and heating and lighting were improved. The library opened an information desk for foreign visitors and extended the hours till 8:00 p.m. An interlibrary loan system was developed, and, for the first time, theses, and *mémoires* (lower degree theses) on microfiches were made available to the public. But there were notable shortcomings. The university of Strasbourg library, which was also the Strasbourg branch of the Bibliothéque nationale and second to Paris, lacked the necessary funds to subscribe to a single daily in English. Its holdings were very inconsistent and some basic scholarly journals were lacking even in French; a great effort was made, however, to make working conditions pleasant. Nanterre had a respectable library of 1,000,000 volumes, but the Parisian libraries had always been far more impressive than most provincial university libraries.

CURRICULUM

Student Life

After 1968, there were modest increases in space for student housing and restaurants. In 1969 the Mallet commission on student life reported that the planning commission envisaged that 20 percent of the students would live in university residences, but by 1970, only 13 percent did so. In 1977, the proportion of students in student housing remained essentially unchanged. Student restaurants, however, were able to serve a large proportion of students, (table 15); there were several types of residence halls: those of the traditional type with strict regulations and no visitation of the opposite sex, those with visitation rights, but some limits and regulations, and others with open visitation at all times. The latter was the case for the majority of residence halls in Paris and to a lesser extent in the provinces. Residence hall fees were raised for 1975-1976 to an average of 180 francs a month ($36.00); students in Paris paid slightly higher rent than did those in the provinces, 215 francs ($43.00). In student restaurants, the price of meals was very modest, 3.30 francs in 1977 (table 16).

Prior to 1963 students had participated in national and regional councils, known as the Conseil national/regional/des oeuvres universitaires et scolaires (CNOUS/CROUS). These organizations were founded in 1955 to look after student interests in matters of housing, restaurants, medical services, social security, xeroxing, and material conditions in general. Student participation was abolished in 1963 but revived in 1970 on the councils of these governmental agencies. Student members were elected by students who were members of this organization. The regional offices obviously had less independence than the national office. The Mallet commission helped achieve more equal representation on the councils: ten administrators, ten students, and ten lay persons, appointed by the minister, of whom five were chosen from a list of fifteen names given him by the students seated on the council. Thus, the council would have fifteen student representatives and fifteen non-student representatives. The CNOUS/CROUS organizations had limited powers and were often in financial difficulties.

In June 1972, Joseph Fontanet requested two survey groups, the Institut français d'opinion publique (IFOP) and Sondage d'opinion français, recherches et études statistiques (SOFRES), to conduct a poll of students for the ministry. The results indicated which problems were of most concern to the students[61] (table 17). These turned out to be much like those preoccupying students in the U.S., although French

CURRICULUM

students complained far more about examinations and the inefficient use of time. Loss of time, as would be expected, was more of a problem in the capital than it would be in the provinces, as were housing and interpersonal relationships. More students mentioned cost of books and xeroxing as a problem than mentioned access to libraries; perhaps because library facilities had been so poor and inaccessible in the past, French students tended to avoid them. They were accustomed to studying from xerox copies of lectures given in the *cours magistraux*, and from outline series (such as the well-known "Que sais-je?" series). Another aspect of the same study revealed that students in Paris were more concerned with world and domestic affairs than were students in the provinces, but oddly enough, students in general seemed to be little concerned with the internal affairs of their universities; only 3 percent indicated such a concern.

Education and the Job Market

One of the overriding goals of the 1968 reforms was to make education more relevant to the needs of modern industrial society. Education was to be a preparation for the job market. The rhetoric in the 1960s and even in the 1970s was that France needed more people trained in technology and sciences. Faure declared that the nation needed 52 percent more technicians; and an OECD study claimed that France needed 100,000 new technicians each year.[62] Other studies on manpower needs and educational planning recognized the difficulty of coordinating the two. One such study made the point that the "social demand" for higher education and the policy of democratization, must not be confused with a country's manpower needs. Even with a policy of democratization, a country had to decide carefully whether its economic resources were adequate to meet demand. Thus the study carefully separated social demand from the country's actual need for manpower. By 1970, a study by the Centre d'études et de recherches sur les qualifications (CEREQ) pointed out that the private sector employed hardly 25 percent of the university graduates, while *Le Monde* indicated that the percentage ought to reach 60 percent, i.e., 20,000 more, annually.

To attempt to plan how many people should be trained to enter the economy was difficult. Employers tended to calculate the personnel needed on the low side, so that if business were slack, the employer would not be reproached. Industry based its plans on the past, for it was

144

CURRICULUM

difficult to look ten years ahead for its manpower needs. The OECD study pointed out that the economic system was a free one. Businesses were independent and hired their personnel freely, just as they bought supplies and built factories. Hence it was difficult to define general tendencies on their part and even harder to fix a universal policy. The study argued that where a system of education was uniform and centralized, as in France, either the industrial sector had to plan ahead rigorously or the educational system had to diversify.[63]

Diversification of the educational system did not necessarily mean that all those who went through an institution of higher learning would necessarily find jobs commensurate with their abilities. This was becoming obvious to people in France, in Europe and in the U.S. In 1976, Saunier-Seité stated that a university graduate could hope to arrive at a lucrative and satisfying career only after a few years had passed.[64]

Employers did not take a university diploma seriously and students from the IUTs tended to get proportionately more jobs. Perhaps the employers preferred to hire staffs with lower qualifications in order to pay them less. A colloquium of the OECD on short-term programs in higher education indicated that a student from an IUT could more easily find a job than a student with a degree in law or a masters of science degree. In England, the reverse was true; a diploma from the selective universities was more valued than one from the polytechnical institutes.[65]

It was not clear that there would be job outlets for graduates holding professional degrees from the universities. The job market in the late 1970s was flooded with graduates at a time when the need for employees had dropped. This slackening was due to 1) massive recruitment in the preceding years, 2) a slowdown in expansion, and 3) increasing pressure, by young employees to become executives after they had acquired further training. Businesses retained their selectivity by hiring graduates of the *grandes écoles* and a much smaller proportion of university graduates. A study of the Besançon region indicated that only 5 percent of the executives came from the universities. Nationally, industry hired only 10 percent of its executives from among university graduates. In commerce, they occupied 5 to 10 percent of the executive positions. Most of the important positions were held by graduates of the *grandes écoles* and the prestigious specialized engineering and commercial schools.[66]

The increasingly competitive job market was reflected in the access to the teaching corps. With greater access to higher education, the market for teaching positions was glutted, and it became increasingly difficult to obtain a teaching position, either at the university or at the secondary school level. The *agrégation* was an asset to anyone wishing to teach at the university, or at the secondary school. While 23.2 percent of the candidates passed in 1967, only 8 percent did so in 1976. Thus, in a sense, it became almost three times harder than it had been only nine years earlier. The CAPES, which was slightly less demanding and was the normal concours required of secondary school teachers, also witnessed comparatively sharper competition. Thus while 43.4 percent succeeded in 1966-1967, only 13 percent did so in 1976 (table 10).

In the case of the *agrégation*, some fields were more prestigious than others, such as the concours in philosophy or the sciences, while the grammar concours was considered less demanding. The success rate for the *agrégation* compared favorably with that of the concours given by the prestigious Ecole nationale d'administration (ENA) which supplied the country's administrative elite. In 1968, while 16.3 percent of the candidates succeeded at the *agrégation*, 9.2 percent (i.e., seventy out of 758 candidates) succeeded at the concours for ENA. Of those who passed the *agrégation*, a large percentage came from the prestigious *grandes écoles* or *écoles normales*. In 1967, the four *écoles normales* (Ulm, Jordan, Fontaney-aux-Roses and Cachan) had 233 *agrégés* out of the 1,149 successful candidates, that is, 20.2 percent of all the *agrégés* in France. Attempts to abolish the *agrégation*, which had been established in 1766 under Louis XV, failed. Criticism was often voiced about the ranking of candidates by examination juries. One individual wrote that jury members often made harsh remarks to candidates and behaved in an intolerant manner toward them. Another wrote that the make-up of the jury was as important a factor in the performance of the candidate as the candidate's own comportment.

While the number of candidates remained high the number of new posts was further reduced, eliciting considerable protest.[67] One possible explanation for this reduction is the stabilizing of the number of pupils in the schools; another is that the government was unwilling to honor its commitment to reduce class size to a minimum of twenty-five pupils.[68] There would naturally be more job openings for teachers if classes were kept small. But, in any case, more teaching positions would provide outlets for university graduates only temporarily. They would not answer the general problem of a disequilibrium between the number of university graduates and the number of positions specifically requiring a university degree.

146

CURRICULUM

Conclusion

In its application, the Faure law of 1968 witnessed the adoption of a number of American practices: the reduction of the multi-university to a human scale and the commensurate growth of the multidisciplinary university; the introduction of teaching and learning units that cut across departmental lines; the use of credit hours and the examination system of midterms and quizzes; the initiation of a relationship between industry and university; and, finally, the creation of the campus.

As the American cultural attaché in Paris commented in 1971, all these elements were adopted in France at a time when their usage was being questioned in the U.S. For example, in the U.S., the credit hour concept was considered too rigid, as was the grading and examination system. Some American universities incorporated the pass-fail concept and others replaced grades with professors' evaluative remarks on student transcripts. Attempts were also made to evaluate a student on the basis of performance in practical and professional work. Relations between industry and universities came under fire, as did the idea of the campus. Moreover, while the French university tried to decentralize, the American university moved in the direction of centralization at the state level. While autonomy was seen as a basic solution for the French university, it did not, argued the cultural attaché, spare the American universities either leftist rebels or financial problems. Both the American and French universities were paralyzed in 1968. Like the French university, the American university found its mission and goals questioned. Those who wanted to reform the American system were looked on with apprehension. The dissatisfaction of alumni and state legislatures, as well as the cutting back of federal funds in the Nixon years, put the financial squeeze on American universities. The problem of student unemployment was also serious in the U.S., but, according to the cultural attaché, "the instability gives rise to a certain dynamism and to experiment." The fact was that education was now a central concern of all modern societies:

> . . . democratization has created financial, political, social, and pedagogical difficulties, and no modern society has been able to master the tensions and contradictions of its educational system. Neither the U.S., nor France has found a solution in that domain, doubtless because there are no solutions. There is no formula or model that will create the desired stability of the educational system.[69]

CHAPTER VI

THE FINANCING OF THE UNIVERSITY

En fait, l'épreuve de mon ministère ne fut ni la loi d'orientation, ni tel ou tel désordre, ce fut le désastre de mon budget.

— Edgar Faure[1]

The 1968 Orientation Act of Higher Education made an important move toward granting financial autonomy.[2] In 1966, the colloquium at Caen had recommended *a posteriori* control to replace *a priori* control, which meant that the universities could decide their own budgetary priorities. Furthermore, the granting of a lump sum to the university gave it freedom to divide up its own budget. This new liberty was limited, however, by the fact that university resources still came from the state.

During and after the debates of 1968, the opportunity was missed to create an organ totally independent of the government for the distribution of funds to the universities. The establishment of an organ similar to the British system's University Grants Committee (UGC) was considered. Such an organ could plead the cause of the universities to the ministry for funds, and, once the budget was voted, it would be responsible for the division of money among all the universities. This idea never left the minds of the presidents; in 1974, they suggested such a plan for reforming the financing of the universities. It was again suggested by the blue-ribbon Bienaymé commission of 1975.[3] Unfortunately, when the opportunity arose to introduce such an organ in France in 1971-1972, the chance was lost, and the CNESER and the Conference of Presidents emerged. The ministry worked with these two groups on deciding important expenditures for vast projects, but essentially the ministry initiated and financed the projects. The presidents were gradually able to make their voices heard, but had to work with the ministry; their group was by no means an independent organ. The failure to introduce an organ independent of the central administration in Paris for financing the universities was perhaps the most crucial shortcoming of the Orientation Act. But France had a centralized administration in all aspects of life, and a move to decentralize would have been foreign to its tradition.

149

Preparation of the Budget

The preparation of the university budget began in January, was voted on by parliament in December, and went into effect the following January. The ministry of finance gave certain deadlines for the budget's preparation to the minister of education. The ministry also appointed a *délégué des affaires budgétaires* from the ministry of finance, to help coordinate drawing up the university budget. Until 1975, two services in the Paris administration dealt with establishing the budget: first, the *Direction des enseignements, de la recherche et des personnels* (DERP), which dealt with all aspects of programs, student life, teaching personnel, statutory and disciplinary matters, and administrative and financial functions in the universities; second, the *Direction des affaires générales et financières* (DAGEFI), which included services in planning, building, and financial affairs. Since 1975, an offshoot of DAGEFI, the offices of the *Groupe d'analyse et de recherche sur les activités et les coûts de l'enseignement supérieur* (GARACES) played an important role also. These departments and the *délégué des affaires budgetaires* informed the universities by circulars of the budget available and requested their proposals.

The preparation of the budget, within limits proclaimed by the minister of finance, filtered from the highest bureaucracy to the lowest:

Ministry of Finance
↓
Secretariat of State for University Affairs
(Ministry of Universities after 1978)
↓
DAGEFI (GARACES)
↓
University Council
↓
UER Councils

Responses from the universities went to the ministry in May or June, indicating budgetary needs for the following year. In July and August, DAGEFI and GARACES examined the university budget requests, cut and trimmed where necessary, and advised the universities of possible alternatives. CNESER and the Conference of Presidents were consulted on new and large-scale propositions, such as the buying of new land or the building of a new laboratory. In October and November, after the budget was established with the agreement of DAGEFI, the minister, and the *délégué des affaires budgétaires*, the minister submitted it to

150

parliament. This was the period of *arbitrage*, when the director of DAGEFI and the *délégué des affaires budgétaires* defended the budget before the ministry of finance. Their role was very important. Any points of dispute not settled at the departmental level were left for the ministers to discuss among themselves, and certain items, known as "reserved" questions, were left to the prime minister for decision. In December of each year, the budget was voted on by parliament, as were all other budgets of state, and the finance law emerged for the following year.[4]

The parliament voted on a lump sum, but the minister of universities divided up the moneys to the universities according to decisions reached by DAGEFI, GARACES, and, when necessary, the Conference of Presidents and CNESER. The universities prepared their draft budgets in the spring according to the framework of expenditures set for them by the central administration; these guidelines stipulated items such as the total number of posts to be created, the amount of appropriations allowed for each heading of expenditures, and any specific provisions made by the government. Thus, each university had to make do with what came to it after the total budget had been voted. The manner in which decisions were reached on budgetary allocations revealed the extent to which centralized control continued: the ministry of universities (or, one might even say, the ministry of finance)[5] exercised real control over the criteria for dividing funds and the execution of these decisions.

Criteria for Dividing Funds Among Universities

The state funded 95 percent of the universities' expenditures. Besides providing funds for equipment and faculty salaries, it provided an operational budget (*crédits de fonctionnement*). After 1971, the operational budget for the upkeep of buildings was based on a formula of payment per square meter (in 1971, 30 francs a square meter). That budget was also based on the number and distribution of students in each university. A flat sum of 100 francs per student was allocated for all students equally, but a second sum varied per student from 40 francs for law, 60 francs for letters, 220 francs for medicine and pharmacy, and 600 francs for the sciences. To all this were added funds for *heures complémentaires*, (additional hours of teaching), and also research funds; the latter were fixed according to the number of researchers and their disciplines, and also took into account the number of theses directed, laboratories associated to the prestigious National Science Research

151

Center, and recent investments. Finally, certain funds could be given for a specific action or program of a university out of a discretionary fund.[6]

When the budget was being drafted, the per capita formula was easy enough to calculate. Requests for additional teaching positions or for the improvement of services, scholarships, or salaries, however, had to be scrutinized by the ministry, since these requests involved policy decisions. It was suggested in a number of interviews that personal commitments or arrangements were sometimes made and those "in favor" could receive extra funding.[7] Although France had a national five-year plan, it is important to note that educational policy was worked out by the education ministry, and not by the Planning Commission (Commissariat de plan). The latter only estimated the amount of resources thought necessary.[8]

In 1968, the cry for autonomy implied *a posteriori* control. The mixed feelings that the idea of total autonomy raised in all segments of the population was discussed in earlier chapters; it was argued that if the universities had to acquire their funds as the American universities did, the ideal of uniformity and equality among universities (which in actuality did not exist) would be abolished. The idea of obtaining money from business groups was also shunned, since it was feared that the universities would then be subjected to the influence of corporations, a fate feared as worse than the central administration. Other options of financing were equally unpromising. Unlike the American universities, France did not perpetuate an alumni system (although it existed for the *grandes écoles*, but not for furnishing funds to the institutions). The Orientation Act allowed universities to establish contracts with business and industry to train people or conduct experiments; funding was to be worked out between the parties concerned. Thus, the IUTs of the eastern region in France were well-endowed, thanks to their link with the industrial sector. When the state gave out funds to universities, it theoretically did not take into account any additional funding received from outside sources, but in fact the ministry supervised all university finances, regardless of the origin of the funds. The funds received from diverse sources were modest in France compared to the U.S., but the practice did enable some universities to gain additional income.

On the whole, the budget tended to favor the scientific universities; they had better faculty-student ratios and more facilities at their disposal.[9] The Parisian universities received about 25 percent more than the provincial universities. This increase had been instituted at one time to compensate for their lack of development, but it remains in effect even

152

FINANCING

now. A small amount was allotted for special projects, 4 percent of the total budget for universities (28 million francs or $5.6 million, in 1975). This sum, it was charged, was too small, and, in 1972, CNESER recommended that the amount reach 40 percent of the budget.[10]

The vast gap between the development of the Parisian universities and that of provincial ones was a constant source of irritation.[11] The problems that faculty and graduate students in the provinces faced with regard to library facilities and laboratory equipment were described earlier; one reason for the flight to Paris was that it was the most developed cultural center. De Gaulle's plan for regional development had tried to counteract this tendency. When Soisson introduced his plan for regional universities, however, it was withdrawn because of opposition from the eastern regions. But the need for regional development remained.

The axiom that the "rich get richer and the poor get poorer" was a valid description of the French universities. While regional disparities existed between universities, nearly all were plagued by varying degrees of penury. One of the commonest complaints made by those concerned with education — and not only higher education — was the lack of funds for faculty, facilities, and modern equipment. One author criticized the government's financial policies, claiming that it spent funds on equipment that brought prestige to the minister; the maintenance of the new equipment was then dropped into the university's operational budget. Hence, telescopes, accelerators, and missile bases were built, but were accompanied with a minimal number of technicians and aides, thus limiting their full use. Allegedly, the government economized in the matter of buildings, equipping them with poor acoustics, heating, study space, and libraries. The universities often were short of personnel. They lacked sufficient auxiliaries, secretaries, technicians, and administrators, so that professors and deans often wasted time doing clerical jobs. The auxiliary staff was badly paid, without much job security or the possibility of promotion. The best people left education and went into the private economic sector.[12]

Presidents and UER directors often complained about the financial situation of their universities.[13] Many resigned in protest, while unions organized strikes of varying lengths. In the spring of 1975, 300 students dramatically marched in a cortege to the Rue de Grenelle, protesting the financial "asphyxiation" of Paris XIII. A coffin, symbolizing the death of the university was labeled, "Morte faute de crédits," and a couple in mourning, "A notre faculté regrettée." The cortege chanted the *De*

FINANCING

Profondis.[14]

France gave a consistent amount for education, as the charts have shown. Edgar Faure said in his memoirs that the French felt relatively comfortable and satisfied with having given moneys to education (table 14) between 1962 and 1965, but the allocations tapered thereafter. Compared to the U.S., U.S.S.R., Japan, and Sweden, France gave a smaller share of its GNP (table 13). France boasted that it spent as much as Germany and Great Britain, but ignored that it had many more students (double the numbers), that the school age population was larger, and that the low density of the French population per square kilometer increased proportionately the expenses for buildings and staffing. As Faure added, "Hence, to pay as much, we have to pay more."[15] Because France had a far larger enrollment of students than any other European country, its per student expenditure was one of the lowest in Europe. Except for the U.S., France had proportionately the largest number of students in higher education. Holland, Germany, Norway, Britain, and the U.S. were all ahead of France in per student expenditure. Holland paid a little more than $4,500 while France paid $1,000. *Le Monde* estimated per student expenditures at 4,996 francs a year. The amount could be broken down as follows:

2,714 — personnel expense
1,369 — operational expense
 833 — social aid
Total 4,966 francs[16]

The cost per student in higher education remained higher than the unit cost at other levels of education. In 1955, it was six times more than the cost for an elementary school child, and in 1968, it was four times more.[17]

Within the existing institutional framework, several suggestions for increasing university budgets were made; these included studying the nation's priorities and reducing military expenditures, instituting a tax on Paris, or increasing the taxes on high incomes. Even in 1968, it was felt that such efforts were not enough and that France would have to make heavy sacrifices over a period of years in order to carry out the Orientation Act and improve the state of the universities. It was also suggested that state financing could be improved by a) saving on unit costs by using an efficient educational technology, b) instituting productive work for the community, c) providing student loans when

FINANCING

necessary, or d) allowing employers to pay for their employees' diplomas. Universities could be supported by regional taxes or by levying tuition fees on university attendance.[18]

French students paid a minimal fee for tuition and housing, unlike their counterparts in Great Britain and the U.S. Moreover, this privilege was extended to all students, including the 104,710 foreign students, who constituted 12.5 percent of the student population in 1977-1978. The student paid a yearly fee of 95 francs ($19), of which $4 went to the rector's office, $12 to the university, and $3 to the library. Students who registered for more than one diploma in the same university paid only the $19, although students who registered for more than one diploma in two universities had to pay an additional 65 francs ($13) for each diploma beyond the first. If a student were registered in several universities, but preparing for only one diploma, he still paid only $19. In addition to these fees, a student had to pay small amounts for medical service 3 francs, student association 30 francs ($6), and social security 20 francs ($4.) Thus a student paid a total of anywhere between 150 and 200 francs ($30 to $40) in fees for the academic year (scholarship students were exempt from all fees, except $6 for the student association and a $2 registration fee). In 1969, when the registration fees were raised to $19, there was a great outcry by students. When the restaurant fees were raised by six cents, there were student strikes.[19] Yet French students still paid far less than their European counterparts. In Britain, fees for students, still relatively low compared to those in the U.S., were increased in 1977 by 300 percent (although the central government in Scotland and the local governments in England reimbursed the tuition fees of all students who were citizens).[20]

While French students who attended foreign universities paid extra amounts, foreign students in France were exempt. The ministry of finance repeatedly considered instituting special fees for foreign students but had to bow to the arguments of the ministries of education, culture, and foreign affairs, which argued that France, as a major cultural force in the world, should attract as many foreign students as possible. France had a special cultural mission, and it was supposed that political advantage would later be reaped by having helped to train the elites of foreign countries.[21] To institute fees for French students went against the grain. It would be a hardship on the poor who had to make large financial sacrifices, and would run counter to the tradition of *égalité*. High fees, it seemed, would not be instituted, however difficult the financial situation of the French universities might be. Since the education

155

budget was — depending on the years — the largest, or second largest, budget of the state, to increase it was asking a great deal. The only alternative was to restrict the number of entrants, but objections that *sélection* was undemocratic had made it politically impossible to impose.

The main problem, given the budget available to the universities, was how to divide the funds. This was a difficult task, for until 1975 a cost analysis of university education had never been conducted. Dissatisfaction with dividing the budget among the universities according to the number of students and the surface allotment caused the ministry to attempt to introduce changes. Olivier Guichard wanted to encourage computer and pedagogical research and innovative programs in continuing, technical, and pedagogical education; to that end, in 1970, he promised additional funds as well as a review of the old system of basic allocations.[22] In 1974, the presidents voiced concern over the ministry's methods of allocation and René Rémond, one of the vice-presidents of the Conference of Presidents, argued that the minister should not grant extra sums to those universities who were merely the most insistent. A new method of dividing funds had to be established.[23] In 1971, seven universities attempted to launch a research program in order to work out a method for cost analysis for buildings, teaching and non-teaching personnel, and the "cost" of a student. The result was inconclusive because of insurmountable methodological problems in the calculations.[24] In January 1975, an OECD conference met in Paris to discuss the cost of higher education, also with limited success. The lack of organized methods of cost analysis meant that the real costs of university education were unknown. The resultant inequities caused some universities to refuse to vote their budgets.[25]

In 1974, Soisson appointed the Bienaymé commission to study university finances. The commission was terminated abruptly a few months later, because it was learned that a study had already been undertaken at the secretariat by a group of researchers. In mid-1973, the director of higher education under Joseph Fontanet, had requested Guy Allain, the bureau chief of a department in DAGEFI, to undertake a study on the cost of university education; the group formed was known as the GARACES. Allain obtained funding from a private research foundation and hired six people to assist him, but in the end, the work was undertaken by himself and two assistants.[26]

GARACES tried to acquire a representative sample of the French universities and used three criteria for selection: 1) the area of specialization, 2) the geographic location, and 3) the number of students. Initially,

156

twenty universities were selected for the study, and their cooperation was elicited. The assistants personally visited the universities and remained long enough to learn the details about them. The first step of the study was to report on the twenty universities and the second step, to send out questionnaires to all universities in France. This was done in June 1975 after authorization was received from the Conference of Presidents. But all these actions took place only after heated debate; the vigorous intervention of president Fresal (Paris V) and René Rémond (Paris X) was necessary to persuade the Conference to agree to the study. Within a month, in July 1975, all the universities had responded. The questionnaire requested information regarding all levels of teaching and the success ratio of students at various levels. It gathered information on the personnel, the amount of used surface, and the number of students enrolled. The data were put into the computer, and, for the first time, a cost analysis of each university existed. The computer print-outs lay on the floors of rented rooms — there were no shelves — while the secretariat sought housing facilities for the operation. Standard questionnaires were sent out each year to update the cost analysis of each university.

Thus, since 1975, the secretariat finally had something concrete with which to discuss finances. The computer print-outs showed that some universities had 10-12 percent of their budgets remaining after all other expenditures. The GARACES report indicated that the ministry should insist that more of the funds be spent on instruction, that the unspent funds be reduced. The report also recommended that 10 percent be put aside for the construction and upkeep of buildings. More universities were built after 1960 than in the entire previous history of the university, but no provision had been made in the budget for upkeep; if that neglect continued, said one official, "we would have to begin building from scratch."[27]

The most important finding of the cost analysis was that about 85 percent of the expenses of a university were fixed costs, spent on faculty and other personnel, as well as on general maintenance and other expenses, regardless of the number of students. Thus, the national criteria that had been used all these years, for payment per student and per student by discipline, were irrelevant. The Bienaymé report stated that the emphasis on student enrollments engendered "a certain amount of fraud" on the part of UERs in the form of falsely inflating their number of registrants.[28] The GARACES study highlighted the inequities of the system of payment by number of students and by discipline. According to GARACES, the national criteria obstructed the proper

157

FINANCING

functioning of university councils. UER councils, rather than making independent decisions on their real needs, demanded their moneys on the basis of national criteria. The UER of medicine, law, and economics at Marseille was in a quandry, because the funds were divided unevenly among the disciplines: the medicine bloc received about ten times as much for the same number of students.[29] Nor were university councils free to divide the total budget according to the priorities they had set for themselves, because the UERs could still claim their share according to the old inequitable national criteria. Rich UERs continued to receive funds, and the poor ones remained poor, because they had to follow a formula set by the national government.

The fact that the ministry had presumably given UERs autonomy to use funds as they saw fit did not change the situation. The GARACES report recommended, however, that henceforth financial powers be centralized in the presidency at the expense of the UERs. The study showed that the 1968 law was not being applied in terms of its multidisciplinary provisions. Power was not vested in the presidents' office and the university councils, but in the directors of the UERs. The study also found that in distributing funds, the universities used exactly the same methods to distribute moneys to the UERs as the central administration used towards the universities, that is, per student, per discipline, per square meter. Faculty-student ratios were thus far better among the rich disciplines; in sciences, it was 1 to 8, while in letters it was 1 to 20. To add insult to injury, UERs with the most faculty members also had the largest number of *heures complémentaires* given, in order to save university funds. These extra hours were considered necessary in a system where "line-positions" were costly. As one official said, it was better to have this kind of system than to fund tenured positions. He gave the example of the science *facultés* that were built after 1968 in Paris, Toulouse, Strasbourg, and other places, where the students who were expected did not show up. "Now," he lamented, "the tenured professors are still there and have to be paid; they cannot be moved to another university where they are most needed, the buildings are not fully utilized, they cannot be reconverted, and the science people will not let them be used for anything else, since they were built for scientists."[30]

The GARACES report noted that the lack of control over the number of entrants subjected the university to "uncontrollable fluctuations, and with increases in numbers, there is a strain on its resources." Therefore, GARACES suggested that a decision be made about each university's capacity to accept more students, and that national policy be set

FINANCING

according to these limits. This was an oblique way of calling for *sélection*. With regard to surface costs, the report recognized that the existing system of allocation was adequate, although it did not always take into account disparities engendered by an expensive heating unit or the need for extra custodial personnel. In 1977 at Limoges, for example, space for the old medical *faculté* tripled from 7,000 to 21,000 square meters, but only one janitorial position was added.[31]

Certain fixed expenses were unavoidable. The personnel paid by the state and known as ATOS (*administratifs, techniciens, ouvriers et service*) also put strain on the university operational budget. Expenses for personnel varied widely, depending on the university. The UERs had some disparities in their employment of staff. Some were over-endowed, while others found it difficult to support personnel on their limited budget.

Therefore, the GARACES report, based on hard facts and figures, recommended a change from allocations per student per discipline and per square meter of surface, to a new system or formula that would take into account the fixed costs that needed funding, regardless of the number of students. Such a plan would neutralize the disparities between disciplines, and would give the universities a chance to reevaluate themselves. It would confirm the universities' autonomy by establishing a saner basis for their relationship with the central administration in Paris. It was hoped that the change would also strengthen the office of the president in the matter of finance. Presumably, the president would no longer be hounded by UER directors for the amount allotted to the university on the basis of number of students in particular disciplines.[32] The president had essentially had no options in deciding a university's priorities, because the funds were predetermined by the formula for distribution. Hence the situation was frozen and the report concluded devastatingly that:

> the universities have not assumed their true autonomy.
> . . . caught in a situation in which they thought they had
> no way out, they were led to play the role of paymaster,
> their room to maneuvre almost nonexistent.[33]

Just as the central administration had attempted to keep a hold on the governance structures (via the quorum and electoral system) and the curriculum (via the national diplomas), it did so also in the case of finances. Funds were not supposed to be earmarked after 1968, but in fact they were as a result of the central administration formula for their

159

allotment; neither the university nor the UER councils had much initiative. This formula may in part have been to blame for the failure of the universities to become multidisciplinary, for the rich wanted to stay rich, while sometimes the poor tagged on in the hope of getting a few crumbs from the rich.

In 1972 CNESER approved plans to reform the system, but not quite in the sweeping manner suggested in the GARACES report three years later. The report was carefully studied after its completion in the summer of 1975, although it was not made public. Perhaps it was kept confidential because of its controversial recommendations on university powers. In October 1975, however, *Le Monde* published some of the main contents of the report on budget allocation.

Attempts were made to institute all of the recommendations. The per student allocation was not totally abandoned; it continued indirectly through staffing, which of course, depended on enrollment. While the number of faculty was supposed to be based on "groups" or "families" of disciplines, it was suggested that the number of administrators and technicians be based on a different criteria, namely the type or structure of the university (mono-, bi-, tri-, or quadridisciplinary) and size.[34] The criteria for surface funding remained. In 1976 the universities received 47 francs per square meter, compared to 46 francs in 1975, and 30 francs in 1971, for upkeep, heating, and cleaning, as well as 0.40 franc per square meter of nonbuilt surfaces such as roads and greens. Soisson abandoned all direct reference to the number of students as a criterion in granting funds but the per student allocation was not totally abandoned; it continued indirectly through staffing, which, of course, depended on enrollment.

The GARACES report was adopted by the committee responsible for financial affairs within the Conference of Presidents during the summer of 1975. The report designed criteria for financing and recognized the need for different faculty-student ratios, depending on the type of discipline. It set the ratio for law and economics at 1 to 35, also taking into account enrollments (1 to 38 for enrollments of 2,000-4,000 students, 1 to 35 for 4,000-8,000 students, and 1 to 33 for more than 8,000 students).[35] In sciences, the ratio was to be 1 to 10, in medicine 1 to 16, again taking account of variations in enrollment. These recommended ratios essentially preserved those prevailing in science and medicine, while improving those for law and economics, which had been 1 to 49 in 1972-1973.

By establishing criteria by groups of disciplines, the GARACES

160

FINANCING

report set guidelines that the UERs could demand be applied. The powers of presidents still depended on the personalities involved, and the establishment of new criteria did not necessarily strengthen the executive. The very existence of criteria also nullified much local university autonomy, which GARACES originally had hoped to strengthen. If the criteria were somewhat more flexible and more generous to certain disciplines, they essentially did not change the method of financing higher education.

Although considerable attention was paid to the problems of dividing up the existing budget for higher education, it was unlikely that the French state would be able to invest a greater proportion of its resources in that area. While in 1967 higher education absorbed approximately 13.5 percent of the education budget, in 1976 this had increased to 15.2 percent. It was hard to think that a greater proportion of the total education budget could be provided for the universities, since the needs of the elementary and secondary schools were at least as urgent. The general education budget itself could hardly be augmented much either; from representing 16.3 percent in 1967 of the state budget, it had increased to represent 18.8 percent in 1976 (table 14), second only to the defense budget.

The French government probably found that it had reached a ceiling for its education expenditures; maybe some sort of selective admissions policy to curb enrollments would allow for an improvement in the condition of the universities with the current funding. Otherwise, a radical departure in government priorities would have to take place. If a left-wing government were to come to power in France in the 1980s, it would not necessarily decide to give higher education a great increase in funds either. Many other social needs are far more pressing and consistent with the programs of the left-wing parties, such as housing, full employment, increases in social security, expansion and improvement of child care centers, and the realization of the welfare state; all these would probably take priority over higher education. It ought to be noted that in countries with advanced welfare state programs, such as Britain, the Scandinavian countries, and all the Communist countries, which also proclaimed a high commitment to social investments, universities had been retained as exclusive elite organizations. Even these countries decided to limit expenditure for universities; but they faced less of a crisis because of their policies of limited admissions.

While some of the causes for conflict between the universities and the central administration, and between various units within universities,

161

could be solved by the introduction of a different method of distributing the funds, the larger questions on the budget were connected with French society in general — its wishes, its priorities, and its image of the role of higher education.

FINANCING

CONCLUSION

*If the goals of a university must dictate its structure,
what determines the goals themselves? Inevitably these
goals and the set of values that underlies them reflect the
values and goals of the society around the university. The
critical question is the nature of the reflection.*

—S. E. and Zella Luria

*Puisque l'état s'est emparé de toute autorité, les Fran-
çais le rendent responsable de tout. Simple citoyens, élus
locaux ou fonctionnaires, rejettent la faute sur le pouvoir
central, dont ils sont les assujettis.*

—Alain Peyrefitte[1]

The adoption of the Orientation Act of Higher Education in November
1968 began a difficult period of adjustment for the French universities.
Some cautiously adapted, and others resisted change. Most were the
scenes of angry confrontations of faculty and students with each other
and among themselves, and in many cases, the innovations were skin-
deep. The new universities were only old facultés under a new name. In a
few cases, however, new universities sprang up that were genuinely
multidisciplinary.

The principle of participation was introduced in 1968. For the first
time, universities possessed elected councils at the unit and university
level, and, in the Conference of Presidents, a representative organ of the
universities to deal with the ministry. Heading the universities were the
newly created presidents, elected by their university councils for five
years.

The Faure law tried to create university autonomy. In matters of
finance, for instance, *a posteriori* control meant that the universities
could theoretically command more of their own budgets than had been
the case prior to 1968. As a result of this greater autonomy, universities
were able to develop more individuality, to excel in different fields of
study, and to attract large enrollments. Paris I, V, VI, VII, VIII, X and
XI, and Toulouse III had more than twice the average university
enrollment (appendix 1). According to a 1977 study, the Parisian universities ranked highest nationally, in fields such as linguistics at Vincennes, in psychology at Paris V, in economics at Paris I and Nanterre.
Yet some of the provincial universities came in a close second and in

163

other fields, provincial universities also made their mark. The time was passed when Paris enjoyed preeminence in all fields.[2]

But the commitment to autonomy was vitiated by ministerial decrees that slowly drained away the autonomy granted by the 1968 law. The central administration in Paris asserted its domination and often obstructed local initiative. Ever since the Ancien Régime, French governments have anxiously sought to preserve their control of education. To prevent the enemies of the regime from taking over educational institutions, asserting opposition, and indoctrinating youth, governments for centuries have exercised a close control over the educational system. This tradition continued after 1968. If anything, the experiences of May 1968 reminded the government how important it was to preserve control over higher education; continued student unrest after 1968 reinforced this determination.

At times the universities themselves requested intervention by the central authorities. Faculty and administrators unable or unwilling to resolve their difficulties relied on the ministry to resolve outstanding disputes. The French universities, even though they were proclaimed autonomous, looked for direction from above; one reform-minded professor called for a "Ralph Nader de la pédagogie" to begin a campaign for a true reform of the educational system in France.[3] Capelle in the National Assembly exhorted the minister of education to take charge of the difficult situation in the universities in 1970, stating in a curious analogy:

> . . . you are the head of an immense herd; the flock questions itself as to its future; while the shepherds do not always know which way to guide their flock. The exalting responsibility comes to you to guide the way toward the star.[4]

A bane of the French centralized system was that its very existence absolved local organs or voluntary groups from making decisions. Knowing that there would be an ultimate authority to act as arbiter, the French often gave themselves over to excessive ideological debates and general wrangling. In turn, this irresponsibility at lower levels of decision making required the central government to intervene.[5] The experience of the universities was no different. Olivier Guichard uttered a truth that continued to be revealing, not only of the educational structures, but of French institutions in general: "In France, centralization is the norm, and a ministry or its minister cannot resist the tempta-

164

CONCLUSION

tion to establish centralized control."[6]

In spite of the announced intentions of the 1968 law to grant the universities autonomy, the ministers actively intervened in the university. They did not hesitate to manipulate the electoral rules in order to achieve university councils or elect presidents favorable to the government. To uphold what they considered academic standards, ministers denied national diplomas to certain university programs, and even denounced others. Urgently desiring to found new universities, ministers did not hesitate at times to ignore rules and regulations, and instead imposed their will and power. After 1974, the ministers increasingly manipulated the university institutions. Student seats on the university councils and university disciplinary councils were restricted, and reelection of student members to the CNESER was deferred indefinitely. Funds were cut to the anti-government student union (the UNEF-ex-Renouveau), while moneys were instead given generously to pro-government student groupings. Dissatisfied with the politics of Nanterre, the secretary dismantled the law unit by not publishing a list of its UERs, thereby preventing students from registering. This matter was taken to the Conseil d'état, and early in 1977, the court ruled against the action of the secretariat.[7]

In the U.S., the university became involved in politics through competition for limited resources and the accountability of public institutions to state legislatures. Politics played a role when, for instance, university presidents were chosen because their political views were compatible with those of the governor or the state legislature. Such politization, however, tended to protect the university from further incursion. In France, the demand for political conformity often went deeper. Faculty of a political coloring favorable to the government gained special appointive positions, and university presidents extra funds. Such politization rewarded political conformity rather than imagination.

The 1968 law did provide, however, the necessary climate for curriculum innovations. Some universities, with their faculty and presidents, took up the challenge and labored selflessly to establish a multidisciplinary type of institution in which new programs were introduced. They made a particular effort to introduce continuing education programs, both in the university and on radio and television. Others attempted to introduce work-study programs to enable students to acquire practical experience outside the university. Attempts were made to provide student counseling, to introduce discussion sections, to cut down class size, and to reduce the number of *cours magistraux*. But the pressure for

165

CONCLUSION

innovation soon subsided, and traditional outlooks and methods reasserted themselves. Innovation in a university is easier when it is tried in one department, college, or university. But the French devotion to centralization and uniformity often meant that untested, expensive, across-the-board changes had to be made. Understandably there was hesitancy about implementing them.

The problems discussed in this study are not peculiar to the French system, but are inherent to the university itself. Organizations adapt to change with difficulty. They are organized mainly to fulfill a specific role, and they find it difficult to redefine their goals and functions. Universities are no exception. In the 1960s, the impetus for change on both sides of the Atlantic came from external stimuli. As Ralph Dungan pointedly observed:

> . . . the fact that major reforms in education have occurred in the past predominantly as a result of external stimuli suggests that there is only limited capacity for internally generated reform, and such actions as are taken come at an agonizingly slow pace.[8]

In most societies, the university has been in a state of crisis for the last two decades or more, depending on the individual country. This is because university education has been recognized as the primary means of social ascension. Knowledge has become power. As a result, the demands of social groups for access to higher education puts the university in the midst of a social confrontation. Because of its expertise, the university has also been looked upon as a reservoir of knowledge, which should be put immediately at the disposal of society. Such functions conflicted with the traditional role of the university as both the recipient and the transmitter of knowledge. The ivory tower concept seemed to have to give way to the notion of the university as the servant of society. Universities in varying degrees attempted to preserve a precarious balance between these two models.[9]

American universities experienced considerable turmoil in the 1960s and attempted to adjust their structures and outlook to the new forces that had been unleashed. On the one hand, the American university was vulnerable in the 1970s, because few powers of repression were available if it again had to face stresses like those in the 1960s. On the other hand, it was a flexible institution, and this was its strength.[10] Although the French university system embarked upon change in 1968, the ministry soon decided to increase its control, and hence reduce the potential

CONCLUSION

vulnerability of the universities. In fact, the university was still very vulnerable, as seen during the strikes of the spring of 1976. But the desire to avoid university vulnerability led to further central control, while reducing the ability of the French university to experiment. The problem was that patterns of authority in the university, which were questioned in the 1960s, broke the old established order without quite giving way to a new consensus. This is a grave problem for universities in most countries. As Clark Kerr stated: "Clarity about functions is becoming essential to sanity in governance now that the consensus which embraced the confusions of the past has disintegrated into conflict."[11]

A number of reformers in France wanted to see more of the Anglo-Saxon model of higher education implanted on French soil. As early as the 1880s, Jules Ferry, the French minister of education, lamented the fact that he had not transplanted the American model to France.[12] In the 1960s, various efforts to emulate the U.S. were also attempted, for instance, in the introduction of American business management techniques. But the passage of time showed that these techniques had not won acceptance. A U.S. management consultant was quoted as having said: "There was a lot of talk about new systems, but in practice things have gone on very much as before. It has been difficult to break down traditional attitudes."[13] Such experiences made reformers realize that there were limitations to transposing institutional models. Alain Peyrefitte, minister of education from 1966 to 1968, declared in the National Assembly that no system was perfect, and that one could not expect to transplant an entire system: ". . . the evolution of universities, like that of all social institutions, has its roots plunged in the specific traditions of a people."[14] The extent to which each university was able to adapt itself to modern needs, depended on limits set by the tradition of a national culture. In the U.S., pluralism and diversity of institutions are valued, but in France uniformity and egalitarianism are the norm.

Ambiguous patterns of authority were accepted in the American university. The French reforms of 1968, for all their desire to bring about a change in spirit and structures, attempted to decree a clear and concise system. Yet the modern university with its many constituencies and diverse functions can probably function best in ambiguity. As Kerr has suggested:

> A new series of consensuses is needed — not one overall "best" solution, not one single preferred form. Variety in solutions should match the variety of situations, and this

167

CONCLUSION

is almost infinite. Many small agreements will come closer to providing effective governance in totality than will any global approach.[15]

Both the American and French university had to adapt to centralization. In the U.S., there was increasing control by the federal government, as well as an attempt to "coordinate" universities at the state level. But all of these efforts were reluctantly accepted. In France, the universities, accustomed to uniformity themselves, often called on the central authority and did not unreservedly uphold their autonomy.

The 1968 reform of the university was instituted as a politically expedient measure to put an end to the student rebellion. It did not come into being because of deeply rooted convictions by university administrators, faculty, or students. In the face of demands by student leaders and the turbulence unleashed in the universities, the government found it necessary somehow to reestablish order in the university. It quickly passed a law, but there was no consistent, organized body inside or outside the university that steadfastly pushed for the realization of the promises of the 1968 law. In fact, it appears that since 1976, the ministers of universities not only flouted the provisions of the Orientation Act of 1968, but also, by repeated speeches aimed against the law, appeared to desire reestablishing the pre-1968 university.[16] With few partisans for the reform law in either the university or at the ministry, it was easy for the university to lapse into its traditional mould.

Sociologist Michel Crozier has argued, that when faced by crisis, French society was able to reform and adjust to new forces. But once the adjustment was made, a new stalemate ensued. Crozier has observed that the French have a dislike of disorder:

> Frenchmen do not dislike change; they dislike disorder, conflict, everything that may bring uncontrolled relationships. . . . What they fear is not change itself, but the risks they may encounter if the stalemate that protects them (and restricts them at the same time) were to disappear. . . . Like players in stalemate . . . they wait for an opening, and when it comes, most probably from the outside, they move in, all at once, thus reconstructing a new stalemate. . . .[17]

What occurred in the French university follows this description. May 1968 was the occasion, the occurrence "from the outside" that shook the

CONCLUSION

foundations of the educational structures. When a new order followed as a result of the Faure law, academe could not tolerate the ambiguity of the unstructured situation that autonomy signified, nor could the ministry or the government exist in an uncontrolled situation vis-à-vis the university. The outcome was an effort to arrive at a new order in which the authority remained centralized in the ministry, and a new stalemate emerged in which many of the traditional values resurfaced.

In the university, the mandarin system returned; although the old mandarins were ousted in 1968, a new set emerged in the decade that followed. The chair system, which was severely attacked in 1968, also returned, as did the *cours magistraux*, even though both systems were abolished by the 1968 law. Neither faculty-student relations nor the faculty-student ratio changed dramatically. Relations continued to be somewhat impersonal.

Those who would like to see more autonomy vested in the university in matters of student recruitment, finance, and even in the development of the competitive university, have been disappointed by the 1968 law, because the granting of autonomy was not pushed to its logical consequence, namely the granting to each university of the authority to select its own students. Perhaps even the universities were a little reticent to see such a measure applied. This was paradoxical, for it was not as if the university was really open; the selection mechanism had already been at work. In spite of repeated efforts to overhaul the baccalauréat, in 1978 it continued to play its double function of lycée diploma and admission examination to the universities. As one report to the minister states: the baccalauréat was a "visceral" issue to the French people.[18] Just as the baccalauréat was an integral part of the educational system, so were the concours, which academics of all political opinions believed essential for selecting the elite of the country.[19]

With their large enrollments, the French universities were overburdened. The 1968 call was for adaptation of the curriculum to the needs of a modern society, and for practical and professional training. Yet the technical institutes founded in 1966 met with limited interest and were not filled to capacity. The big question was how the universities could accomplish their goals of quality education without restricting the numbers. For many, the issue of *sélection* was considered a false problem. They argued that it was unrealistic to cut enrollments of 800,000 down to, for instance, 400,000 like the British. Rather, more diversity of institutions was required. One attractive option was to increase the funding for higher education, but this would entail higher

CONCLUSION

taxation. Like taxpayers around the world, Frenchmen were wary of additional taxes. Such economic sacrifices might be made, however, if the university diploma assured one of employment, but it did not. While the trend increasingly was to see the university as a training ground for the job market, it had mixed success in fulfilling this function. It could be surmised that when a system of higher education was pluralistic, it could more successfully prepare young people for the job market. In France, until the 1970s, the university dispensed theoretical knowledge, while practical training was relegated to a few other institutions outside it and usually was considered inferior. Universities did not take into account local or regional needs, and diversity was not fostered.

Moreover, the universities were not the high road to success in France in any case. The *grandes écoles* with their 80,000 students provided the country with its ruling class.[20] The 800,000 in the universities entered the job market in positions that were often below their qualifications, found jobs by luck or family contacts, or joined the band of the unemployed. Since the *grandes écoles* were not integrated into the university system, governments were able to elude facing many of the problems of higher education. They could somewhat neglect the universities, knowing that France would always be assured of a well-trained elite through the *grandes écoles*. Their assimiliation into the universities might lead to greater solicitude for the universities and to the development of competitive universities, but, for better or worse, the public resisted the idea of competitive universities. In France, competition in general, as Peyrefitte has argued, was resisted. Speaking of the French economy, he noted:

> Our administration believes only very little in the advantages of a market economy. It prefers to set prices, fix quotas, create new establishments, rather than to make sure that the laws of competition are faithfully followed.[21]

If the competitive university were introduced, the *grandes écoles* could be integrated in a fully competitive system of higher education. It was suggested that admission to the *grandes écoles* be restricted to university graduates, that such a plan would end the rivalry of these schools with the university and would transform them into graduate institutions.[22]

In the 1970s, however, values of French families and employers have remained the same as they were prior to 1968. The *grandes écoles* were most highly esteemed; then came the universities and finally the IUTs.

CONCLUSION

Career patterns and social mobility continued to be limited by the origin of a person's diploma. The competitive university (at least at the under-graduate level) is unlikely to appear, in view of the traditional non-mobility of French students, as well as the strongly held values of *égalité* and uniformity.

The results of the 1968 university reforms were disappointing in light of the promise and rhetoric accompanying their adoption. By 1974, authority had been consolidated in Paris, creating a new stalemate within the university. It was likely that the pattern of student strikes, and particularly the aftermath of 1976, allowed the government to regain its centralized power, and thereby reverse the liberating trend that the Orientation Act — despite some shortcomings — gallantly attempted to bring to the universities. Education is but one field in which the Fifth Republic after having attempted reforms seems to have reached a new stalemate. The possibility of further innovations also seems bleak in other sectors of French society.[23]

The French university system, however, was changed by the May events and the reforms of 1968. It was not what it had been in 1968. Compared to the Italian and German universities, the French universi-ties have proven themselves to be better organized and adapted to the needs of society and students. A start in the direction of autonomy and self-government developed at the university level. University administrators and faculty did not hesitate to challenge the ministries when they deemed that rules and regulations had been broken. Faculty members who desired to innovate sometimes found a favorable climate for experiment. And at the level of the Conference of Presidents, a collective university voice was heard. Curriculum change has not gone as far as hoped, but nevertheless, major changes have occurred. Greater diversity of educational institutions also developed. Student facilities were greatly improved and sums of scholarships increased for the needy. Within the universities, forces of change were instituted, which potentially could continue. Based on the acquired reforms, a vast new program of imaginative restructuring of the French universities might develop, in spite of centralization. But educational reforms are not readily realized by the signing of a law. Their success or failure is tied to the prevailing values and experiences of a whole society. Only to the extent that French society itself will change its structures and values can one expect a true transformation of the French university.

CONCLUSION

NOTES

Chapter I

[1]Emile Durkheim, in Jacques Fournier, *Politique de l'éducation* (Paris, 1971), p. 128.

[2]Félix Ponteil, *Histoire de l'enseignement 1789-1965* (Paris, 1966), pp. 126-127; Pierre Silvestre, "Les vingt-trois nouveaux ministères de l'éducation nationale," *Le Monde*, 30 October 1970; the provision that no institution was to exist outside the university was difficult to fulfill in view of the number of independent and religious establishments which had already existed prior to the Napoleonic reorganization of the educational system, Jacques Minot, "L'organisation du ministère de l'éducation," *Les Cahiers de l'INAS* (Paris, 1975), p. 2.

[3]Ponteil, *Histoire*, p. 25.

[4]John E. Talbott, *The Politics of Educational Reform in France, 1914-1940* (Princeton, N.J., 1969), p. 7.

[5]Theodore Zeldin, "Higher Education in France, 1848-1940," *Journal of Contemporary History*, 2 (1967): 54-60.

[6]Ibid., p. 70; Alain Peyrefitte, *Rue d'Ulm. Chroniques de la vie normalienne* (Paris, 1963), p. 28.

[7]Zeldin, "Higher Education," p. 70; Georges Pompidou, "Introduction," in Peyrefitte, *Rue d'Ulm*, p. 1.

[8]Rapport du groupe d'études au Premier Ministre [26 September 1963], "Recueils et Monographies. Les conditions de développement, de recrutement, de fonctionnement et de localisation des grandes écoles en France," *La Documentation française*, 45 (1964): 32. The study indicated that half of those wishing to enter were admitted to preparatory classes for the *grandes écoles*.

[9]Charles Frankel, "Examiners' Report" in Charles Frankel *et al.*, *Reviews of National Policies for Education. France* [Organization of Economic Cooperation and Development (OECD)] (Paris, 1971), p. 71.

[10]Zeldin, "Higher Education," p. 69; Antoine Léon, *Histoire de l'enseignement en France* (Paris, 1972), pp. 37-38.

[11]George Dupeux, *La société française 1789-1970* (Paris, 1972), p. 216.

[12]UNESCO, Conférence des ministres de l'éducation des états membres d'Europe sur l'accès à l'enseignement supérieur [Vienna, 20-25, November 1967], *Données statistiques comparatives sur l'accès à*

173

l'enseignement supérieur en Europe [Mineurop 3 b] (Paris, 1967), p. 3.

[13]Comité du personnel scientifique et technique [OECD], *Examen des politiques nationales en matière d'éducation. France*, Vol. I: *La planification du système d'enseignement* (Paris, 1969), p. 382; Alfred Sauvy, *La révolte des jeunes* (Paris, 1970), pp. 41-42.

[14]Claude Grignon and Jean-Claude Passeron, *The French Experience Before 1968* [OECD] (Paris, 1970), p. 46.

[15]Daniel Singer, *Prelude to Revolution* (London, 1970), p. 52; Jean Capelle, *Tomorrow's Education: The French Experience* [Transl. by W. D. Halls] (New York, 1967), p. 30.

[16]All tables are at the end of the book.

[17]Dieter Berstecher and Ignace Hecquet, "Coût et financement de l'enseignement universitaire" in Berstecher *et al.*, *L'Université de demain* (Brussels, 1974), p. 94.

[18]Emile Boutmy, in Talbott, *Politics*, p. 12.

[19]Ibid., pp. 114-115, 175.

[20]Edmond Goblot, *La Barrière et le niveau* (Paris, 1925), p. 9.

[21]Vivien Isambert-Jamati, *Crises de la société, crise de l'enseignement* (Paris, 1970), p. 296.

[22]Pierre Bourdieu and Jean-Claude Passeron, *Les héritiers* (Paris, 1964), p. 25.

[23]Raymond Boudon, *L'Inégalité des chances* (Paris, 1973); Capelle, *Tomorrow's* p. 107; Bourdieu and Passeron, *Les héritiers, passim*; Idems, *La réproduction* (Paris, 1970), *passim*; Maurice Garnier and Lawrence Hazelrigg, "La mobilité professionnelle en France comparée à celle d'autres pays," *Revue francaise de sociologie*, 15 (1974): 363-378; also Idem, "Father-to-Son Occupational Mobility in France. Evidence from the 1960s," *American Journal of Sociology*, 80 (September 1974): 478-502; and various OECD studies cited in this study; Noëlle Bisseret, *Les inégaux ou la sélection universitaire* (Paris, 1974), especially pp. 61-73; Idem, "La sélection à l'université et sa signification pour l'étude des rapports de dominance," *Revue française de sociologie*, 9, (1968): 463-495; Idem, "La 'naissance' et diplôme. Les processus de sélection au début des études universitaires," *Revue française de sociologie*, 9, numéro spécial (1968): 186-207; Pierre Bourdieu and Monique de Saint-Martin, "Les catégories de l'entendement professoral," *Actes de la recherche en sciences sociales*, 3 (May 1975): 68-75. (The whole issue of *Actes* is devoted to the inequality of educational opportunity in France.)

NOTES

UNESCO and OECD studies since 1967 have pointed to several factors which determine access to higher education: 1) social stratification, 2) sex, and 3) characteristics of specific regions in France; thus for example, the most unpopulated and most rural areas have the least number of youngsters attending secondary schools, and the reverse is true of the populated and industrialized areas. Also while women have 8 out of 100 chances of reaching higher education, the difference is greater among lower classes where the female's chances are less than for the female in the upper social stratum, Conférence des ministres de l'éducation des états membres d'Europe sur l'accès à l'enseignement supérieur, "Accès à l'enseignement supérieur du point de vue de l'origine sociale, économique et culturelle des étudiants," [Mineurop, 4], *UNESCO* (Paris, 1967), *passim.*, especially pp. 5, 30, 33, 41-42, 69, 81-82.

[24]Bourdieu and Passeron, *Héritiers*, pp. 39-40, the cultural advantages of the upper classes is by no means unique in France. Other studies on the inequality of educational opportunity have been widely discussed on both sides of the Atlantic, Rémi Clignet, *Liberty and Equality* (New York, 1974); Donald M. Levine and M. J. Bane, eds., *The "Inequality" Controversy* (New York, 1975); M. A. Matthijssen and C. E. Vervoort, eds., *Education in Europe, L'éducation en Europe* (Paris, 1969); Bryan Wilson, ed., *Education, Equality and Society* (London, 1975).

[25]Grignon and Passeron, *French Experience*, p. 71.

[26]Frankel, *Review of National Policies*, p. 53.

[27]Capelle, *Tomorrow's*, p. 172; France, Ministère de l'éducation nationale, service d'information économiques statistiques, *Tableaux de l'éducation nationale 1958-1968* (Paris, 1969), pp. 40-41.

[28]Jean-Raymond Tournoux, *Le Mois de mai du Général* (Paris, 1969), p. 51.

[29]Conférence des ministres de l'éducation des états membres d'Europe sur l'accès à l'enseignement supérieur [Mineurop 3b, 4] (Paris, 1967), also "Accès à l'enseignement supérieur du point de vue des besoins actuels et prévisibles du développement de la collectivité," Vienna, 20-25 November, 1967 [Mineurop 5] (Paris, 1967), Deuxième conférence des ministres de l'éducation des états membres d'Europe, Bucarest, 26 November-4 December, 1973 [Mineurop II, Ref. I] (Paris, 1973); OECD conference, "Towards Mass Higher Education; OECD Conference on Policies for Educational Growth, Educational Policies for the 1970s,"

175

General Report, Paris, 3-5 June, 1970; Frankel, *Reviews of National Policies*; Grignon and Passeron, *French Experience*; OECD, *Examen des politiques nationales*, vol. I; Union des étudiants de France (UNEF), "Manifeste pour une réforme démocratique de l'enseignement supérieur" (Paris, 1967); "Colloque national de Caen," *L'Expansion de la recherche scientifique, Revue trimestrielle de l'association d'études pour l'expansion de la recherche scientifique*, no. 23-24, May 1967; "Recommandations du colloque national d'Amiens, 15-17 mars 1968" in Ibid., special no., May 1968.

[30]"Les doyens des facultés des sciences veulent élaborer des propositions sur la sélection à l'entrée des universités," *Le Monde*, 27 January 1968; "Nouvelles prises de position pour l'entrée en faculté," *Syndicalisme universitaire*, no. 255 (29 February, 1968), p. 6; "L'entrée dans les facultés," *Education nationale*, no. 850 (8 February, 1968), p. 6, the reporting in the various journals was slanted to suit political points of view and portrayed the confusion that reigned with regards to the issue of *sélection*.

[31]Jean Cornec, *Pour et contre le baccalauréat* (Paris, 1968), pp. 36-37; "Les communistes et l'enseignement supérieur," *Ecole et la nation*, no. 131 (August 1964), p. 3.

[32]Tournoux, *Le mois*, pp. 45-46. Tournoux claimed that Fouchet opposed *sélection* fearing that it would be tantamount to *numerus clausus*, however, not all evidence supports this interpretation.

[33]Antoine Prost, "Trop d'étudiants," *Syndicalisme universitaire*, no. 449 (January 11, 1968), p. 8.

[34]OECD, "Towards Mass Higher Education," p. 186; Vladimir Kourganoff, *La face cachée de l'université* (Paris, 1972), p. 69; Pierre Bartoli, "L'université de Paris et son avenir," in Jean-Louis Crémieux-Brilhac, ed., *L'éducation nationale* (Paris, 1965), pp. 539-546, the author explains that the faculty-student ratio was worse in Paris than in the provinces, p. 541.

[35]Berstecher *et al.*, *L'Université*, p. 96.

[36]Antoine Prost, "Les enseignants," Crémieux-Brilhac, ed., *L'éducation nationale*, p. 580.

[37]Guy Michaud, *Révolution dans l'université* (Paris, 1968), p. 102; on the subject of the *cours magistral*, see also Raymond Aron, *La révolution introuvable* (Paris, 1968), pp. 60-61; Charles Debbasch, *L'université désorientée* (Paris, 1971), p. 68; Paul-Henri Chombart de Lauwe, *Pour*

NOTES

l'université avant, pendant et après 1968 (Paris, 1968), pp. 28-31; Fernand Robert, *Un mandarin prend la parole* (Paris, 1970), pp. 161-166.

[38]A model case study of the traditional mandarin system found in Terry N. Clark, *Prophets and Patrons: The French University and the Emergence of the Social Sciences* (Cambridge, Mass., 1973); the mandarin system as it exists in Italy in Burton R. Clark, *Academic Power in Italy* (Chicago, 1977); see tables 7 and 8.

[39]Prost, "Les enseignants," p. 584; and on the poor working conditions of the junior faculty, see the union journal *Bulletin du syndicat national d'enseignement supérieur*, for example the article by A. G., "Pleins temps," *Bulletin du SNE-Sup*, no. 154 (February, 1968), p. 1.

[40]Guy Herzlich, "Comment enseigner la gestion moderne des entreprises. I. L'école amérique," *Le Monde*, 15 March 1968. Herzlich cited McNamara as saying that the economic differences between Europe and the U.S. were not due to varying levels of technology, but rather to that of business administration.

[41]Monique de Saint-Martin, *Les fonctions sociales de l'enseignement scientifique* (Paris, 1971), pp. 60, 157, 161.

[42]Sauvy, *Révolte*, p. 240.

[43]Grignon and Passeron, *French Experience*, p. 121.

[44]Prost, "Trop d'étudiants," p. 8, and Saint-Martin, *Fonctions sociales*, p. 157.

[45]*Tableaux, 1971* (Paris, 1971), p. 422; Sauvy, *Révolte*, p. 240.

[46]Catherine Valabrègue, *La condition étudiante* (Paris, 1970), p. 123. The book is useful in giving a full description of student life in French universities.

[47]The Mallet Commission, "Commision nationale paritaire de la vie de l'étudiant," *La Documentation Française* (Paris, 1969), p. 32.

[48]OECD, "Examen des politiques nationales," vol. I, p. 395; *Tableaux, 1974* (Paris, 1974), p. 11; Jean-Charles Asselain, *Le budget de l'éducation nationale 1952-1967* (Paris, 1969), p. 86, the figures for higher education cited in the text exclude expenditures on research, libraries and central administration connected with higher education. See table 12.

[49]Ibid., p. 130; Kourganoff, *Face cachée*, p. 69; Pierre Daumard, *Le prix de l'enseignement en France* (Paris, 1969), p. 54.

[50]See table 12.

[51]OECD, "Towards Mass Higher Education," p. 208.

[52]Berstecher *et al.*, *L'université*, p. 98. The graph indicates national expenditures in the same order as the OECD study.

[53]Sauvy, *Révolte*, pp. 49-50, John Cairns, *France* (Englewood Cliffs, N.J., 1965), p. 84; France, National Assembly, 2nd séance, 9 November 1971, *Journal officiel* (10 November 1971), p. 5545. For figures on student population age-group 19-24 years, see Grignon and Passeron, *French Experience*, p. 47, Table 3.

NOTES

Chapter II

[1]Alfred Fabre-Luce, *Le Général en Sorbonne* (Paris, 1968), p. 7; Claude Lefort, "Le désordre nouveau," in Edgar Morin *et al.*, *Mai 1968: La bréche* (Paris, 1968), p. 59; Philippe Labro, *Les barricades de mai* (Paris, 1968), n. p.

[2]Michel Crozier, *The Bureaucratic Phenomenon* (Chicago, 1964), *passim*.

[3]Singer, *Prelude to Revolution*, p. 36.

[4]Aron, *Révolution introuvable*; Morin *et al.*, *La bréche*, p. 66; Lefort, in Ibid., p. 81; Roger Caillois, "La révolution cachée," *Le Monde*, 13 June 1968. For the many views held by prominent observers, see Claude Fohlen, ed., *Mai 1968, révolution ou psychodrame?* (Paris, 1973); André Malraux viewed May 1968 as a "crisis of civilization," André Barjonet viewed it as a revolutionary situation; Waldeck Rochet, the Communist Party leader, did not think it was a revolution. For Erick Hobsbawm, the British historian on revolutions, May 1968 was somewhere in between, while for Adrien Dansette, clergyman-historian, May 1968 symbolized a new era of instability for France, ibid., pp. 22-23. Mathilde Niel, "A propos de la révolte de mai, réponse à Raymond Aron," *Combat*, 6 June 1968.

[5]Jean-Paul Sartre, "L'idée neuve de mai 1968," *Le Nouvel Observatuer*, 26 June 1968, pp. 21-24.

[6]"Student Clashes," *The Observer*, 10 March 1968, p. 1.

[7]"Why Those Students are Protesting," *Time*, 10 March 1968, pp.

178

24-25.

[8]Theodore Roszak, *The Making of a Counter-Culture* (New York, 1968), p. 27. Roszak said that "in American as in a number of European countries a bit more than 50% of the population is under twenty-five years of age"; Kenneth Kenniston, "Sources of Student Dissent," in Edward E. Sampson and Harold A. Korn, eds., *Student Activism and Protest* (San Francisco, 1970), p. 184.

[9]"Les étudiants italiens réclament une réforme profonde et rapide des universités," "Le difficile combat de l'université espagnole," *Le Monde*, 17 February 1968.

[10]The Sorbonne had been built in 1900 to accommodate 15,000, in 1967 it had 50,000. Mattei Dogan, "Causes of the French Student Revolt in May 1968," in Stephen D. Kertesz, ed., *The Task of Universities in a Changing World* (South Bend, Ind., 1972), p. 307; Singer, *Prelude*, p. 118.

[11]Passing the *concours d'agrégation* gave one the title of *agrégé*, thus an individual in secondary school would be known as a *professeur agrégé* which assured one of a senior position and other special privileges. Those who pass the concours de CAPES became known as *professeurs certifiés* in secondary schools and so came second to the *agrégés* in rank. There are a number of less prestigious echelons in the hierarchy of secondary school teachers. To prepare for a CAPES or an *agrégation*, an individual has a choice of two routes. One can acquire the *licence* (undergraduate degree) and then prepare for the CAPES examination, or one can take the *licence*, the master's, and then prepare for the *agrégation*. The *agrégation* gives access to either secondary school or university teaching, Conseil de l'Europe, Conseil de la coopération culturelle, *Réforme et développement de l'enseignement supérieur en Europe* (Strasbourg, 1967), pp. 91-92.

[12]Dogan, "Causes," p. 313.

[13]In 1968, 450,000 people were unemployed in France of whom 40 percent were young people; Singer, *Prelude*, p. 110; Dogan, "Causes," p. 313.

[14]Dogan, "Causes," p. 314.

[15]Ibid., p. 308; also A. Belden Fields, *Student Politics in France* (New York, 1970), p. 71, reiterated this view when he said that "it was natural that student activists direct both positive demands and expressions of discontent to the government."

[16]Ibid., p. 77.

[17]For a coherent comparative analysis of student activism see Sampson and Korn, eds., *Student Activism*, and especially Richard Flacks, "Social and Cultural Meanings of Student Revolt," Ibid., pp. 118-141; with regards to student rebellion against the established authority pp. 122-133; Stephen R. Graubard and Geno A. Ballotti, eds., *The Embattled University* (New York, 1970), especially Erik H. Erikson, "Reflections on the Dissent of Contemporary Youth," Ibid., pp. 154-176, and Stanley Hoffmann, "Participation in Perspective?" Ibid., pp. 177-221.

[18]Dogan, "Causes," pp. 318-319; Tournoux, *Mois de mai*, p. 369.

[19]The roots of UNEF organization date back to 1877, Fields, *Student Politics*, pp. 16, 37-38; Tournoux, *Mois de mai*, p. 375; Frédéric Gaussen and Guy Herzlich, "Les étudiants entre l'apathie et la violence," Part III, *Le Monde*, 9 May 1968; Dogan, "Causes," p. 316; Frédéric Gaussen, "Les congrès universitaires," *Le Monde*, 9 April 1968; Sylvain Zegel, *Les idées de mai* (Paris, 1968), p. 14.

[20]For discussions of political parties and groups, Tournoux, *Mois de mai*, pp. 371-374; Jean-Pierre Mouchon, *La crise estudiantine et les émeutes de mai 1968* (Paris, 1969), pp. 21-23; "Petit lexique de group-uscules," *Le Monde*, 9 May 1968. The name of the "Movement of March 22" was an imitation of Fidel Castro's "Movement of July 26," see brochure in the 3rd of a series on the New Left by Claude Harmel, "La crise de l'enseignement supérieur en France," *Centre international de documentation et d'information* (The Hague, 1970), p. 9.

[21]Sauvy, *Révolte des jeunes*, p. 79; Dogan, "Causes," p. 317.

[22]For general discontent during the months preceding May 1968, regarding dormitory regulations, restaurants, curriculum, see *Le Monde*, especially "Interdiction d'un débat sur le Vietnam à la Sorbonne," *Le Monde*, 26 January 1968; B. G. A., "Des jeunes filles occupent un pavillon de garçons dans une cité universitaire de Nantes," *Le Monde*, 25 January 1968; "Grève des étudiants en sociologie de Tours"; J. P. Quelin, "Antony le rouge," *Le Monde*, 16 February 1968, and *Le Monde*, 6 February 1968, and the president of the Federation of university residences in France declared "Il fallait bousculer un état de fait pour forcer au dialogue" (We had to upset the apple cart in order to encourage a dialogue); "Le retard dans le paiement des allocations de troisième cycle," *Le Monde*, 21 February 1968; "Grève à la faculté de

NOTES

médecine de Paris," *Le Monde*, 24 April 1968; "Un projet de réforme des réglements des cités universitaires va être examiné par le comité des oeuvres," *Le Monde*, 11-12 February 1968; for Alain Peyrefitte's views on the troubles and reform of university residence regulations, Gaussen, "La manifestation des étudiants et des enseignants au quartier latin," *Le Monde*, 29 March 1968; *Bulletin du SNE-Sup* no. 155 (February 1968). For discussion of protests against the Fouchet plan of 1966 on curriculum reorganization, "Manifestations d'étudiants à Besançon," *Le Monde*, 2 March 1968; Jacqueline Romilly, *Nous autres professeurs* (Paris, 1969), p. 43; Jean Chardonnet, *L'université en question* (Paris, 1968), p. 20 ; Aron, *Introuvable*, pp. 61, 63; Dogan, "Causes," p. 320; J. Perret, *Inquiète Sorbonne* (Paris, 1969), p. 20.

[23]Frédéric Gaussen, "Les étudiants entre l'apathie et la violence," Part II, *Le Monde*, 8 May 1968.

[24]Nanterre had 12,000 students of whom 1,500 were residents. The campus consisted of a *faculté* of letters, and a *faculté* of law which was an annex to the Paris law *faculté*; there was a student restaurant and a dormitory complex, "Nanterre," *Le Monde*, 10 January 1968 and "Nanterre," *Le Monde*, 4 May 1968; Tournoux, *Mois de mai*, p. 15; Michel-Antoine Burnier and Bernard Kouchner, *La France sauvage* (Paris, 1970), pp. 28-36.

[25]Fields, *Student Politics*, p. 80.

[26]"Incidents à la faculté de Nanterre," *Le Monde*, 27, 28-29 January 1968; "A Nanterre," *Le Monde*, 3 April 1968; "Après l'occupation des locaux," *Le Monde*, 29 March 1968; Zegel, *Idées*, pp. 25-36; Tournoux, *Mois de mai*, pp. 347-350; the term "enragés" was used during the French Revolution of 1789 for a group of political extremists.

[27]With regards to the disciplinary hearing of the March 22 group, university authorities thought the affair would take time and would not be concluded before the spring vacation. Moreover, the rector and several deans were about to embark on a study mission to the U.S. It was agreed to delay the hearing till after the end of April; it was set for May 6, Tournoux, *Mois de mai*, p. 349.

[28]Zegel, *Idées*, p. 28; "Paris: un groupe d'étudiants pratique des méthodes de partisans," *Le Monde*, 30 March 1968; "Nanterre: les 'prochinois' Empêchent M. Juquin de parler," *Le Monde*, 27 April 1968; "Les cours de la faculté des lettres reprendaient progressivement à Nanterre," *Le Monde*, 4 May 1968; "Le communiqué du doyen," *Le*

181

Monde, 4 May 1968; Tournoux, *Mois de mai*, pp. 19, 349; Alain Geismar in Hervé Bourges, ed., *The French Student Revolt, The Leaders Speak* (Paris, 1968), p. 31.

[29]The date was symbolic for ten years earlier, on May 13, 1958, the revolt against the Fourth French Republic had broken out bringing Charles de Gaulle back to power.

[30]Singer, *Prelude*, especially pp. 119, 130, 147; Tournoux, *Mois de mai*, pp. 62, 83-84, 93, 379; Jean-Louis Monneron *et al.*, *Politique et prophétisme, mai 1968* [Centre catholique des intellectuels français] (Paris, 1969), especially Michel Crozier, "Réponses d'un témoin," in Ibid., pp. 75-78; René Rémond, "Evénement ou avénement? Etait-ce une révolution?" Ibid., pp. 81-89; Joseph Thomas, "Procès d'une civilisation," Ibid., pp. 119-132; Maurice Clavel *et al.*, *Que faisaient-ils en avril?* (Paris, 1969), notably Edgar Pisani, "Une révolution de privilégiés," Ibid., pp. 183-184; François Mauriac, "La société de consommation . . . un point de départ," Ibid., pp. 177-179; Guy Michaud, *Révolution*; B. G. A., "Les violentes échauffourées du quartier latin ont parfois pris l'allure d'un combat du rue," *Le Monde*, 8 May 1968; "Près de six cents interpellations au cours des violents incidents du quartier latin," *Le Monde*, 8 May 1968; "Le gouvernement ne peut admettre la fanatisme et la violence," *Le Monde*, 9 May 1968.

[31]Tournoux, *Mois de mai*, p. 162.

[32]Bourges, *French student*, pp. 7, 65, 76, 81.

[33]The revolution in China had its roots in the Sin-Kiang region; Raymond Aron, "La crise de l'université," *Le Figaro*, 13 June 1968.

[34]Alain Geismar speaking of the ideas expressing hope for a new society added: "Many people refer to Marcuse. I must say that, to my knowledge, none of the militants in my union, in the UNEF or in any other organization, with the possible exception of one in a thousand, has ever read a line of this author who is presented to us as the great precursor to the struggles taking place in the universities in the world over; which is not to reject his influence, for he has apparently been the first to put into writing analyses of a number of social phenomenon; we have put them into action," Bourges, *French Student*, pp. 36-37; Aron, *Introuvable*, recorded a meeting with Herbert Marcuse in which Aron said to him: "In short your philosophy is violence in order to arrive at a new peaceful society," and Marcuse is reported to have answered, "It is exactly that," Ibid., p. 119; Reich had written on the sexual alienation of

182

NOTES

workers; Edgar Morin, "La commune étudiante," in Morin *et al.*, *La bréche*, p. 15; Guy Herzlich, "Les étudiants entre l'apathie et la violence," Part I, *Le Monde*, 7 May 1968.

[35]Fabre-Luce, *Le Général*, p. 7; Aron, *Introuvable*, p. 31.

[36]Aron, *Introuvable*, p. 143.

[37]Bourges, *French Student*, p. 34.

[38]"Le doyen Zamanski souligne l'absence de formation professionnelle pour les étudiants," *Le Monde*, 8 May 1968; "La contestation des structures," *Le Monde*, 15 May 1968; B. G. A., "Dans les facultés et les grandes écoles les principes d'autonomie et de cogestion sont approuvés à la quasi-unanimité," *Le Monde*, 21 May 1968; Michaud, *Révolution*, pp. 53-65.

[39]Alain Schnapp and Pierre Vidal-Naquet, eds., *Journal de la commune étudiante, Novembre 67-Juin 68* (Paris, 1969).

[40]Roger Duchène, *A la recherche de l'université* (Paris, 1972), p. 6.

[41]"Les communistes et l'enseignement," *L'école et la nation*, no. 131 (August, 1964), pp. 3-23; "Propositions du parti communiste français pour une réforme démocratique de l'enseignement," 1967 deuxième édition, *L'école et la nation*, special no. 185-186 (January-February 1970), p. 53.

[42]For examples of the reform movement see "M. Pompidou promet que les étudiants participeront à l'élaboration de la réforme de l'université," *Le Monde*, 16 May 1968; "Le mouvement de contestation s'étend à Paris et en province, un 'pouvoir étudiant' cherche à s'affirmer," *Le Monde*, 17 May 1968; "Dans les universités de province et de l'étranger," *Le Monde*, 18 May 1968.

[43]Rector Antoine had visited American universities and had been impressed by the American professor. He harshly criticized the French professor whom he said was "often a proud and egotistical individual." "Combien de maîtres de l'enseignement supérieur se contentent de donner leur cours? déclare le recteur Antoine à la télévision d'Orléans," *Le Monde*, 19-20 May 1968.

[44]There were those who disapproved of the anarchical method of discussions going on during this time. Raymond Aron found that the propositions that were made by the various communes or commissions showed that their "imagination was not very imaginative," often discussing petty issues, some were resolved by a "cooperative spirit," others by "utopic anarcho-syndicalist" methods. It was questionable, he argued,

how anything constructive could result from an assembly of four hundred people, Aron, *Introuvable*, p. 110.

[45]Bourges, *French Student*, p. 73.

[46]Singer, *Prelude*, p. 152.

[47]Ibid., p. 92. In 1968 there were 15 million wage earners in France. Less than a quarter were unionized, much less than in Britain, Germany or the Scandinavian countries.

[48]Richard F. Hamilton, *Affluence and the French Worker* (Princeton, N.J., 1967); Dupeux, *Société française*; Morin, in Morin *et al.*, *La brèche*, p. 70; Alain Touraine, *Le mouvement de mai ou le communisme utopique* (Paris, 1968), pp. 25-26 (transl. in English by Leonard F. X. Mayhew, *The May Movement, Revolt and Reform* (New York, 1971)).

[49]Singer, *Prelude*, p. 84; Fohlen, *Mai 1968*, p. 34.

[50]Singer, *Prelude*, p. 159; Tournoux, *Mois de mai*, p. 337; Fohlen, *Mai 1968*, p. 12; Fabre-Luce, *Le Général*, p. 23; "Répercussions économiques," *Le Monde*, 22 May 1968.

[51]Jesse Pitts, "Continuity and Change in Bourgeois France," in Stanley Hoffmann, ed., *In Search of France* (New York, 1965), pp. 235-304, note section by Pitts entitled "The Delinquent Community," pp. 254-259; Crozier, *Phenomenon*.

[52]Morin, Lefort in Morin *et al.*, *La brèche*, pp. 54, 75.

[53]Tournoux, *Mois de mai*, pp. 97, 112; Singer, *Prelude*, p. 69; Mouchon, *La crise*, p. 62.

[54]Mouchon, *La crise*, p. 66.

[55]Fohlen, *Mai 1968*, p. 47.

[56]The first draft of the Grenelle Accord gave an increase of hourly wages from 44 U.S. cents to 66 cents, this applied to some 200,000 workers earning the 44 cents minimum and to about 600,000 earning less than 60 cents. The rest of the labor force was promised a 10 percent wage increase for the year, "Le protocole d'accord entre le syndicat, le patronat et le gouvernement est soumis aux grévistes," *Le Monde*, 28 May 1968. The final concessions granted 2-3 percent more than the original offer in wages, and agreed in some cases to pay the full wages for the days of the strike, Singer, *Prelude*, pp. 182-208.

[57]"La situation dans l'université," *Le Monde*, 5 June 1968.

[58]"Les mesures envisagées par le premier ministre," *Le Monde*, 21 June 1968; "Dans un appel au ministre de l'éducation nationale," *Le Monde*, 30 June 1968.

NOTES

NOTES

Chapter III

[1]Edgar Faure, Minister of Education, at his investiture to office on 24 July 1968, 1st séance, 24 July 1968, *Assemblée nationale débats, J. o.* (25 July 1968), p. 2525; Olivier Guichard, Minister of Education, *Un chemin tranquille* (Paris, 1975), p. 165; for translation of the full text of the Orientation Act of Higher Education of 1968 see Appendix 4.

[2]Pierre Viansson-Ponté, "Le Général de Gaulle envisage de consulter le pays en juin par référendum sur 'la participation," *Le Monde*, 22 May 1968. De Gaulle later withdrew his decision to hold a referendum and promised a general election instead.

[3]Gilles Plazy, "M. Ortoli hérite d'un ministère empoisonné," *Combat*, 2 June 1968.

[4]Quoted in Pierre Viansson-Ponté, "Le premier conseil des ministres," *Le Monde*, 14-15 July 1968.

[5]Faure, *Crois*, pp. 19-24; a detailed description of de Gaulle's new cabinet, Jacques Fomerand, "Policy-Formulation and Change in the Fifth Republic: the 1968 Orientation Act of Higher Education," (Ph.D. dissertation City College of New York, 1973), pp. 101-106.

[6]B. G. A., "M. E. Faure confie une mission de coordination au recteur Antoine," *Le Monde*, 18 July 1968. For list of collaborators, see Faure, *Crois*, pp. 40-46, and Fomerand, "Policy-Formulation," p. 292. Antoine has also co-authored a book with André Passeron, *La réforme de l'université* (Paris, 1966).

[7]Fomerand, "Policy-Formulation," p. 99; Jacques de Chalendar, *Une loi pour l'université avec le manuscrit inédit d'Edgar Faure* (Paris, 1970), p. 32; Faure, *Crois*, p. 44.

[8]Zeldin, "Higher Education," pp. 60-62.

[9]"Un colloque sur la formation des maîtres va se tenir à Amiens," *Le Monde*, 23 January 1968; "Au colloque d'Amiens," *Le Monde*, 16 March 1968; Charles Fourrier, *Les institutions universitaires* (Paris, 1971), p. 9.

[10]Bertrand Girod de l'Ain, "Un colloque sur l'enseignement supérieur en Europe," *Le Monde*, 27 March 1968.

[11]Zeldin, "Higher Education," pp. 57, 60, 62.

[12]Fourrier, *Institutions*, p. 9; Mouchon, *La crise*, p. 26; Capelle, *Education et politique*, p. 160.

[13]Jacques Chevallier, *L'enseignement supérieur* (Paris, 1971), p. 7; Kourganoff, *La face cachée*, p. 22; Frankel, in Frankel *et al.*, *Reviews of National Policies*, p. 71.

[14]"L'exposé des motifs du projet de loi," *Le Monde*, 29-30 September, 1968; for issues of decentralization towards the regional level, "Les débats à l'assemblée nationale," *Le Monde*, 26 July 1968.

[15]Fomerand, "Policy-Formulation," p. 63.

[16]Schnapp and Vidal-Naquet, *Journal*, pp. 240-241, 248, 703; Fomerand, "Policy-Formulation," p. 76.

[17]Chalendar, *Une loi*, p. 197.

[18]Schnapp and Vidal-Naquet, *Journal*, pp. 707-708; "Structures et autonomie des facultés, comité de liaison interfacultés," *Le Monde*, 4 July 1968.

[19]Association d'étude pour l'expansion de l'enseignement supérieur, ed., *De l'université aux universités, octobre 1968-janvier 1971* [Cahiers des universités françaises, I (Paris, 1971)]. For the full account of the introduction and application of the Orientation Act of Higher Education, see this comprehensive account with the texts of Edgar Faure's speeches in parliament and the texts of the laws as well as the directives given to the universities in their restructuring.

[20]George Bourjac, "L'administration locale," in Crémieux-Brilhac, ed., *L'éducation nationale*, pp. 519-525.

[21]With regards to the membership of the university council, some feared that they would grow too large, so it was decided in parliament to reduce them to less than 100 members, and the figure of eighty was agreed upon, 1st séance, 9 October 1968, *Assemblée nationale, débats, J.o.* (10 October 1968), p. 3143.

[22]Chalendar, *Une loi*, p. 212; proposals to make the rector of the academy also the rector of the university did not materialize, Guy Herzlich, "Le ministre reçoit les représentants des universités de province," *Le Monde*, 6 September 1968.

[23]Chalender, *Une loi*, pp. 209-210.

[24]Schnapp and Vidal-Naquet, *Journal*, p. 704; Chalendar, *Une loi*, pp. 198-199, 258.

[25]"Un bureau permanent de liaison groupant universitaires et étudiants est créé à Amiens," *Le Monde*, 24 January 1968; "Dans les académies — Amiens," *Education nationale*, no. 849 (1 February 1968), p. 8; "A quand des structures nouvelles dans les facultés (à propos d'une

NOTES

expérience lilloise)," *Syndicalisme universitaire*, no. 461 (2 May 1968), p. 6; Hervé Bourges, *French Student Revolt*, p. 14.

[26]Fohlen, *Mai 1968*, pp. 37-38.

[27]A hellenist professor at the Sorbonne asserted: "The Germans occupied Paris, I did not collaborate; the students occupied the Sorbonne, I shall not collaborate," Schnapp and Vidal-Naquet, p. 643.

[28]Chalendar, *Une loi*, pp. 98, 105; Schnapp and Vidal-Naquet, *Journal*, pp. 117, 643, 645, 722; Michelle Perrot *et al.*, *La Sorbonne par elle même Mai-Juin 1968* (Paris, 1968), pp. 374-380, for debates on the subject of parity on councils.

[29]For de Gaulle's attitude towards participation, see the issue devoted to the subject in *Espoir*, 5 (December 1973-January 1974). "Participation" was not always considered very seriously by Pompidou who in 1963 was quoted as having said to his fellow cabinet members: "Participation, do you know what that is? No one has ever explained it to me." Alain Peyrefitte, *Le mal français* (Paris, 1976), p. 399.

[30]Chalendar, *Une loi*, pp. 109, 260-261; 1st séance, 3 October 1968, *Assemblée nationale, débats, J.o.* (4 October, 1968), p. 3004. When necessary a university was to have a scientific council alongside the university council which was to be responsible for laboratory and research funds.

[31]Chalendar, *Une loi*, p. 110; "L'exposé des motifs du projet de loi," *Le Monde*, 29-30 September 1968.

[32]B. G. A., "Le projet de loi d'orientation universitaire," *Le Monde*, 18 September 1968.

[33]"Les réactions au projet de loi d'orientation . . ." *Le Monde*, 26 September 1968; G. H., "Le SGEN approuve avec quelques réserves les réformes des enseignants secondaires et supérieurs," *Le Monde*, 2 October 1968; "Durant l'élaboration de la loi d'orientation," *Syndicalisme universitaire*, no. 470 (3 October 1968), pp. 11-12; 1st séance, 24 July 1968, *Assemblée nationale, débats, J.o.* (25 July 1968), p. 2529; Jacques Monod, "L'étrange alliance," *Le Monde*, 8 October 1968; Debbasch, *L'université désorientée*, p. 98, thought that the Faure law was admirable in that it included all segments of the university community as well as lay persons; for a conservative view of the law, Fernand Robert, *Mandarin*, p. 223.

[34]1st séance, 3 October 1968, *Assemblée nationale, débats, J.o.* (4 October 1968), p. 3003, 1st séance, 9 October 1968, *Assemblée nationale*,

débats, J.o. (10 October 1968), p. 3144.

[35]For arguments on obligatory voting in university elections, debates in the National Assembly, for example, 2nd séance, 3 October 1968, *Assemblée nationale, débats, J.o.* (4 October 1968), p. 3032; 1st séance, 9 October 1968, *Assemblée nationale, débats, J.o.* (10 October 1968), p. 3156 (Borscher); pp. 3157-8 (Duhamel, Falala, Dupuy); pp. 3154-55 (Faure); and 2nd séance, 9 October 1968, *Assemblée nationale, débats, J.o.* (10 October 1968), p. 3167 (Fanton, Capelle).

[36]Burnier and Kouchner, *France sauvage*, pp. 77-79.

[37]"Les propositions d'amendement du projet de loi d'orientation," *Le Monde*, 3 October 1968; 1st séance, 3 October 1968, *Assemblée nationale, débats, J.o.* (4 October 1968), p. 3003; 1st séance, 9 October 1968, *Assemblée nationale, débats, J.o.* (10 October 1968), p. 3172.

[38]Frédéric Gaussen, "Les projets de réformes des universités et des facultés," *Le Monde*, 4 July 1968.

[39]2nd séance, 25 July 1968, *Assemblée nationale, débats, J.o.* (26 July 1968), p. 2611.

[40]Maurice Duverger, "La politique dans l'université," *Le Monde*, 14 August 1968; B. G. A., "Le projet de loi d'orientation universitaire," *Le Monde*, 19 September 1968; B. G. A., "Réforme de l'enseignement supérieur . . ." *Le Monde*, 12 September 1968.

[41]With regards to disciplinary councils for faculty and students, see article 38 of the law; on the subject of liberty of expression, Pierre Viansson-Ponté, "Les projets de réforme de l'université," *Le Monde*, 13 September 1968; "Les réactions au projet de loi . . .," *Le Monde*, 26 September 1968; Frédéric Gaussen, "Une ou deux politiques," *Le Monde*, 9 August 1968; Dean Georges Vedel wrote Edgar Faure an open letter on the subject of freedom of expression in which he disapproved of the liberal interpretation the law allowed, *Le Monde*, 11-12 August 1968; Chevallier, *L'enseignement supérieur*, p. 17; Burnier and Kouchner, *France sauvage*, p. 80 (my italics and my translation of the articles of the law, since it is more literal than the official translation in the appendix).

[42]For a history of continuing education in France and experiments made in various institutions, L. Weil *et al.*, "Elargissement du cadre éducatif. Vers l'éducation permanente," in Crémieux-Brilhac, ed., *L'éducation nationale*, pp. 238-257; the current situation is conveniently summarized in *Education permanente*, 27 (January-February 1975): 3-109.

188

NOTES

[43]"La commission des affaires culturelles," *Le Monde*, 27 September 1968; "L'exposé des motifs du projet de loi," *Le Monde*, 29-30 September 1968; B. Bemians, "Le monde de l'économie, 'job' ou carrière?" *Le Monde*, 27 August 1968, Supplement I; "L'orientation universitaire," *Bulletin du SNE-Sup*, no. 160 (27 May 1968), p. 6; *Education nationale*, no. 866 (27 June 1968), pp. 25-27; "La loi d'orientation sur l'enseignement supérieur," *Education nationale*, nos. 1-2 (26 September 1968), p. 72.

[44]Schnapp and Vidal-Naquet, *Journal*, p. 705. One of the most influential documents that emerged in June 1968 came from the Commission nationale inter-disciplines (CNID), an offshoot of the Comité de liaison inter-facultés (CLIF), seated in the Paris law *faculté* on Rue d'Assas. This commission gathered faculty and students from all over France and studied the works of many commissions of the various general assemblies, and then itself drafted an elaborate document regarding the new university. Michel Alliot, professor of the law *faculté* played an important role on this committee; the outline of the reform plans were to be followed in many aspects in the drafting of the Orientation Act of Higher Education. For the full document, see Schnapp and Vidal-Naquet, *Journal*, pp. 699-708.

[45]Chalendar, *Une loi*, p. 90; Capelle, *Politique*, p. 176.

[46]"L'accès aux enseignements supérieurs," *Education nationale*, no. 849 (1 February 1968), pp. 6-7; "La réforme de l'orientation," *Education nationale*, no. 853 (29 February 1968), pp. 13-17; "Le plan d'Alain Peyrefitte sur la rénovation pédagogique," *Education nationale*, no. 854 (7 March 1968), pp. 6-7; "La formation donnée par les facultés," *Le Monde*, 21 January 1968; "Au conseil des ministres, M. Alain Peyrefitte fait approuver les grandes lignes du projet réformant l'orientation péda-gogique et professionnelle," *Le Monde*, 11 January 1968. For a lengthy discussion of the Peyrefitte plan, Tournoux, *Mois de mai*, pp. 49-53; B. G. A., "L'information et l'orientation scolaire," *Le Monde*, 21 December 1968.

[47]For Faure's statement that he did not intend the university to be a placement service, 1st séance, 3 October 1968, *Assemblée nationale, débats, J.o.* (4 October 1968), p. 3018; Deputy Poujade spoke of "supple orientation," instead of authoritarian orientation, p. 3008; for the setting up of a national office of information ONISEP, and the problems of career opportunities, 1st séance, 25 July 1968, *Assemblée nationale,*

débats, J.o. (26 July 1968), p. 2582; 1st séance, 28 October 1968, *Assemblée nationale, débats, J.o.* (29 October 1968), p. 3634.

[48]Chalendar, *Une loi*, p. 85, citing the vice president of the senatorial commission for cultural affairs; also in Fomerand, "Policy-Formulation," p. 69; Alain Geismar, "Mise au point," *Bulletin du SNE-Sup*, no. 159 (April 1968), p. 161; "Nouvelles prises de position sur l'entrée en faculté," *Syndicalisme universitaire*, no. 455 (29 February 1968), p. 6.

[49]Chalendar, *Une loi*, p. 85.

[50]Minot, *Entreprise éducation nationale* (Paris, 1970), pp. 322-323; Frédéric Gaussen, "Universitaires sans carrière, II. Le retour des mandarins," *Le Monde*, 14 February 1973; Suzanne Citron, *L'école bloquée* (Paris, 1971), p. 6; Ponteil, *Histoire*, p. 387. For debate in the National Assembly regarding the retention of the national faculty recruiting organ, the CCU, 1st séance, 10 October 1968, *Assemblée nationale, débats, J.o.* (11 October 1968), p. 3227; Capelle, a UDR deputy and head of the Assembly's cultural affairs commission stated: "There exists a complementary organ at the national level which in spite of the call for decentralization, must be preserved, and that is the *Comité consultatif.*"

[51]P. Baquet, "Thèse de doctorat ès-lettres," *Le Monde*, 11 July 1968; Chombart de Lauwe, *Pour l'université*, p. 110.

[52]"Les propositions du projet de loi d'orientation," *Le Monde*, 3 October 1968; J. P. Colin, "Propos pour une université nouvelle," *Le Monde*, 19 June 1968; "Lignes directrices d'une réforme," *Syndicalisme universitaire*, no. 464 (13 June 1968), pp. 19-20; "L'exposé des motifs du *L'étudiant périmé* (Paris, 1968), p. 44; 1st séance, 24 July 1968, *Assemblée nationale, débats, J.o.* (25 July 1968), p. 2528.

[53]Duchène, *A la recherche*, p. 13.

[54]Fourrier, *Institutions*, p. 9; Frédéric Gaussen, "Les projets de réforme de l'université, III. Cogestion," *Le Monde*, 4 July 1968; C. Pietri, "Conférence de presse, propositions du SGEN," *Syndicalisme universitaire*, no. 464 (13 July 1968), pp. 19-20; "L'exposé des motifs du projet de loi," *Le Monde*, 29-30 September 1968.

[55]Schnapp and Vidal-Naquet, *Journal*, p. 660.

[56]1st séance, 24 July 1968, *Assemblée nationale, débats, J.o.* (25 July 1968), pp. 2525, 2528; Edgar Faure, *L'éducation nationale et la participation* (Paris, 1968), p. 50; 1st séance, 3 October 1968, *Assemblée nationale, débats, J.o.* (4 October 1968), p. 3004.

190

NOTES

[57]Conversation with a professor from Poitiers during his visit to Indiana University, 1973-1974.

[58]Barny et al., "Projet de plateforme syndicale," *Bulletin du SNE-Sup.*, no. 162 (July, 1968), pp. 1-8; Fourrier, *Institutions*, p. 21; S. Gibara and P. Viguerois, "Le néo-réformisme de l'enseignement par petits groupes," *Le Monde*, 19 June 1968 (both authors had attended Harvard Business school and taught at commerce schools in France, H.E.C.'s); Schnapp and Vidal-Naquet, *Journal*, pp. 730-733; 1st séance, 10 October 1968, *Assemblée nationale, débats, J.o.* (11 October 1968), p. 3223.

[59]C. M. Vardot, "Les facultés nouvelles poussent comme des champignons," *L'Aurore*, 21-22 September 1968; "Le centre de Vincennes décernera les mêmes diplômes que les autres," *L'Aurore*, 24 October 1968; "Vincennes, Antony, Dauphine," *Combat*, 2 October 1968; "M. E. Faure annonce la création de trois établissements expérimentaux," *Le Monde*, 16 September 1968; "Dans les centres expérimentaux de la région parisienne," *Le Monde*, 2 October 1968; Y. de Gentil-Baichis, "Les nouveaux centres, un propos attirant," *La Croix*, 9 October 1968.

[60]Some went so far as to suggest that students should participate in decisions about examinations and even sit on exam juries. This idea was rejected by Faure, for he said: "It might give the public the impression that examinations were not serious and hence lead to devaluation of the diploma," 2nd séance, *Assemblée nationale, débats, J.o.* (11 October 1968), p. 3232.

[61]"Document: réflexion sur la mutation de l'université," *Education nationale*, no. 866 (27 June 1968), pp. 10-14; proposals by the famous Commission nationale inter-discipline (CNID) made on 6 June 1968, in Schnapp and Vidal-Naquet, *Journal*, pp. 707-798.

[62]Frédéric Gaussen, "Les projets de réforme des universités. II. Financement des universités," *Le Monde*, 4 July 1968.

[63]1st séance, 10 October 1968, *Assemblée nationale, débats, J.o.* (11 October 1968), pp. 3215-3216.

[64]1st séance, 3 October 1968, *Assemblée nationale, débats, J.o.* (4 October 1968), p. 3005 [Jean Charbonnel, reporter for the finance commission of the draft of the new law]; for a discussion on the views of the reformers and the contradictions of their ideas, Fomerand, "Policy-Formulation," p. 84.

NOTES

[65]A. Ballet, "L'assemblée nationale a entamé la discussion des articles," *Le Monde*, 10 October 1968.

[66]Ibid.

[67]M. O. F., "La loi devant l'assemblée," *Education nationale*, no. 5 (17 October 1968), pp. 7-9 (referring to debates at the National Assembly on 3-4 October 1968).

[68]Ibid.

[69]Particulary useful for the different views held regarding the Orientation Act of Higher Education after the drafting stage, "Après l'adoption de la loi d'orientation," *Le Monde*, 15 October 1968; Frédéric Gaussen, "Les universités face au mouvement de mai," *Le Monde*, 16 November 1968, supplement; Guy Michaud, *Révolution dans l'université*.

NOTES

Chapter IV

[1]Edgar Faure, *Philosophie d'une réforme* (Paris, 1969), p. 21; Bloch-Lainé, *Le Figaro*, 17 March 1973 cited in M. Boret, "La réforme des établissements publics," *Education et gestion*, no. 37 (June 1973), p. 28; J. Bousquet, "Pour l'éducation de l'an 2,000, prospectives et programmation," *Education*, no. 43 (30 October 1969), p. 8.

[2]For a list of ministers, Debbasch, *L'université désorientée*, pp. 42-47.

[3]B. G. A., "Le changement de ministère de l'éducation nationale," *Le Monde*, 29-30 June 1969; Edgar Faure, *Crois*, pp. 100-101; Olivier Guichard, *Chemin*, p. 63.

[4]1st séance, 12 November 1969, *Assemblée nationale, débats, J.o.* (13 November 1969), p. 3582.

[5]Guichard, *Chemin*, pp. 93, 131-139, has told the story of how in 1958 de Gaulle supposedly called Pompidou and said: "Pompidou, Guichard is a nobody. He must become something." A few days later Guichard was appointed *préfet* at the ministry of interior; and later held several cabinet posts.

[6]F. G., "Un homme simple," *Le Monde*, 10-11 September 1972.

[7]"Après la nomination de M. Haby," *Le Monde*, 30 May 1974; F. G.,

"Un ministre 'technicien' ou exécutant?" *Le Monde*, 6 June 1974.

[8]Robert, *Mandarin*, p. 237.

[9]"Université, 'gigantisme oblige'," *Université moderne*, no. 53 (November-December 1974), pp. 9-10; BOEN, 27 (4 July 1974): 2128; "Les présidents des universités et leur secrétariat d'état," *Le Monde*, 28 June 1974.

[10]Frédéric Gaussen, "Mme Alice Saunier-Seité," *Le monde de l'éducation*, no. 16 (April, 1976), pp. 43-44.

[11]Alfred Grosser, "L'université mal administrée," *Le Monde*, 3 October 1968; Pierre Silvestre, "L'éduction nationale mal administrée," *Le Monde*, 19 December 1968; Jacques Duhamel, 1st séance, 3 October 1968, *Assemblée nationale, débats, J.o.* (4 October 1968), p. 3011.

[12]Jean-Louis Crémieux-Brilhac, "Conclusion," in Crémieux-Brilhac, ed., *Education nationale*, pp. 699-703.

[13]Faure, *Crois*, p. 15.

[14]"Mise en oeuvre de la réforme," *AUPELF*, 6,3 (Winter, 1968): 36-37.

[15]"Exposé des motifs du projet de loi d'orientation de l'enseignement supérieur," Part V, *Le Monde*, 29-30 September 1968.

[16]B. G. A., "La création d'universités autonomes et pluridisciplinaires," *Le Monde*, 4 February 1969.

[17]*Le Monde*, 5 November 1968.

[18]Calendar of events: There were approximately 100 *facultés* in twenty-two universities, which were to be cut up by the new law into approximately 600 UERs in sixty-five universities. On 31 December 1968, a list of the provisional UERs was established by the ministry. In the summer and autumn of 1969, twenty-one provincial universities were created, others were in the process of organizing themselves. By March 1970, the thirteen Parisian universities had been established. On 24 December 1970, the last university statute was approved by the ministry. Early 1971, the last university presidents were elected. 31 March 1971, elections held for CNESER, those for CRESER were delayed till April 1972. 1969-1970 was considered the year I in the life of the new universities. Thus it took from November 1968 to November 1971 before the new structures were completed and functioning (three years). For a calendar of events for each academy, as well as decrees pertaining to the implantation of the structures in each academy, L'Association d'étude pour l'expansion de l'enseignement supérieur,"

NOTES

"Mises en place des structures," *De l'université aux universités, Octobre 1968-Janvier 1971* [*Cahiers des universités françaises 1*]: 759-774.

[19]Frédéric Gaussen, "L'université, de l'ancien régime au nouveau," *Le Monde*, 8 December 1970; Maurice Duverger, "Une course contre la montre," *Le Monde*, 26 February 1970; "L'application de la loi d'orientation, la période transitoire de mise en place des universités est achevée," *Le Monde*, 2 January 1971.

[20]M.-A. Burnier and B. Kouchner, *France sauvage*, p. 329.

[21]"L'agitation dans les facultés, les dix C.H.U. de la région parisienne sont maintenant touchés par la grève," *Le Monde*, 11 November 1969; Frédéric Gaussen, "Les grèves universitaires sont les signes d'un profond désarroi," *Le Monde*, 17 February 1970.

[22]"Tension à Nanterre où les entrées sont contrôlées," *Le Monde*, 17 December 1969; B. G. A., "Deux cent soixante-dix interpellations à la suite des incidents du quartier latin et de Vincennes," *Le Monde*, 25 January 1969; "Protestations contre l'augmentation des droits d'inscription universitaire," *Le Monde*, 5-6 October 1969; "Boycottage dans plusieurs facultés," *Le Monde*, 3 October 1969; "Incidents à la faculté des lettres d'Aix-en-Provence . . ." *Le Monde*, 5 November 1969. Gabrielle Russier was a high school teacher who had fallen in love with a young pupil and arrested for seducing a minor. She committed suicide, see Mavis Gallant, *The Affair Gabrielle Russier* (New York, 1971); Capelle, *Politique*, pp. 199-201; "Les universitaires ne peuvent plus faire régner l'ordre, déclare le doyen de la faculté des lettres," *Le Monde*, 30 May 1970.

[23]Décret no. 71-66 du 22 Janvier 1971 relatif à l'ordre dans les locaux et enceintes universitaires, in *J.o., Enseignement supérieur, loi d'orientation et textes d'application* (Paris, 1972), pp. 99-102.

[24]Décret no. 71-216 du 24 mars 1971 relatif à la juridiction disciplinaire exercée par les conseils des universités et des établissements publics à caractère scientifique et culturel, indépendants des universités, in *J.o., Enseignement supérieur*, pp. 103-118; and in *BOEN*, 13 (1 April 1971), pp. 857-863; "Les conseils d'université seront souverains en matière disciplinaire," *Le Monde*, 26 March 1971.

[25]"L'écho de l'actualité universitaire en France," *AUPELF*, 7, 1 (1969): 121; Fourrier, *Institutions universitaires*, pp. 10-11.

[26]Burnier and Kouchner, *France sauvage*, pp. 74-75; B. G. A., "La création en France d'universités autonomes et pluridisciplinaires," Part

III, *Le Monde*, 6 February, 1969; Chalendar, *Une loi*, p. 175.

[27]Debbasch, *L'université désorientée*, p. 68; G. H., "Le SGEN approuve avec quelques réserves les réformes des enseignements secondaire et supérieur," *Le Monde*, 2 October 1968.

[28]Capelle, *Politique*, p. 165; B. G. A., "La création en France d'universités autonomes et pluridisciplinaires," *Le Monde*, 6 February 1969.

[29]Frankel, *Reviews of National Policies. France*, p. 74, and citation on the multidisciplinary universities, Capelle, *Politique*, p. 170.

[30]Capelle, *Politique*, p. 169; interview with a member of the university council at Paris V, 25 July 1975.

[31]For instance at Paris and Strasbourg.

[32]B. G. A., "La création d'universités autonomes et pluridiscipli-naires," *Le Monde*, 5 February 1969 and 6 February 1969; "L'université de Paris éclate," *La Vie Française*, 18 October 1968.

[33]"Création d'universités . . ." *Le Monde*, 21 June 1969 and 27 June 1969; "Le découpage des universités suscite de vives protestations," *Combat*, 12 June 1969; "Protestations contre la constitution d'univer-sités pluridisciplinaires, Toulouse: Pour une université dominante juridique,," *Le Monde*, 25 June 1969; Jean Capelle and Pierrre Mazeaud, 1st séance, 12 November 1969; *Assemblée nationale, débats, J.o.* (13 November 1969), pp. 3577, 3592; for the full content of programs offered by each of the Parisian universities see "Paris de I à XIII," *Combat*, 21 March 1970; and Y. de Gentil Baichis, "Les facultés parisiennes regroupées en 13 universités,' *La Croix*, 22 March 1970.

[34]B. G. A., "Treize universités dans la région parisienne. Plus de divorces que de mariages," *Le Monde*, 22-23 March 1970; "Les 13 universités de Paris au microscope," *Paris Presse*, 17 June 1970.

[35]"La commission paritaire propose de diviser la faculté en plusieurs universités," *Le Monde*, 14 December 1968.

[36]"M. Mallet a remis à M. Guichard un projet de constitution des universités de la région parisienne," *Le Monde*, 12 March 1970; "Divergences sur la répartition des locaux et des enseignants de la faculté des sciences," *Le Monde*, 26-27 April 1970; Fourrier, *Institutions universitaires*, p. 46, praised the law for giving the freedom of choice as to which university in Paris the faculty could opt for.

[37]"Grève d'étudiants en droit et économie à Clermont-Ferrand," *Le Monde*, 19 February 1976; Guy Porte, "Le lecteur interdit la fermeture

de l'université de Provence," *Le Monde*, 28-29 November 1976.

38"La loi d'orientation de l'enseignement supérieur," *AUPELF*, 8, 1 (1970): 89.

39Pierre Bartoli, "L'université de Paris et son avenir," in Crémieux-Brilhac, ed., *Education nationale*, p. 541; Guy Herzlich, "L'agitation universitaire," *Le Monde* [weekly issue], 4-10 March 1976. More than 60 percent of all foreign students go to Paris, and 12.5 percent of all students in higher education in France are foreign students, i.e., 104,710 in 1977-1978.

40Pierre Silvestre, "Les vingt-trois nouveaux ministères de l'éducation nationale," *Le Monde*, 30 October 1970; G. Antoine, "Le campus d'Orléans est un échec," *Le Monde*, 8 August 1971.

41*Note d'information*, no. 77-07 (18 February 1977), pp. 5-6.

42"Les étudiants parisiens pourront s'inscrire dans l'université de leur choix," *Le Monde*, 20 April 1977; "Les principales filières," *Le Monde de l'éducation*, no. 40 (June 1978), pp. 16-18.

43"La carte de l'enseignement supérieur. M. Soisson envisage de créer sept régions universitaires," *Le Monde*, 21 December 1974; "Un project de secrétariat d'état aux universités. Les sept grandes régions universitaires," *Le Monde*, 24 January 1975; Y. Agnés, "Après l'intervention du premier ministre. Le projet de carte universitaire est remis en question," *Le Monde*, 29 January 1975.

44B. G. A., "Le travail reprend dans les facultés de province," *Le Monde*, 29 November 1968; "Les modalités des élections et l'institution de conseils transitoires font l'objet de deux décrets," *Le Monde*, 10 December 1968.

45"Les élections universitaires. La plupart des universités ont choisi des formules identiques pour désigner leurs conseils," *Le Monde*, 13-14 December 1970.

46Fourrier, *Institutions universitaires*, p. 109; Burnier and Kouchner, *France sauvage*, p. 79.

47Pierre Mazeaud, 2nd séance, 12 November 1969, *A.n.*, *débats*, *J.o.* (13 November 1969), p. 3592.

48"Après avis du conseil d'état, l'administration propose une réduction de la participation étudiante aux conseils d'université," *Le Monde*, 26 April 1975; the lowering of the quorum for students from 60 percent to 50 percent for elections to the UER councils and the implication that there would be a quorum restriction for elections to

NOTES

university councils found in Loi no. 75-573 du 4 juillet 1975, and in *BOEN* 28 (17 July 1975), pp. 2233-2234.

[49]Conversation regarding student participation in elections with professor from Paris V, 12 March 1977; interviews with university presidents, 13 April 1977 and 4 May 1977.

[50]2nd séance, 21 June 1971, *Assemblée nationale, débats, J.o.* (22 June 1971), p. 3179.

[51]Yves Agnès, "Un test pour les futures élections universitaires, le 'coup' de Toulouse," *Le Monde*, 21 January 1975; "Les élections à l'université de Toulouse-le-Mirail," *Le Monde*, 24 January 1975; "Les élections ont été empêchées par l'intervention d'étudiants d'extrême-gauche," *Le Monde*, 13 February 1975; "La démission des administrateurs provisoires est refusée par le lecteur," *Le Monde*, 29 January 1975; Jean-Pierre Amalric, "Non aux urnes truquées de M. Soisson," *Syndicalisme universitaire*, no. 643 (January 1975), p. 7.

[52]Frédéric Gaussen, "Une année de cogestion dans les trois universités," *Le Monde*, 1 April 1970.

[53]C. Arditti, "Les élections dans les universités," *Le Monde*, 10 December 1975.

[54]Isabel Boussard, "La participation aux élections universitaires en France, 1970-1973," *Revue française de science politique*, 24 (October 1974): 940-965; "Bilan des élections dans les UER," *Education*, no. 27 (17 April 1969), p. VIII; Frédéric Gaussen, "Le bilan des élections universitaires est encourageant pour M. E. Faure," *Le Monde*, 3 April 1969; D. Dhombres, "Les élections universitaires à Amiens," *Le Monde*, 23 December 1975. In 1969, students participated according to disciplines as follows: letters 42.02 percent voted; sciences 43.39 percent; law, economics and political science 59.46 percent; medicine, pharmacy and dentistry 65.36 percent; in IUTs 77.36 percent voted. Student participation was higher for the provinces than for Paris in UER elections. In 1974 17 percent voted in Paris compared to 28.4 percent in the provinces. Philippe Boggio, "Les premiers résultats des élections universitaires," *Le Monde*, 11 December 1976.

[55]For an excellent treatment of the election control commissions, their powers, responsibilities and limitations, D. Chabarol, "La commission de contrôle des élections universitaires," *La revue administrative*, no. 140 (March-April 1971), pp. 159-163; Boussard, "La participation," pp. 942-943; Frédéric Gaussen, "L'université de l'ancien régime au nouveau,

197

IV, L'enjeu politique," *Le Monde*, 11 December 1970; idem, "Cogestion dans trois universités," Robert, *Mandarin*, p. 217; A.-M. V. et M. G., "Le malaise du supérieur," *Education*, no. 34 (5 June 1969), p. 25; Capelle, *Politique*, p. 154; J.-P. Clerc, "L'indifférence des étudiants à l'égard des élections universitaires se confirme," *Le Monde*, 23-24 December 1973; interview with a member of the university council of Paris V, 25 July 1975.

[56]J. Beaujeu, "La politique dans l'université," *Le Monde*, 23 January 1970.

[57]C. Arditti, "Les élections"; "La suppression de la subvention de l'UNEF," *Le Monde*, 20 August 1976.

[58]B. Frappat, "Après le départ des étudiants du PSU," *Le Monde*, 21 January 1971; Guy Herzlich, "Les UNEF ou la vie à deux," *Le Monde*, 28 September 1972; Frédéric Gaussen, "Les élections au CNESER. Les syndicats de gauche remportent la moitié des sièges," *Le Monde*, 25-26 April 1971; "Les élections universitaires ont connu un faible taux de participation," *Le Monde*, 23-24 December 1973; "L'indifférence des étudiants à l'égard des élections se confirme," *Le Monde*, 23-24 December 1973; "L'UNEF-ex-Renouveau veut faire des élections universitaires la principale bataille du trimestre," *Le Monde*, 17 October 1974; A. Meury, "L'état et les organisations voudraient enrayer la désaffection croissante des étudiants à l'égard des élections universitaires," *Le Monde*, 7 January 1975.

[59]"La suppression de la subvention de l'UNEF," *Le Monde*, 20 August 1976; Guy Herzlich, "Le secrétariat d'état aux universités envisage de modifier la composition des conseils de discipline," *Le Monde*, 3 December 1976.

[60]"Les représentations des personalités extérieures," *Le Monde*, 6 February 1975; "A Caen le secrétaire d'état aux universités empêche l'élection d'un président membre du SNE-Sup.," *Le Monde*, 20 February 1975; "A Caen l'université est impuissante à se donner un président," *Le Monde*, 13-14 April 1975.

[61]"La nouvelle université technique de Compiègne est créé," *Le Monde*, 4 October 1972; Guy Herzlich, "Compiègne: les difficultés d'un prototype," *Le monde de l'éducation*, no. 6 (May 1975), pp. 45-46.

[62]2nd séance, 14 November 1970, *Assemblée nationale, débats, J.o.* (15 November 1970), p. 5559.

[63]Frédéric Gaussen, "Les nouveaux 'patrons" des universités:

NOTES

négociateurs, planificateurs, animateurs," *Le Monde*, 12 May 1971; also Gaussen's interview with a former president of Grenoble, on the duties of a president as well as the powers and limitations of the conférence des présidents, "L'université abandonnée," pp. 5-7.

[64]For a full study of the British University Grants Committee, the fund dividing agency in Britain, Raymond Gibson, *Block Grants for Higher Education* (Iowa, 1972); document drawn up by UGC, "The University Grants Committee," in France: Secrétariat d'état aux universités, rapport de la commission (Bienaymé commission), *Le financement des universités* [La documentation française] (Paris, 1976), pp. 112-115; F. G., "La formation du conseil national de l'enseignement supérieur. Assemblée unique ou bicamérisme," *Le Monde*, 25 December 1970; B. G. A., "Les universités seront représentées 'au sommet' par deux conseils," *Le Monde*, 27 January 1971; "Les élections au CNESER," *Le Monde*, 27 March 1971; for application of the law, décret no. 71-140 du 19 février 1971, relatif au conseil national de l'enseignement supérieur et de la recherche in *J.o., Enseignement supérieur*, pp. 23-32, also in *BOEN*, no. 29 (22 July 1971), pp. 1788-92; and in *BOEN*, no. 31 (26 August 1971), pp. 1993-1994.

[65]P. Boggio, "Un autre rapport de force," *Quotidien de Paris*, 4 February 1975; "Les renouvellements du Conseil national de l'enseigne-ment supérieur et de la recherche," *Le Monde*, 6 January 1976; *Le Monde*, 26-27 February 1978.

[66]J. Minot, "Le conseil national de l'enseignement supérieur et de la recherche," *La revue administrative*, no. 141 (June 1971), pp. 318-319.

[67]Interviews with university presidents, 13 April and 4 May 1977; Frédéric Gaussen, "A quoi sert le CNESER?" *Le Monde*, 10-11 December 1972; Jean-Louise Quermonne, "L'université abandonnée," (interviewed by Frédéric Gaussen), p. 7; "Mme Saunier-Seité rappelle que le CNESER 'n'est pas un organe de décision," *Le Monde*, 18 September 1976; les cahiers de l'INAS (Institut national d'adminis-tration scolaires et universitaires), *Conférence des présidents* (Paris, 1975), p. 6. Introduction by René Rémond, historian and former president of Nanterre university.

[68]Interview with a university president, 13 April 1977.

[69]For a discussion of the role of the rector, G. Bourjac, "L'adminis-tration locale," in Crémieux-Brilhac, ed., *Education nationale*, p. 519, and in Fourrier, *Institutions universitaires*, pp. 36-38.

199

[70]Conversation reported first hand to me in December 1976.

[71]Circulaire no. IV, 68-494 du 6 décembre 1968, *BOEN*, 44 (12 December 1968): 3331; arrêté, 100-1, 26 November 1968, *BOEN*, 11 (20 February 1969): 616-617; arrêté du 10 mars 1972, *BOEN*, 11 (16 March 1972): 797; circulaire no. 72-338, 15 September 1972, *BOEN*, 35 (21 September 1972): 3141-3142; Anon, "Pouvoirs des recteurs d'académie," *Education*, no. 22 (27 February 1969), p. 22.

[72]For discussion of CRESER, "Pour une politique d'enseignement supérieur," *Education*, no. 52 (19 February 1970), pp. i-iii; 2nd séance, 8 October 1968, *Assemblée nationale, débats, J.o.* (9 October 1968), p. 3179; ministerial decrees for the application of the regional councils were made on 5 July 1972 and 5 September 1973.

[73]P. Boggio, "La géographie de la concertation," *Quotidien de Paris*, 21 January 1975.

[74]Burnier and Kouchner, *France sauvage*, p. 81; G. Lapassade, *Procès de l'université* (Paris, 1969), p. 82.

[75]Alain Peyrefitte, minister of education, went to the U.S. in 1970 for two weeks and returned declaring the merits of that system of education; "M. Peyrefitte: L'université américaine n'est pas faite pour les professeurs, mais pour les étudiants," *Le Monde*, 5 May 1970; J. Vuillemin, *Rebâtir l'université* (Paris, 1968), p. 51; Charles Debbasch, "L'université et les contradictions de la société," *Le Monde*, 3 August 1972; Debbasch recognized that neither extreme centralization nor full autonomy pushed to its fullest limits would be suitable, but that somehow there must be reform within the existing structures, Debbasch, *L'université désorientée*, p. 80.

[76]Debbasch citation in Capelle, *Politique*, p. 177.

[77]Henri Hatzfeld, "Ici on ne discute pas," *Le Monde*, 14 April 1973.

[78]Paul Valéry, cited by Poujade, a U.D.R. deputy, in 2nd séance, 10 October 1968, *Assemblée nationale, débats, J.o.* (11 October 1968), p. 3252. It is customary in the French parliament for members to engage in learned quotations — this in itself a tribute to the elitism of the educational system.

[79]Efforts by British minister of education to bring about more uniformity in the secondary school curriculum brought a loud outcry from local school authorities, Anne Corbett, "Des programmes scolaires sur contrat," *Le Monde de l'éducation*, no. 15 (March, 1976), p. 23.

[80]F. Goblot, former director of the review *Cahiers pédagogiques*, "Il faut supprimer l'inspection générale," *Le Monde*, 6 November 1968.

NOTES

NOTES

Chapter V

[1]Faure quoted in Capelle, *Education et politique*, p. 15; Claustre, vice-president of Grenoble II quoted in D. Granet and J. Linares, "Etudiants en quête d'emploi," *L'Express* (1-7 July 1974), p. 57.

[2]Maurice Duverger, "Les contradictions de l'université nouvelle," *Le Monde*, 12 September 1969; Olivier Guichard, "L'université après la loi," *Education*, no. 43 (30 October 1969), p. 21.

[3]Fourrier, *Institutions universitaires*, p. 95, university diplomas existed before 1968, and while some called for their abolition, the Faure law retained them in the name of university autonomy. The list of national diplomas can be found in Capelle, *Politique*, p. 181; Olivier Guichard, 7th séance, 14 April 1970, *Assemblée nationale, débats, J.o.* (15 April 1970), p. 1001; Faure quoted in Capelle, *Politique*, pp. 179-180, also Faure's speech before the Assemblée nationale on 8 October 1968 in *Association d'étude pour l'expansion de l'université*, p. 55; and in Faure, *Philosophie d'une réforme* (Paris, 1969), p. 92, my italics.

[4]Claude Guichard, 1st séance, 14 November 1970, *Assemblée nationale, débats, J.o.* (15 November 1970), pp. 5549-50; Jean-Philippe Lecat, 1st séance, 21 June 1971, *Assemblée nationale, débats, J.o.* (22 June 1971), p. 3151.

[5]Debbasch, *L'université désorientée*, p. 109; Frédéric Gaussen, "Les universités disposeraient d'une plus large autonomie dans la préparation des diplômes nationaux," *Le Monde*, 21 January 1972; Jean Capelle, 2nd séance, 14 November 1970, *Assemblée nationale, débats, J.o.* (15 November 1970), p. 5559.

[6]"La rentrée universitaire," *Education*, no. 13 (30 October 1969), pp. 29-30; "Le nombre d'étudiants boursiers augmenterait légèrement," *Le Monde*, 21 October 1969. Jean-Pierre Soisson, *Six principes et un projet politique; présentation du projet de budget pour 1975 du secrétariat d'état aux universités* (Paris, 1974), p. 12; "Nouvelles modalités d'application des bourses," *Education*, no. 19 (6 February 1969), p. 21; France, secrétariat d'état aux universités, *Tableaux statistiques 1975-1976* (June, 1976), pp. iii and 6; "Le système d'attribution des bourses d'enseignement supérieur est modifié," *Le Monde*, 31 May 1969; D. Dhombres, "Qui peut être boursier," *Le monde de l'éducation*, no. 5

201

(April, 1975), p. 47.

[7]*Note d'information*, no. 75-35 (17 October 1975), p. 2; "Le montant des bourses d'enseignement supérieur," *Le Monde*, 30 April 1974. On the average, a student needed about 110-120 dollars (550-600 francs) a month to attend university, "Les bourses," *Dernières Nouvelles d'Alsace*, 21 April 1976; "La rentrée universitaire," *Education*, no. 43 (30 October 1969); *Tableaux, 1976*, pp. 550-551; *Tableaux statistiques 1976*, pp. iii, 2; statistics for 1977 based on personal information. Of the seven categories of 'needy' students eligible for a scholarship, the sixth category (i.e., the group in nearly the greatest need) contained the largest number of scholarship holders, while the seventh which was the most needy category of all had the low number. The reason for this was not that the government did not give scholarships to the most needy, but probably that that group was least aware or had no interest in applying, or simply that their families could not afford to lose a working member. Most likely it was a combination of all the above. The university was still foreign ground to this category of the population.

[8]"Le nombre des étudiants boursiers augmenterait légèrement cette année," *Le Monde*, 21 October 1969; "M. Soisson entreprend une délicate réforme de l'aide aux étudiants," *Le Monde*, 9 August 1974; Bosc, "Les bourses de l'enseignement supérieur," p. 71; *Tableaux statistiques 1975-1976*, pp. iii, iv, 2, 6, and personal information for 1977 figures; *Tableaux, 1970*, p. 14; *Note d'information*, no. 75-41 (28 November 1975), p. 3; *Le Monde*, 9 August 1974; "La rentrée universitaire," *Education*, no. 43 (30 October 1969), p. 29; Chardonnet, *L'université en question*, pp. 38-39, 108.

[9]J.-C. Passeron, "Les problèmes et les faux problèmes de la 'démocratisation' du système scolaire," *Education et gestion*, no. 28 (1972), p. 20.

[10]"M. Edgar Faure: Planifier la démocratisation de l'enseignement," *Education*, no. 22 (27 February 1969), pp. 17-18; René Rémond, *Vivre notre histoire* (Paris, 1976), p. 243, Rémond noted that, depending on the region, students from humble background composed 10 to 20 percent of their universities' population.

[11]Frédéric Gaussen, "Une protestation symbolique," *Le Monde*, 11 March 1972; *Le Monde*, 15-16 February 1976.

[12]Raymond Barre and Jean-Louis Boursin, "De l'enseignement secondaire à l'enseignement supérieur, expériences étrangères et

NOTES

problèmes français," *La Documentation française, Rapport à M. le ministre de l'éducation nationale* (Paris, 1974), p. 15; "Statistiques des diplômes universitaires délivrés en 1974, *Note d'information*, no. 75-39 (14 November 1974), p. 1; Soisson, *Six principes*, p. 8; Secrétariat d'état aux universités, *Données statistiques sur le développement des effectifs de l'enseignement supérieur en France depuis 1960* [*Etudes et documents*], no. 31 (1975), pp. 38-39; D. Granet and J. de Linares, "Etudiants en quête d'emploi," p. 56; "Une enquête auprès de cinq mille anciens étudiants," *Le Monde*, 23 February 1974; Rémond, *Vivre*, pp. 242-243.

[13]C. Arditti, "L'application de la réforme Haby dans les lycées pourrait être retardée de trois ans," *Le Monde*, 21-22 November 1976; "La réforme Haby dans le second cycle," *Le Monde*, 24 November 1976; "Les premiers textes d'application de la réforme Haby sont publiés," *Le Monde*, 5 January 1977; Kourganoff, *Face cachée*, p. 71; J. Thomas, "Universités françaises et universités étrangères," in Crémieux-Brilhac, ed., *L'éducation nationale*, p. 149; the drop out rate in the British universities was 14 percent during the course of studies; "L'orientation et la sélection"[Forum organisé par le Syndicat national de l'enseignement supérieur, Paris 12 février 1977], *Bulletin du SNE-Sup*, no. 75, n.s., January 1977, p. 7; P.-P. Pellegrin, "Admission policies in postsecondary education," in OECD, *Towards Mass Higher Education*, pp. 79, 84; on the German universities, "La loi cadre sur les universités," *Le Monde*, 18 December 1975; Jean Royer, 3rd séance, 9 November 1971, *Assemblée nationale, débats, J.o.* (10 November 1971), p. 5563.

[14]*Le Monde*, 1 November 1974; "L'origine socio-professionnelle des étudiants, situation dans les universités en 1974-75," *Note d'information*, no. 76-15 (30 April 1976), p. 2; *Note d'information*, no. 77-07 (18 February 1977), p. 6.

[15]Capelle, *Tomorrow's*, p. 166; Capelle, 3rd séance, 9 November 1970, *Assemblée nationale, débats, J.o.* (10 November 1970), p. 4952; Capelle, 1st séance, 14 November 1970, *Assemblée nationale, débats, J.o.* (15 November 1970), p. 5544; Guichard in ibid., p. 5583; Saint-Martin, *Fonctions sociales*; Kourganoff, *Face cachée*, p. 71.

[16]*Le Monde*, 25-26 March 1973; "La conférence des présidents d'université approuve le projet de réforme des diplômes du premier cycle," *Le Monde*, 2 June 1972; *Le Monde*, 6 April 1973.

NOTES

[17]"Deux ans d'études pour les sept nouveaux diplômes (DEUG) à la rentrée 1973-1974," *France-Soir*, 10 March 1973, the diagram for distribution requirements is useful; "La réforme du premier cycle des enseignements supérieur et la création du DEUG en France," AIISUP. *Informations universitaires et professionnelles internationales* (August-September 1973), p. 35; "Que Faire avec le baccalauréat," *Le Monde de l'éducation*, no. 40 (June, 1978), p. 16.

[18]D. Dhombres, "La grève 'dure' des étudiants de Nantes," *Le Monde*, 15 January 1976.

[19]Guy Herzlich, "La réforme du second cycle universitaire. Professionalisation et sélection," *Le Monde*, 17 February 1976; "Les marginaux des campus," *Le Monde* weekly, 4-10 March 1970; J. Ségard, "Le rôle des enseignants et la réforme du 2ème cycle," *Le Monde*, 15 April 1976; "Journée nationale de manifestation contre la réforme," *Le Monde*, 16 April 1976; "L'université: la cassure," *Dernières Nouvelles d'Alsace*, 16 April 1976; D. Brison and J. English, "L'université en question," *Dernières Nouvelles d'Alsace*, 16 April 1976; "Nouvelle journée d'action le 23," *Dernières Nouvelles d'Alsace*, 19 April 1976; Guy Herzlich, "Après le succès des manifestations d'étudiants," *Le Monde*, 17 April 1976; "Université: pas de nouveau mai 68," *Dernières Nouvelles d'Alsace*, 23 April 1976; "La conférence des présidents demande le 'retrait' d'une réforme malthusienne," *Le Monde*, 17 April 1976.

[20]Interview with a university president, 13 April 1977.

[21]Council of Europe, *La réforme et le développement de l'enseignement supérieur en Europe (France)*, p. 78.

[22]"A Lille, le premier enseignement universitaire en alternance," *Le Monde*, 27 November 1974.

[23]"Un colloque à Rennes sur l'enseignement en alterance," *Le Monde*, 21 September 1973; G. Barbey, "Université des ondes," *Education*, no. 38 (September 1969), pp. 28-29; some of the courses were designed for preparation of the two-year DEUG, others for the concours d'agrégation and CAPES. Instruction for registration was given, see an example of a program "La radio universitaire," *Le monde de l'éducation*, no. 15 (March, 1976), pp. 44-46.

[24]R. B., "La faculté des lettres de Montpellier offre un enseignement d'esthétique et d'histoire du cinéma," *Le Monde*, 6-7 April 1969; "Nouvelles formations et expériences pédagogiques," *Le Monde*, 21 October 1970; "Les universités de Toulouse créent un diplôme

204

d'éducation sexuelle," *Le Monde*, 8 January 1975. Katie Breen, "L'essor des études feministes," *Le monde de l'éducation*, no. 40 (June, 1978), pp. 54-58; "Enseignement supérieur," *Syndicalisme universitaire*, no. 569 (27 January 1972), p. 8; "Motions présentées par les chercheurs CNRS à l'A.G. de la section," *Syndicalisme universitaire*, no. 521 (19 March 1970), pp. 4-6; "Une université expérimentale sera créée en 1973 à Compiègne," *Le Monde*, 28-29 May 1972; Guy Herzlich, "Les instituts d'administration des entreprises veulent prouver que les universités peuvent enseigner la gestion," *Le Monde*, 2 May 1974; "Les universités de la capitale. Paris VII: développer au maximum la pluridisciplinarité," *Le Monde*, 26 June 1970; "Victime de son succès, l'université de Paris VII a dû refuser plus de 500 inscriptions," *Le Monde*, 23 August 1974; "Université Paris IX (Paris-Dauphine)," *AUPELF* 8, 2 (1970): 133, "A la faculté des sciences de Paris," *Le Monde*, 8-9 October 1970; "Les nouvelles maîtrises de sciences et techniques ne seront plus agréées comme diplôme national," *Le Monde*, 19 October 1974.

[25]"A l'université de Paris-Nord, les étudiants de lettres pourront préparer des maîtrises des techniques et communications," *Le Monde*, 3 December 1972; *AUPELF*, 6, 3 (1969): 151: 8, 2 (1970): 133, 8, 1 (1970): 90. George Suffert and Jean Lesieur, "Université: L'enlisement," *Le Point*, no. 242 (9 May 1977), pp. 115-116.

[26]J. Fontanet, "Colloque national sur l'éducation. Réflexions finales," *Discours* (23 November 1973). This is part of a file entitled, "Discours, J. Fontanet," item no. 52, Ministry of education library; Chalendar, *Une loi pour l'université*, p. 257.

[27]M. Rollant and M. Rivoire, "Université, économie, éducation permanente: conception de la CFDT," *AUPELF* 12, 1 (Spring, 1974): 173; the sum to be paid by the employers was 0.8% of all salaries in 1972 and 1973, and was increased to 1% for 1974. "Quarante-cinq universités reçoivent des subventions pour la formation continue," *Le Monde*, 28 October 1972; L. Cros, "Permanence de l'éducation," *Education nationale*, no. 3 (3 October 1968), pp. 16-17; "Le compte économique de l'éducation et des formations: la formation professionnelle continue," *Note d'information*, no. 76-07 (27 February 1976), p. 1; the total French education budget for 1975-76 was 47 billion francs ($9.4 billion); France, Secrétariat d'état aux universités, "Budget," 1976, m.s.

[28]"La rentrée universitaire — promotion sociale et éducation permanente," *Education*, no. 43 (30 October 1969), pp. 29-30. At Stras-

205

[26]J. Fontanet, "Colloque nationale sur l'éduction. Réflexions finales," *Discours* (23 November 1973). This is part of a file entitled "Discours, J. Fontanet," item no. 52, Ministry of education library; Chalendar, *Une loi pour l'université*, p. 257.

[27]M. Rollant and M. Rivoire, "Université, économie, éducation permanente: conception de la CFDT," *AUPELF* 12, 1 (Spring, 1974): 173; the sum to be paid by the employers was 0.8% of all salaries in 1972 and 1973, and was increased to 1% for 1974; "Quarante-cinq universités reçoivent des subventions pour la formation continue," *Le Monde*, 28 October 1972; L. Cros, "Permanence de l'éducation," *Education nationale*, no. 3 (3 October 1968), pp. 16-17; "Le compte économique de l'éducation et des formations: la formation professionnelle continue," *Note d'information*, no. 76-07 (27 February 1976), p. 1; the total French education budget for 1975-76 was 47 billion francs ($9.4 billion); France, Secrétariat d'état aux universités, "Budget," 1976, m.s.

[28]"La rentrée universitaire — promotion sociale et éducation permanente," *Education*, no. 43 (30 October 1969), pp. 29-30. At Strasbourg, an effort was made to train 30-50 year old women as bilingual secretaries and as hospital aides, 1st séance, 10 November 1972, *Assemblée nationale, débats, J.o.* (11 November 1972), p. 5001; M. Caire, "Nanterre," *Education et gestion*, no. 43 (1974), pp. 3-15; J.-Y. Guérin, "L'éducation permanente à Paris X," *Syndicalisme universitaire*, no. 639 (3 December 1974), p. 19; Fourrier, *Institutions universitaires*, p. 92; Fournier, *Politique de l'éducation*, p. 113; *Education permanente*, 27 (January-February 1975): 3-110.

[29]Guérin, "L'éducation permanente à Paris X," p. 19; "Université Paris IX-Dauphine," *AUPELF* 12, 1 (Spring, 1974): 147.

[30]Fournier, *Politique de l'éducation*, pp. 114-116; Université et formation continue," *AUPELF*, 12, 1 (Spring, 1974): 98-142, *Tableaux VII* entitled "financement," demonstrated that out of thirty-eight centers responding to a questionnaire regarding their financing, only nine of them received a part of their funding from the state. The rest of the funds came from other public or private sources, pp. 128-129; "Création multipliée de centres d'enseignements supérieurs en liaison avec les municipalités," Circulaire no. 73-260 du 15 juin 1973, *BOEN*, no. 25 (21 June 1973), pp. 1971-72; Faure, *Ce que je crois*, p. 186; F. G., "Un colloque à Rennes," *Le Monde*, 27-28 October 1974; Rollant and Rivoire, "Education permanente," p. 173.

206

NOTES

[31]Bertrand Girod de l'Ain, "Une université expérimentale cinq ans après. Dauphine à travers un entretien avec B. G. de l'Ain, Octobre 1973," *Education et gestion*, no. 43 (1974), p. 27.

[32]Marie-Odile Fargier, "Vincennes huit jours après," *Combat*, 18 December 1968; "Vincennes," *Le Monde*, 14 December 1968; "Les enseignants du centre universitaire de Vincennes vont enfin être nommées," *Le Monde*, 22 January 1969; Burnier and Kouchner, *France sauvage*, pp. 20-24; Michel Debeauvais, *L'université ouverte: les dossiers de Vincennes* (Grenoble, 1976).

[33]"Près de la moitié de non-bacheliers parmi les étudiants de Vincennes," *Le Monde*, 26 December 1969; Jean-Pierre Velis, "Vincennes: Renaissance de l'université?" *Education*, no 18 (30 January 1969), pp. 9-11; "Le président de l'université de Vincennes et le bureau du conseil donnent leur démission," *Le Monde*, 12 June 1971; P. Boggio, "La révolution du possible," *Quotidien de Paris*, 29 October 1974; idem, "La peur du début de la fin," *Quotidien de Paris*, 28 October 1974; Michel Beaud, *Vincennes, an III. Le ministère contre l'université* (Paris, 1971), p. 10; "Mme Saunier-Seité: Vincennes n'a pas l'exclusivité des non-bacheliers," *Le Monde*, 29 April 1977.

[34]"La licence de philosophie . . .," *Le Monde*, 16 January 1970; "La licence de philosophie restera diplôme 'libre' en 1970-71," *Le Monde*, 27 August 1970.

[35]In October 1969, there was a big raucous as to how easily students were able to obtain academic credit (unités de valeur); while students were expected to take ten UVs (or thirty credit hours), it was rumored that about a third of the students acquired fifteen UVs (or forty-five credit hours). This was seen as lowering the quality of the diploma. Hence a commission was set up to study the situation; later it was revealed that the university council defended the university, saying that far fewer students took more than twelve UVs (thirty-six credit hours) than had been suspected earlier: "Les UV obtenues l'an dernier ne seront pas toutes automatiquement validées," *Le Monde*, 3 October 1969; "Rentrée difficile au centre de Vincennes," *Le Monde*, 11 November 1969; "La situation des non-bacheliers à Vincennes," *Le Monde*, 27-28 October 1974; "Non-bacheliers de Vincennes," *Le Monde*, 6 November 1974; "Le diplôme de premier cycle . . .," *Le Monde*, 22 November 1974; "Dans certaines disciplines seulement les diplômes de premier cycle de l'université de Vincennes sont reconnus nationalement," *Le Monde*, 29

207

May 1975.

[36]J. P. Clerc, "Vincennes: la fin du 'folklore.' Une université expérimentale cinq ans après," *Le Monde*, 18 April 1974; Boggio, "La peur du début de la fin"; D. Dhombres, "Vincennes dans l'entassement," *Le Monde*, weekly issue, 20-26 November 1975.

[37]Beaud, *Vincennes, passim*; C.-F. Jullien, "Le blocus de Vincennes," *Le Nouvel Observateur*, 1 November 1971, p. 46; "Rentrée difficile à l'université de Vincennes," *Le Monde*, 8 November 1975.

[38]"Paris VIII: rupture pédagogique," *Le Monde*, 26 January 1977; Guy Herzlich, "L'université Paris VIII (Vincennes) sera transférée à Marne-la Vallée," *Le Monde*, 27-28 February 1977; Michel Beaud, "L'etouffement," *Le Monde*, 17 March 1977.

[39]Bertrand Girod de l'Ain, "La rentrée dans les universités de Paris, en province. Le nouveau centre universitaire Dauphine ouvrira avant la fin de novembre," *Le Monde*, 30 October 1968; idem, "Une université expérimentale cinq ans àpres: Dauphine," p. 27; "L'expérience de Dauphine," *Le monde de l'éducation*, no. 1 (December, 1974), p. 49.

[40]Guy Herzlich, "Compiègne: Les difficultés d'un prototype," *Le Monde de l'éducation*, no. 6 (May, 1975), pp. 45-46; for a diagram of studies offered at Dauphine, J.-L. Lescene, "Au centre universitaire Dauphine," *Education nationale*, no. 9 (14 November 1968), pp. 13-14; Debeauvais, *L'université ouverte*, p. 11; *Note d'information*, no. 77-07 (18 February 1977), p. 6.

[41]The breakdown of numbers of students and faculty by university is not available for the same years for other than 1969-70. Information could only be obtained for that year, *Tableaux 1972*, pp. 366-69.

[42]Kourganoff, *Face cachée*, pp. 99, 101.

[43]Granet and Linares, "En quête d'emploi," p. 57; Capelle, *Politique*, p. 152; Aron, *Introuvable*, p. 60; Kourganoff, *Face cachée*, pp. 286, 74; Jean-Pierre Richardot, "Une semaine à Tolbiac," *Le Monde de l'éducation*, no. 28 (May, 1977), p. 37.

[44]Circulaire no. 72-278, 22 June 1972, *BOEN*, no. 30 (27 July 1972), pp. 2145-46; "La difficulté pour un universitaire de résider dans la ville où il enseigne," *Le Monde*, 26 August 1972. It was reported in 1977 that between 33-40 percent of the teaching faculty at Saint-Etienne for example did not reside in that town, Yves Agnès *et al.*, "Les universités dans leurs régions," p. 7; Fourrier, *Institutions*, p. 120; Université Louis Pasteur, "Obligation de résidence et accidents de trajet," *ULP Info*, no.

NOTES

188 (19 November 1976) lists Strasbourg and the suburbs which are permitted as residence to those teaching at the universities of Strasbourg; faculty needed special permission to reside outside these limits from the president of their university.

[45]Two conversations with professors at Strasbourg in October and November 1976; Capelle, *Politique*, p. 158.

[46]Georges Innocent, "Le syndicat à l'université," *Le Monde*, 7 August 1970; C. Arditti, "Au congrès de Lyon," *Le Monde*, 17-18 June 1973; "Selon le SNE-Sup. la grève des enseignants des universités est largement suivie," *Le Monde*, 24 January 1974; Paul Didier, "La réconciliation inachevée," *Le Monde de l'éducation*, no. 8 (July-August 1975), p. 36; "Les maîtres-assistants de sciences juridiques, économiques, politiques et de gestion demandent des garanties sur leur statut," *Le Monde*, 20-22 December 1975; as an example of career blockage, in 1975-76 there were only five positions for full professors in chemistry in all of France; J. Cattegno, "Nos carrières — Il y a des préalables," *Syndicalisme universitaire*, no. 619 (10 June 1974), pp. 34-35; Saunier-Seité, in Suffert and Lesieur, "L'enlisement," p. 122.

[47]Francis de Baecque, *La situation des personnels des universités, éléments de réflexion pour une réforme* (Paris, 1974), pp. 9, 22-26; "Le rapport Baecque sur les carrières des universitaires," *Le Monde*, 3 October 1974; Faure, 2nd séance, 4 October 1968, *Assemblée nationale, débats, J.o.* (5 October 1968), p. 3071.

[48]Suffert and Lesieur, "L'enlisement," p. 118.

[49]Catherine Arditti, "L'enseignement féminin," *Le Monde*, 3 May 1977.

[50]"Le comité consultatif des universités," *Le Monde*, 13 May 1969; "Réforme du comité consultatif des universités," *Education*, no. 32 (22 May 1969), p. 22; décret no. 72-1016, 6 November 1972, "Comité consultatif des universités," *BOEN*, no. 44 (23 November 1972), pp. 3797-3801; Frédéric Gaussen, "Universitaires sans carrières," *Le Monde*, 15 February 1973; Minot, *Entreprise*, pp. 332-335; *Baecque Report*, pp. 9, 26; Institut national de recherche et de documentation pédagogiques, *L'organisation de l'enseignement en France* [Cahiers de documentation, no. 1 CD] (Paris, 1973), pp. 62, 120-121 (henceforth will refer to this as INRDP, *Organisation de l'enseignement*). Interview with university president, 13 April 1977.

[51]Frédéric Gaussen, "Michel Butor: L'université française est plus

209

fermée sur elle-même aujourd'hui qu'avant 1968," *Le monde de l'éducation*, no. 14 (February 1976), pp. 35-37; Michel Butor, renowned author and former professor at Columbia, who received a doctorat d'état, applied to the CCU for placement on the *liste d'aptitude* so that he could teach in a French university. The CCU turned him down stating that his research was not based on a broad synthesis of a literary work.

[52]"Echos d'actualité universitaire," *AUPELF*, 8, 1 (1970): 75; "La réorganisation de l'orientation scolaire et professionnelle," *Le Monde*, 29 September 1970; 2nd séance, 9 November 1971, *Assemblée nationale, débats, J.o.* (10 November 1971), p. 5558; Arrêté, 5 July 1972, "Organisation des services de l'ONISEP modifiés," *BOEN*, no. 31 (24 August 1972), p. 2216.

[53]3rd séance, 10 November 1972, *Assemblée nationale, débats, J.o.* (11 November 1972), p. 5030; "La réforme de l'orientation dans l'enseignement secondaire," *Le Monde*, 10 February 1973; interview with the director of the CIO (Centre d'information et d'orientation) of the 6ème arrondissement in Paris, 11 July 1975; "Informer les étudiants et influencer les établissements. Les cellules d'orientation dans les universités," *Le Monde*, 7 May 1975; "Les secrétaires généraux face à certains problèms de gestion," *Education et gestion*, no. 43 (March, 1974), p. 56; interview with secretariat official, 25 July 1975, who stated that most universities offered a counselling service, and on 4 March 1977, the same official said that all universities now had a *cellule d'orientation*, but that funds for expansion were frozen. A counsellor at one university said that counselling services existed generally, but that most programs were incomplete and had limited services, 18 January 1977.

[54]Arrêté, 20 December 1973, création de centres d'information et d'orientation, *BOEN*, no. 2 (10 January 1974), pp. 86-87; Arrêté, 19 September 1974, création de CIO, *BOEN*, no. 36 (3 October 1974), p. 2858; inadequacies of counselling centers described by Citron, *L'école bloquée*, p. 28, and by deputy Ernst Rouxel in 1st séance, 14 November 1970, *Assemblée nationale, débats J.o.* (15 November 1970), p. 5552.

[55]Burnier and Kouchner, *France sauvage*, p. 85; "Examen ou contrôle continu des connaissances," *Le Monde*, 9 April 1969; Mathé J.-M. Daniels and J. Schowten, *L'éducation en Europe. La sélection des étudiants*, series I, *Enseignement supérieur et recherche*, no. 8 (Paris, 1970), pp. 69, 72; "Une conférence de presse de M. E. Faure," *Le Monde*, 26 April 1969; Capelle, *Politique*, p. 77; "Les examens dans les facultés,"

NOTES

Le Monde, 22 October 1969; Boscher, 2nd séance, 12 November 1969, *Assemblée nationale, débats, J.o.* (13 November 1969), p. 3604; Olivier Guichard, ibid., p. 3655; Robert, *Mandarin*, p. 179; conversation with a *maître-assistant* from Paris, who was also member of the university council, 28 July 1975; Dauphine returned to traditional examinations, *Le Monde*, 16 July 1977.

[56]M. Roulland, "L'évolution des charges administratives des universités," *Education et gestion*, no. 43 (1974), p. 53; Fourrier, *Institutions*, p. 85; F. G., "La rentrée dans l'enseignement supérieur," *Le Monde*, 27 October 1971. An example of transfer problems was witnessed at Strasbourg where the law university continued the system of annual examinations whereas the humanities university introduced the unité de valeur (credit hour system). Hence agreements had to be worked out between the two administrations.

[57]Faure, 1st séance, 24 July 1968, *Assemblée nationale, débats, J.o.* (25 July 1968), p. 2527; and in Faure, *Education nationale*, p. 38.

[58]"A Créteil les premiers bâtiments de l'université de Paris Val-de Marne . . .," *Le Monde*, 26 January 1971; Pierre Citron, "La danse sur le volcan," *Le Monde*, 4 March 1971; Maurice Duverger, "Paris sans université," *Le Monde*, 7 April 1971; Suffert and Lesieur, "L'enlisement," p. 122.

[59]Louis Odru, 2nd séance, 14 November 1970, *Assemblée nationale, débats, J.o.* (15 November 1970), p. 5576, speaking on Créteil and Villetaneuse; Granet and Linares, "En quête d'emploi," p. 57; Henri Claustre, *Vivre dans l'université* (Grenoble, 1973), p. 156; J. A., "L'université de Villetaneuse s'implante avec lenteur," *La Croix*, 6 April 1975.

[60]Paul Bourcier, "Université: l'an II de la réforme," *Les nouvelles littéraires*, 18 June 1970, pp. 6-7; Maurice Duverger, "Des universités en papier," *Le Monde*, 3 July 1970; "M. M. Duverger démissionne du conseil de Paris I," *Le Monde*, 5 October 1973; "Démission en série dans les universités," *Le Monde*, 11 October 1973; "Chauffage, papier et difficultés financières" *Le Monde*, 1 November 1974; "A Rennes II," *Le Monde*, 8-9 February 1976; Suffert and Lesieur, "L'enlisement," p. 118.

[61]Jacques Bouzerand, "Etudiants: le grande peur," *Le Point*, no. 1 (25 September 1972), pp. 91-92; the student poll conducted by SOFRES was also cited in Soisson, *Six principes*, pp. 20-21, but that report gave the date of the study as being July 1973.

NOTES

[62]Faure, *Ce que je crois*, p. 194, citing OECD *Examen des politiques nationales d'éducation*, pp. 63-64; J. Vuillemin, *Rebâtir l'université*, (Paris, 1968), pp. 25-26.

[63]OECD, "Organizational problems in planning educational development," [OECD, study group in the economics of education] (Paris, 1966), pp. 89-90; Guy Herzlich, "Professionalisation et sélection," *Le Monde*, 17 February 1976; OECD, *L'enseignement supérieur court* (Paris, 1973), pp. 327-328.

[64]Frédéric Gaussen, "Mme Alice Saunier-Seité — Les universités doivent partir à la conquête des débouchés," *Le monde de l'éducation*, no. 16 (April, 1976), pp. 43-44; for employment difficulties facing young people, see Marc Mangenot *et al.*, *Les jeunes face à l'emploi* (Paris, 1972).

[65]Frédéric Gaussen, "Un colloque de l'OECD," *Le Monde*, 25 November 1971.

[66]J. Vincens, "La société et ses diplômes," *Le Monde*, 3 August 1971; J.-B. Ettori, "Besançon," *Education et gestion*, no. 43 (1974), pp. 33-39; "La marelle de M. Soisson," *Le Monde*, 15 March 1975; France, ministère de l'éducation nationale, Bureau d'informations et de prévisions économiques (BIPE), "Les relations entre les emplois de cadre et les formations supérieurs," *Document de travail*, no. 8 (January, 1973), pp. 2-5.

[67]Pierre Silvestre, "La réussite à l'agrégation," *Education et gestion*, no. 19 (January, 1970), pp. 33-35; Jean Vincens, "Que faire des littéraires?" *Le Monde*, supplement, 13 June 1972; M. Declaux and J. Minot, "A propos des jurys," *Education et gestion*, no. 2 (April, 1970), p. 23; "Nouvelles réductions des postes aux concours de l'agrégation et du CAPES," *Le Monde*, 23 January 1976; "Les protestations contre la réforme du deuxième cycle," *Le Monde*, 6 February 1976.

[68]Guy Herzlich, "Un plan socialiste pour 'réconcilier l'école avec ses usagers et avec la nation'," *Le Monde*, 14 September 1976.

[69]Roger Masters, "L'université sans murs. Un modèle contesté," *Le Monde*, 23 February 1971; Masters was a political science professor from Dartmouth College serving as cultural attaché in Paris when he wrote the article.

212

NOTES

NOTES

Chapter VI

[1]Faure, *Ce que je crois*, p. 163.

[2]Jacques Vivies, "L'autonomie financière des universités," *Education et gestion*, no. 18 (October, 1969), p. 63.

[3]Robert, *Mandarin*, p. 230; Gibson, *Block Grants*, passim; "L'assemblée générale de la conférence des recteurs européens," *Le Monde*, 11 September 1974; France, secrétariat d'état aux universités, *Le financement des universités. Rapport de la commission chargée de proposer une meilleure répartition des crédits de l'état.* Bienaymé commission [La documentation française] (Paris, 1976), pp. 111-115.

[4]INRDP, *Organisation de l'enseignement*, pp. 68-70; interview with official at the secretariat on 16 July 1975.

[5]For the pervasive influence of the ministry of finance see for instance Robert Buron, *Le plus beau des métiers* (Paris, 1963), pp. 214-217, reprinted in François Goguel and Alfred Grosser, "Le terrible ministre des finances," *La politique en France*, third edition (Paris, 1964), pp. 248-249.

[6]Yves Agnès, "Les difficultés financières des universités," *Le Monde*, 28 July 1971; Guy Herzlich, "Une commission suggère une transformation progressive du système de répartition des crèdits d'état aux universités," *Le Monde*, 2 July 1975.

[7]Of course, it has been suggested that sometimes "difficult" political groups have been appeased by rewards, Marcel Signac, "Vive l'université napoléonienne!," *Rivarol*, 22 February 1973.

[8]OECD, *Educational Policy and Planning. France* (Paris, 1972), pp. 577-79; Annex II, "The procedure for drawing up the budget of the ministry of education."

[9]See appendix 3.

[10]Herzlich, "Une commission."

[11]Kourganoff, *Face cachée*, p. 73; *Propositions du parti communiste français pour une réforme démocratique de l'enseignement* [*L'école et la nation*, no. 185-86] (January-February, 1970), p. 151.

[12]Kourganoff, *Face cachée*, pp. 75-76; "Les problèmes financiers des universités," *Education et gestion*, no. 43 (1974), p. 59.

[13]"La conférence des présidents des universités," *Le Monde*, 4-5 June

213

1972; "Les difficultés financières des universités," *Le Monde*, 26 January 1977; L. P., "Difficultés financières à Toulouse-Le Mirail," *Le Monde*, 7 May 1977; C. F., "Les difficultés financières des universitès de province," *Le Monde*, 15-16 May 1977; Suffert and Lesieur, "L'enlisement," pp. 117-118.

[14]"A l'assemblée nationale, la commission des affaires culturelles émet un avis sur le budget des universités," *Le Monde*, 31 October 1974; "Manifestations et protestations contre le budget du secrétariat d'état," *Le Monde*, 18 November 1975; "Strasbourg," *Le Monde*, 7 November 1974; "Les universités de Paris III, XIII manifestent devant le secrétariat d'état," *Le Monde*, 16-17 March 1975.

[15]Faure, *Ce que je crois*, p. 163.

[16]"Un étudiant 'coûte' . . .," *Le Monde*, 11 August 1970; J. Hallack, *The analysis of educational costs and expenditures* [UNESCO], translated by International Institute for Educational Planning (Paris, 1969), p. 27; OECD, *Towards mass higher education*, p. 208.

[17]Daumard, *Prix de l'enseignement*, pp. 141-142.

[18]Jacques Monod, "L'étrange alliance," *Le Monde*, 8 October 1968; D. Najman, *L'enseignement supérieur pour quoi faire* (Paris, 1974), pp. 180-181; Berstecher *et al.*, *L'université*, p. 109; Vuillemin, *Rebâtir*, p. 42; interview with a university president, 4 May 1977.

[19]"La petite guerre des loyers a commencé dans les résidences universitaires," *Le Monde*, 24 December 1975; "Les universités percevront désormais la totalité des droits payées par les étudiants," *Le Monde*, 26-27 September 1971; B. Frappat, "Les droits de scolarité dans les facultés," *Le Monde*, 28-29 September 1969; INRDP, *Organisation de l'enseignement*, p. 69; "Le budget moyen," *Dernières Nouvelles d'Alsace*, 21 April 1976.

[20]*Le Monde*, 4 March 1977; interview with Dean John Hargreaves of the Faculty of Arts and Social Sciences, Aberdeen University, 14 May 1977.

[21]Interview with an official at the secretariat of university affairs, 4 March 1977; interview with Dean John Hargreaves.

[22]Frédéric Gaussen, "L'université de l'ancien régime au nouveau, III. Evoluer ou dépérir," *Le Monde*, 10 December 1970.

[23]"Les présidents des universités demandent une subvention de 50 millions de francs pour 1975," *Le Monde*, 23 November 1974.

[24]Bienaymé commission, "Note sur les études menées au sein d'un groupe de travail," pp. 117-118.

NOTES

[25]Bertrand Le Gendre, "Une conférence de l'OECD. Le prix des universités," *Le Monde*, 28 January 1975; Yves Agnès, "Les difficultés financières des universités, Reims, Paris I, Saint-Etienne," *Le Monde*, 28 July 1971.

[26]The twenty universities studied by GARACES were: Amiens, Bordeaux I, Bordeaux II, Brest, Grenoble III, Limoges, Montpellier I, Montpellier II, Nantes, Orléans, Paris V, Paris X, Paris XI, Reims, Strasbourg I, Strasbourg II, Toulon, Toulouse II, Toulouse III, and Valenciennes. The report of the Bienaymé commission was published in 1976; according to some reports, Soisson promised to hold a press conference with GARACES in September 1975, and indicated that parts of the confidential report might be published. This was never done. But recommendations of the GARACES report have been influential in the secretariat's financial policies and were implemented; interviews with two officials at the secretariat, 11 and 12 August 1975.

[27]Quermonne, former president of Grenoble I and ex-director of the division of DERP at the secretariat during the Soisson administration, expressed concern over the lack of provisions for the upkeep of new constructions; "L'autonomie va changer profondément la physionomie des universités," *Le Monde*, 22 February 1972; the same point was made by officials interviewed at the secretariat on 11 and 12 of August 1975. The system of cost-analysis introduced by GARACES also pointed to areas of wastage, misuse of telephone and computer privileges, lack of organized systems of buying supplies, and heat wastage, Suffert and Lesieur, "L'enlisement," p. 116.

[28]Bienaymé commission, pp. 22, 86.

[29]Guy Herzlich, "L'université d'Aix-Marseille II est sur le point d'éclater," *Le Monde*, 22 December 1971.

[30]Interview with official at the secretariat, 11 August 1975.

[31]Groupe d'analyse et de recherche (GARACES), "Analyse et recherche sur les activités et les coûts de l'enseignement supérieur," Paris, August 1975 (report at the secrétariat d'état aux universités), pp. 331-32; Suffert and Lesieur, "L'enlisement," p. 117.

[32]GARACES, "Analyse," pp. 345-347, 357.

[33]Ibid., p. 358.

[34]Ibid., p. 143.

[35]After 1976, law and economics were separated administratively into two distinct fields of study. In law, faculty-student ratio worsened from

215

the previous year, while it improved for economics, interview with a university president, 13 April 1977; France, Secrétariat d'état aux universités, "Fiche technique sur les critères de répartition des crédits de fonctionnement pour 1977," m.s.

NOTES

Conclusion

[1]S. E. and Zella Luria, "The Role of the University: Ivory Tower, Service Station, or Frontier Post?" in Graubard and Ballotti, eds., *Embattled*, p. 75; Peyrefitte, *Le mal français*, p. 302.

[2]Frédéric Gaussen, "Le palmarès des universités," *Le monde de l'éducation*, no. 19 (July-August 1976), pp. 3-21; Yves Agnès, "Les universités dans leur régions," pp. 7-8.

[3]D. Najman, *L'enseignement supérieur*, p. 9.

[4]Capelle, 1st séance, 14 November 1970, *Assemblée nationale, débats, J.o.* (15 November 1970), pp. 5544-45.

[5]In various ways this theme has been developed in Crozier, *Bureaucratic*, and *La Société bloquée*, (Paris, 1970); Pitts, "Continuity and Change," Peyrefitte, *Le mal*; Schonfeld, "Towards understanding the bases of democratic political instability. A case study of French social authority patterns," and idem, *Obedience and Revolt: French Behavior toward Authority* (Beverly Hills, California, 1976); Nathan Leites, *House without Windows* (Stanford, California, 1955).

[6]Olivier Guichard writing in *Le Nouvel Observateur* (September, 1970), cited in Beaud, *Vincennes*, p. 19.

[7]Guy Herzlich, "La désectorisation de Nanterre a provoqué un imbroglio administratif," *Le Monde*, 21 October 1976; "Les suites de la 'désectorisation' de Nanterre," *Le Monde*, 10 November 1976; "Après la décision du Conseil d'état," *Le Monde*, 15 February 1977.

[8]Ralph A. Dungan, "Higher Education: The Effort to Adjust," in Graubard and Ballotti, eds., *Embattled*, p. 152.

[9]Stanley Hoffmann, "Participation in Perspective?" p. 198; for an analysis of the role of the university in society see S. E. and Zella Luria, "The Role of the University," p. 81.

216

[10]Masters, "Université sans murs"; for other views concerning the vulnerability of the American university and alternatives for coping with the problem, Martin Trow, "The Transition from Mass to Universal Higher Education," in Graubard and Ballotti, eds., *Embattled*, pp. 38-40.

[11]Clark Kerr, "Governance and Functions," in Graubard and Ballotti, eds., *Embattled*, p. 121.

[12]Alain Peyrefitte, 7th séance, 14 April 1970, *Assemblée nationale, débats, J.o.* (15 April 1970), p. 1007.

[13]Jonathan Story and Michael Parrott, "An essay on Management in France," *International Herald Tribune* [an Economic Report] (Paris, May 1977).

[14]Alain Peyrefitte, see footnote 12.

[15]Charles Perrow, "The Analysis of Goals in Complex Organizations," in Amitai Etzioni, ed., *Readings on Modern Organizations* (Englewood Cliffs, N.J., 1969), p. 74. The author, while focussing on goals in a hospital as his model, found that in the absence of a single authority the organization could tolerate considerable ambiguity of goals and achievements as long as standards remained high in most areas, occupancy was sufficient to operate with a minimum deficit, and a favorable public image was maintained; Kerr, "Governance," p. 121.

[16]In the speeches of the secretary of university affairs, attacks were made: on the faculty of the political left, the small classes at the expense of the *cours magistraux*, the system of *unité de valeur*, as well as the experimental university of Vincennes, and the electoral system established by the 1968 law, Philippe Boggio, "Les enseignants 'autonomes' accentuent leur offensive contre la loi d'orientation de l'enseignement supérieur," *Le Monde*, 26 April 1977; Guy Herzlich, "La longue préparation de la réforme universitaire," *Le Monde*, 27 April 1977; "Mme Saunier-Seité: Vincennes n'a pas l'exclusivité des non-bacheliers," *Le Monde*, 29 April 1977; "Les députés souhaitent une réforme de la loi d'orientation de l'enseignement supérieur," *Le Monde*, 7 May 1977; "Mme Saunier-Seité: des assistants sont livrés à eux-mêmes," *Le Monde*, 8-9 May 1977; "Au sénat violente diatribe de Mme Saunier-Seité contre la politisation des universités, 'Vincennes c'est l'Italie' affirme le secrétaire d'état," *Le Monde*, 28 May 1977.

[17]Crozier, *Bureaucratic*, p. 226.

[18]Barre and Boursin, *De l'enseignement secondaire à l'enseignement*

217

supérieur, p. 15.

[19]Philippe Boggio, "Un 'forum' du SNE-Sup: Le rôle social de l'enseignement supérieur," *Le Monde*, 15 February 1977.

[20]The overwhelming number of higher civil servants are graduates of the *grandes écoles*, for the authoritative study of the higher French civil service, Ezra N. Suleiman, *Politics, Power and Bureaucracy in France — The Administrative Elite* (Princeton, 1974); also Pierre Birnbaum, *Les sommets de l'état* (Paris, 1977).

[21]Alain Peyrefitte cited in David Cudaback, "Happiness decreed from on high — The French Illness," *International Herald Tribune* [an Economic Report] (Paris, May 1977).

[22]Interview with a university president, 4 May 1977.

[23]This was the overall assessment of the Conference on "Two Decades of Gaullism — The Impact of the Fifth Republic on France," held at State University of New York College at Brockport, June 9-11, 1978. Especially significant were Michel Crozier, "France's Cultural Anxieties under Gaullism," Stanley Hoffmann, "Government and Society," and comments by Jesse R. Pitts. The proceedings of the Conference will be published.

NOTES

GLOSSARY

TABLES

APPENDICES

BIBLIOGRAPHY

GLOSSARY

Academy: Educational administrative unit of France. There are twenty-seven academies each administered by a rector.

Agrégation: Competitive examination leading to teaching posts at university or secondary school.

Agrégé: An individual who has succeeded in the *agrégation* examination.

Assistant: Lowest rank in the teaching faculty. Responsibilities vary.

Baccalauréat: Secondary school diploma giving automatic access to university.

CAPES: (Certificat d'aptitude au professorat de l'enseignement du second degré) Competitive examination leading to teaching in secondary school. An individual who has passed the CAPES is known as a *professeur certifié*.

CCU: (Comité consultatif d'université) National committee on recruitment and promotion of faculty.

CNESER: (Conseil national de l'enseignement supérieur et de la recherche) A national representative organ of higher education and research.

CNOUS/CROUS: (Centre national/regional des oeuvres universitaires et scolaires) National and regional student services organisation.

Concours: Competitive examinations at any level or within various organisations.

Conference of Presidents: An organisation comprising all university presidents.

CRESER: (Conseil régional de l'enseignement supérieur et de la recherche) A regional representative council of higher education and research which has remained a dead letter.

DEA: (Diplôme d'études approfondi) Intermediary graduate degree emphasizing research.

DESS: (Diplôme d'études supérieures specialisées) Intermediary graduate degree emphasizing professional training.

DEUG: (Diplôme d'études universitaires générales) Two year undergraduate diploma.

Doctorat d'état: Most advanced degree, above the American Ph.D.

Doctorat de troisième cycle: Graduate degree, approximates the American Ph.D.

DUEL/DUES: (Diplôme universitaire d'études littéraires/scientifiques) Two year undergraduate diploma phased out in 1974 in favor of the more general diploma, the DEUG.

220

DUT: (Diplôme universitaire de technologie) Two year diploma from an IUT.

Faculté: Traditional academic unit. A university could have one or several facultés — letters, law, sciences, medicine and pharmacy. The faculté structure was abolished in 1968.

GARACES: (Groupe d'analyse et de recherche sur les activités et les coûts de l'enseignement supérieur) A committee in the secrétariat of state of universities which issued the first cost-analysis of French universities in 1975.

Grandes écoles: Elitist institutions of higher education.

IUT: (Institut universitaire de technologie) University technical institutes founded after 1966.

Licence: Undergraduate diploma after three years of study.

Liste d'aptitude: Ranked national list drawn up by the CCU of faculty for recruitment and promotion purposes.

Maître assistant: Faculty rank approximately equivalent to American assistant professor.

Maître de conférences: Faculty rank approximately equivalent to American associate professor.

Maîtrise: Master's degree.

ONISEP: (Office national d'information sur les enseignements et les professions) National office providing academic and career information.

Orientation Act of Higher Education: The reform law passed in 1968 restructuring the universities (also known as the Faure Law after its sponsor, the minister of education, Edgar Faure).

Rector: The government's representative in each academy co-ordinating all levels of education.

Sélection: Restrictive admission practices.

UER: (Unité d'enseignement et de recherche) Unit of teaching and research founded by the 1968 law which can include one or several disciplines.

GLOSSARY

TABLE 1

GROWTH PATTERN OF STUDENT POPULATION 1936-1978 AND AVERAGE ANNUAL INCREASE

Year	Average Annual Increase Percent	University/I.U.T.
1936-1937	[4.6]	72,000
1945-46		123,313
1950-51	[2.4]	139,593
1955-56		157,489
1958-59	2.4	202,128
1959-60	5.0	213,062
1960-61	0.7	214,672
1961-62	12.0	244,814
1962-63	14.0	285,614
1963-64	12.0	326,311
1964-65	11.0	367,701
1965-66	10.0	413,756
1966-67	10.0	458,409
1967-68	10.0	508,119
1968-69	11.0	576,000
1969-70	8.0	625,551
1970-71	3.8	650,231
1971-72	6.8	697,791
1972-73	5.0	735,418
1973-74	0.8	741,137
1974-75	2.5	760,590
1975-76	6.7	811,258
1976-77	1.3	821,591
1977-78	2.0	837,680

SOURCES: H. Rachou, "La direction des enseignements supérieurs," in Crémieux-Brilhac, ed., *Education nationale*, p. 375; *Tableaux, 1958-1968*, p. 40 and subsequent volumes; *Note d'information*, no. 75-41 (28 November 1975), p. 3; *Note d'information*, no. 77-07 (18 February 1977); *Note d'information*, no. 78-23 (9 June 1978).

TABLE 2

STUDENT ENROLLMENT (DECEMBER 1976)

UNIVERSITIES	LAW	ECONO-MICS	LETTERS	SCIEN-CES	MEDI-CINE	PHAR-MACY	DENTIS-TRY	ENGI-NEERING	PHYS. ED.	SOC.SCI. & SOC.AM. FLO.AMN.	I.N.T.	TOTAL	PREVIOUS YEAR 1975-76
AIX I			10052	3621						128		13801	13023
AIX II		1918	454	1300	10242	2176	770		547	477	759	18643	17837
AIX III	7283	1149	701	1473				103		513	576	11798	11423
AVIGNON			879	307								1186	1137
LA REUNION	804	85	618	213								1720	1623
TOTAL	8087	3152	12704	6914	10242	2176	770	103	547	1118	1335	47148	45043 +4,67
AMIENS	1474	635	2435	1170	1907	629					814	9064	9472
COMPIEGNE				743								743	542
TOTAL	1474	635	2435	1913	1907	629					814	9807	10014 -2,06
BESANCON	1157	288	3458	1442	2378	483		236	143	60	1117	10762	10605 +1,46
BORDEAUX I	7525	2333	2177	4209				195			1227	15489	15314
BORDEAUX II				392	8137	2180	848		407		551	14141	13877
BORDEAUX III			7601	92						27	54	8244	7944
PAU	2042	535	1663	737								5058	4532
TOTAL	9567	2868	11441	5430	8137	2180	848	195	407	27	1832	42932	41667 +3,03
CAEN	1555	1080	4040	1527	1660	880		210	287	58	624	11921	11767 +1,30
CLERMONT I	2441	938		48	2324	1039	350				581	7721	
CLERMONT II			3375	2034				60	371		341	6381	
TOTAL	2441	938	3375	2082	2324	1039	350	60	371		922	14102	14419 -2,19
DIJON	2393	754	3320	2093	2051	554		104	323	245	887	12724	12954 -1,85
GRENOBLE I			273	5058	3168	1031			430		1199	11159	10371
GRENOBLE II	4569	2275	2603	320						432	1477	11676	11552
GRENOBLE III			4355	90						58		4445	4232
CHAMBERY	498		942	470							266	2203	2119
I.N.P.				439				1179				1649	1491
TOTAL	5067	2275	8173	6377	3168	1031		1179	430	490	2942	31132	29765 +4,59
LILLE I			770	5891		1647		83		242	2004	10699	10961
LILLE II	4166	1951			6844		780		507		105	14291	13365
LILLE III			9249							312	288	10166	10414
VALENCIENNES	303	61	460	402	256						758	1923	1813
TOTAL	4469	2012	10479	6293	7100	1647	780	83	507	554	3155	37079	37053 +0,08
LIMOGES	1280	420	1298	959	1531	580				63	889	7020	7092 -1,02
LYON I				6229	9968	2324	802		344	52	1948	21667	20362
LYON II	1037	1780	8639							274		11720	11024
LYON III	4992	587	1626	168						422		7795	7191
SAINT-ETIENNE	598	837	1635	694	1364					114	764	6006	5697
TOTAL	6627	3204	11900	7091	11332	2324	802		344	862	2712	47198	45174 +4,48
MONTPELLIER I	4341	1501			6978	3084	782		235	436		17357	17525
MONTPELLIER II	122			5214				102			1677	7115	7104
MONTPELLIER III		69	6707		342					175		7293	7687
PERPIGNAN	993	297	799	391							188	2668	2670
TOTAL	5456	1867	7506	5605	7320	3084	782	102	235	611	1865	34433	34991 -1,59
NANCY I				3497	5420	1191	359	361	340		835	12003	11993
NANCY II	2417	1235	4796							78	772	9320	9467
METZ	1213	40	2055	1108						111	754	5281	5092
I.N.P.				532				1126				1658	1483
TOTAL	3630	1275	6851	5137	5420	1191	359	1487	340	189	2361	28262	28035 +0,80

TABLE 2 (continued)

NANTES	1913	871	4209	2207	2977	1089	665	408			1187	15526	16357
ANGERS	941	210	997	470	1849	538				98	594	5697	5549
LE MANS	766	337	896	441						94	483	3017	2989
TOTAL	3620	1418	6102	3118	4826	1627	665	408		192	2264	24240	24895 −2,63
NICE	3715	1240	5045	2420	2783		177				818	16198	15770
TOULON	1018	175		218						93	600	2104	2051
TOTAL	4733	1415	5045	2638	2783		177			93	1418	18302	17821 +2,69
ORLEANS	1202	332	974	1650						111	916	5185	5456
TOURS	1356	431	4068	1045	3257	909				194	988	12248	12194
TOTAL	2558	763	5042	2695	3257	909				305	1904	17433	17650 −1,22
PARIS I	8422	8935	8459	687						428		26931	27635
PARIS II	13225	1965	115							160		15465	16992
PARIS III			16027									16027	15427
I.N.L.C.O.			8037									8037	7304
PARIS IV			18611									18611	18862
PARIS V	649		6548		14680	3245	2165		846	62	1069	29264	28575
PARIS VI				18283	16193			144				34620	34110
PARIS VII			10661	9117	10594		2075		78	852		33377	32619
PARIS VIII	1835	1345	26170	2646								31996	31958
PARIS IX	402	4498		416						234		5550	5533
PARIS X	5742	3032	12340						121	295	432	21962	21811
PARIS XI	3886			7961	2370	3983					2240	20440	20095
PARIS XII	3083	950	2260	298	3121					71	734	10517	9948
PARIS XIII	1917	1140	4185	1637	1795					174	1654	12502	11846
I.E.P.	3476	654										4130	4307
TOTAL	42637	22519	113413	41045	48753	7228	4240	144	1045	2276	6129	289429	287022 +0,83
POITIERS	2566	718	3149	1941	1422	567		263	415	264	1246	12551	12794 −1,90
REIMS	2289	680	2412	1203	2204	954	479			18	1614	11853	11409 +3,89
RENNES I	3037	1454	121	3099	3740	870	619	104		294	1552	14890	14462
RENNES II			6162	29					372	301	399	7263	7230
BREST	1366	328	1682	1195	1179					565	1377	7692	7499
TOTAL	4403	1782	7965	4323	4919	870	619	104	372	1160	3328	29845	29191 +2,24
ROUEN	1879	529	3669	1694	2416	519				187	1031	11924	11540 +3,32
STRASBOURG I		952	1278	2830	4891	1064	449	112		60		11636	11441
STRASBOURG II			6291						89			6380	6687
STRASBOURG III	4010	325	211								496	5042	4829
MULHOUSE			532	305				129			786	1752	1605
TOTAL	4010	1277	8312	3135	4891	1064	449	241	89	60	1282	24810	24562 +1,00
TOULOUSE I	6346	3309		23						518		10196	10406
TOULOUSE II			10663							72	74	10809	10195
TOULOUSE III				7518	7627	1938	886		392		2498	20859	20768
I.N.P.								1230				1230	1119
TOTAL	6346	3309	10663	7541	7627	1938	886	1230	392	590	2572	43094	42488 +1,42
ANTILLES-GUYANE	2129	429	695	289	48							3590	3367 +6,62
T O T A L	130373	55607	253447	122707	147716	33474	12206	6149	6247	9422	44243	821591	811258 +1,27
Previous Year 1975–76	129485	57353	252636	121510	143423	33510	11258	5896	5136	7525	43526	811258	

SOURCE: *Note d'information*, no. 77-07 (18 February 1977).

TABLE 3

GROWTH RATE OF STUDENT POPULATION
IN OECD COUNTRIES
1961-1970 (in percent)

Australia	9.3
Belgium	10.2
Canada	17.7
Denmark	8.7
France	13.6
Federal Republic of Germany	9.7
Japan	15.4
Netherlands	10.2
Norway	12.0
Sweden	13.2
U.K.	9.9
U.S.A.	6.6
Average	11.3

SOURCE: Conference on Future Structures of Post-Secondary Education, *Towards Mass Higher Education, Issues and Dilemmas* [OECD] (Paris, 1974), p. 182.

TABLES

TABLE 4

AVERAGE LENGTH OF UNIVERSITY STUDIES
AND APPROXIMATIVE RATE OF SUCCESS
A COMPARATIVE TABLE

Country	Theoretical no. of Years	Real no. of Years	Success Rate % 1960-1965
Germany	4-5	5	52
Austria...........	4	5	47
Belgium	4	5	66
Denmark	6	7	55
Spain	4-5	6	45
Finland...........	4	5	66
France	4	5	44
Greece	5	6	62
Ireland	3-4	4	83
Italy	4	6	56
Norway	4-5	5	54
Holland	4-6	7	60
U.K...............	3-4	3-4	86
Sweden...........	4	6	68
Yugoslavia........	4	6	41
U.S.	4	4-5	70
Japan	4	4	91

SOURCE: Soisson, *Six principes*, p. 8.

TABLE 5

SOCIAL ORIGIN OF FRENCH STUDENTS
BETWEEN 1961-1962 AND 1965-1966
(in percent)

Social Origin	1961-62	1962-63	1963-64	1964-65	1965-66
Farm workers	0.6	0.5	0.6	0.7	0.6
Farmers..................	5.6	6.5	5.4	5.5	5.8
Service industries	0.9	1.0	1.0	1.2	1.1
Workers	6.4	7.9	7.6	8.3	9.4
Total working class	13.5	15.9	14.6	15.7	16.9
Craftsmen-tradesmen	13.7	13.4	12.3	13.3	12.2
Office workers	7.9	7.4	8.6	8.2	8.6
Middle management	17.8	17.4	17.8	17.7	16.7
Total middle class	39.4	38.2	38.7	39.2	37.5
Professions, Senior executives, businessmen............	32.5	29.3	32.5	33.1	31.5
Not gainfully employed (other categories)	14.6	15.1	14.2	13.0	14.1
Totals	100%	100%	100%	100%	100%

SOURCE: Grignon and Passeron, *French Experience*, p. 70.

TABLES

TABLE 6

OCCUPATION OF STUDENTS' PARENTS 1964-1975, AND PERCENTAGE OF EACH CATEGORY IN THE ACTIVE POPULATION

Occupation	1964-65	1967-68	1973-74	1974-75	1968 Active Population	1976 Active Population
Farmers	5.5	6.3	6.1	6.0	12.1	10.4
Farm Workers	0.7	0.7	0.6	0.7	2.9	1.7
Employers in Industry and Commerce	15.2	15.4	11.9	11.7	9.6	10.2
Professions and top Executives	30.2	34.5	32.6	32.9	4.9	7.0
Middle Management	17.7	17.4	16.2	16.4	9.8	13.3
Office Workers	8.2	9.3	9.4	9.2	14.7	17.0
Workers	8.3	11.1	12.5	12.6	37.8	36.9
Service Personnel	1.2	0.8	0.8	0.8	5.7	6.3
Other Occupations	6.5	3.0	8.1	7.0	2.5	1.9
No Profession	1.1	1.5	1.8	2.7		
Total	100	100	100	100	100	100

SOURCES: *Note d'information*, no. 76-15 (30 April 1976), p. 1; "La démocratisation de l'enseignement supérieur depuis 1964," *Le Monde*, 29 August 1974. The 'other categories' on the table included army, police and artists; figures of the active population were found for 1968 in the above article in *Le Monde*, and in Institut national de la statistique et des études économiques (INSEE), *Annuaire statistique de la France, résultats de 1972*, 79 (1974): 57; figures for the active population in 1976 were found in B. Seys and P. Lauthé, *Enquête sur l'emploi de 1976* [Les collections de l'INSEE, 48 D] (November 1976), p. 31.

229

TABLE 7

GROWTH PATTERN: FACULTY IN THE FRENCH UNIVERSITIES — NUMBERS AND PROPORTIONS BY RANKS 1960-1977.

Rank	1960-61	1965-66	1966-67	1967-68	1968-69	1969-70	1970-71	1971-72 a	1972-73	1974-75	1975-76 b	1976-77
Professors	3,585	5,218	6,082	2,293	2,451	2,610	8,772	9,060	2,672	2,777	2,788	4,800
%	45.4%	38.5%	29%	10%	9%	8%	25%	24%	7%	7.3%	7.3%	12.2%
Maîtres de Conférences				3,964	4,525	4,964			5,887	7,182	7,209	5,500
%				18%	16%	16%			16%	18.8%	19.0%	13.8%
Maîtres-Assistants/Disc. and Lab.	4,316	11,521	4,700	5,194	6,315	7,032	8,932	9,434	8,931	11,145	11,281	14,500
%	54.6%	61.5%	22.5%	23%	23%	23%	25%	25%	24%	29.2%	29.7%	36.4%
Assistants			10,182	11,062	12,974	13,818	15,919	16,613	15,476	16,762	16,339	15,000
%			48.5%	49%	46%	44%	45%	45%	41%	43.9%	43.0%	37.6%
Other Categories including all Ranks in IUTs	—	—	—	—	1,609	2,874	2,056	2,075	4,885	—	395	—
%					6%	9%	5%	6%	12%	0.8%	1.0%	—
Total	7,901	18,739	20,964	22,513	27,874	31,302	35,679	37,182	37,851	38,220	38,012	39,800
%	100%	100%	100%	100%	100%	100%	100%	100%	100%	100%	100%	100%

SOURCES: Asselain, *Budget*, pp. 130-31; *Tableaux 1970*, p. 416; *Tableaux 1976*, p. 319; Statistics for 1975-76, personal communication; 1976-77, Suffert and Lesieur, "L'Enlisement," p. 122.

aCategories for 1972-73 differed in the 1974 edition of *Tableaux* from earlier editions. Thus, there were some apparent declines in the number of *assistants*. Statistics in the Baecque report on faculty do not concur with those of the ministry of education statistics, Baecque, "Situation," p. 33; the *Annuaire statistique, 1976* gave a total of 38,499 for 1972-73, INSEE, *Annuaire statistique de la France, 1976*, 81 (Paris, 1976):108.

bStatistics for 1975-76 were categorized somewhat differently from previous years, thus IUT faculty was no longer included in a separate category.

230

TABLES

TABLE 8

NUMBER OF FACULTY AND STUDENTS
AND THEIR RATIO 1951-1977.

Year	Teaching Faculty	Students	Ratio
1951-52	2,960	137,000	46.3
1953-54	3,280	146,000	44.5
1955-56	3,750	152,000	40.5
1957-58	5,300	175,000	31.1
1959-60	6,600	195,000	29.6
1960-61	8,300	203,000	24.5
1961-62	9,800	233,000	23.8
1962-63	12,700	271,000	21.3
1963-64	14,700	326,000	22.2
1964-65	17,700	368,000	20.8
1965-66	19,300	413,000	21.4
1966-67	20,700	440,000	21.2
1967-68	22,513	508,119	22.5
1968-69	27,874	576,000	20.6
1969-70	31,302	625,551	19.9
1970-71	35,679	650,231	18.2
1971-72	37,182	697,791	18.7
1972-73	37,851	735,418	19.4
1973-74	———	741,137	———
1974-75	38,220	760,590	19.9
1975-76	38,012	811,258	21.3
1976-77	39,800	821,591	20.6

SOURCES: Calculations based on Asselain, *Le budget*, pp. 130-131, and on statistics acquired from the ministry of education, *Tableaux 1970*, p. 433; *Tableaux 1971*, p. 396; *Tableaux 1972*, p. 365; *Tableaux 1974*, pp. 404-405; *Tableaux 1976*, p. 319; various *Notes d'information*; the figures include university and IUT students and faculty. Figures for 1975-76 total faculty did not include all categories, and hence were not quite accurate, obtained from personal source. Figures of total faculty for 1976-77 differed in two sources, from 40,600 to 39,800, "Mme Saunier-Seité: des assistants sont livrés à eux-mêmes," *Le Monde*, 8-9 May 1977; Suffert and Lesieur, "L'enlisement," p. 122.

231

TABLE 9

STUDENT MEMBERSHIP IN UNEF 1945-1976

Year	Number of Students in Higher Education	Members UNEF (approx.)	Members % of Total Student Population
1945	123,000	25,000	20%
1950	170,000	42,000	25%
1957	212,000	88,000	42%
1963	328,000	85,000	26%
1964	384,000	85,000	22%
1967	460,000	49,000	11%
1976	821,591	50,000	6%

SOURCE: Fields, *Student Politics*, p. 102; membership after 1957 includes members of the Union des grandes écoles which affiliated with UNEF in 1957-58. The figures above are often approximated. For example, Belden Fields calculated the 49,000 figure for membership in 1967, while an official of UNEF thought the figure was more like 70,000.

232

TABLES

TABLE 10

SUCCESS RATE IN THE COMPETITIVE EXAMINATIONS:
AGREGATION AND CAPES

Year	Agrégation				CAPES			
	Candidates	Posts	Passed	Success in %	Candidates	Posts	Passed	Success in %
1967	7,087	—	1,645	23.2	866	—	385	43.4
1970	12,087	—	1,924	15.9	20,005	5,282	3,000	15.0
1971	14,637	—	1,979	13.5	26,644	6,367	3,808	14.3
1973	19,106	2,200	1,959	10.2	37,551	6,398	4,078	10.9
1974	18,650	2,200	1,911	10.2	36,977	6,363	4,033	10.9
1975	18,563	1,800	1,586	8.5	—	6,000	—	—
1976	18,661	1,600	1,504	8.0	34,138	4,439	4,429	13.0
1977	—	—	—	—	—	4,000	—	—
1978	—	1,200	—	—	—	3,250	—	—

SOURCES: *Tableaux, 1968*, pp. 310-11; "Statistiques des concours de l'agrégation et du certificat d'aptitude au professorat de l'enseignement du second degré," *Note d'information*, no. 79 (2 December 1970), no. 121 (17 December 1971), no. 73-42 (7 December 1973), no. 74-38 (22 November 1974); *Le Monde*, 7 March 1978.

TABLE 11

EVOLUTION OF THE NUMBER OF SCHOLARSHIPS AND FUNDS ALLOCATED TO HIGHER EDUCATION
1965-1978

Year	Number of Scholarships	Funds Allocated in Francs
1965-66	94,739	230,114,000
1966-67	104,433	263,170,000
1967-68	112,337	300,248,000
1968-69	129,140	397,926,000
1969-70	140,036	434,113,000
1970-71	144,036	447,981,000
1971-72	137,614	443,391,000
1972-73	139,648	470,893,000
1973-74	131,449	496,879,000
1974-75	115,313	494,000,000
1975-76	101,000	472,989,000
1976-77	100,720	522,000,000
1977-78	92,460	534,500,000

SOURCES: Soisson, *Six principes*, p. 12; *Note d'information*, no. 75-35 (17 October 1975), p. 2, gives slightly different figures for number of scholarships, for example only 112,713 scholarships for 1974-75 compared to 115,313 given in *Six principes*; C. Bosc, "Les bourses de l'enseignement supérieur," *Education et Gestion*, no. 43 (1974), pp. 70-76; and personal information.

TABLES

TABLE 12

STATE EXPENDITURES FOR ALL LEVELS OF EDUCATION
IN FRANCE FROM 1952-1967
(In millions of francs)

	1952[a]		1957[a]		1962		1967	
	A	B-%	A	B-%	A	B-%	A	B-%
Primary.....	1,075	52.9%	1,692	50.2%	2,914	38.3%	4,933	32.5%
Special education...	3	0.1%	3	0.1%	11	0.1%	31	0.2%
Secondary...	719	35.5%	1,204	35.7%	2,772	36.9%	6,078	40.0%
Technical training	15	0.7%	29	0.9%	50	0.7%	106	0.7%
Higher education...	135	6.6%	236	7.1%	700	9.2%	1,727	11.4%
Research	32	1.6%	80	2.4%	300	4.0%	732	4.8%
Libraries	8	0.4%	11	0.3%	27	0.4%	55	0.4%
Common expenditures ..	8	0.4%	35	1.0%	128	1.7%	309	2.0%
Central Administration.	12	0.6%	19	0.6%	31	0.4%	74	0.5%
Other expenditures not connected with public education...	24	1.2%	60	1.7%	587	7.8%	1,141	7.5%
Totals		100%		100%		100%		100%

SOURCE: Asselain, *Budget*, p. 86.

[a]The amounts have been converted into post-1958 francs.

TABLE 13

EXPENDITURES ON HIGHER EDUCATION
— A COMPARATIVE TABLE
(In millions of dollars and as percentage of GNP)

Country	1961	% GNP	1970	% GNP
Australia	97.0 (1958)	0.3	278.3	0.8
Belgium	35.5	0.2	231.4 (1969)	1.0
Canada	201.3	0.5	1,960.0	2.7
Denmark	25.7	0.3	216.0	1.2
France (univer- sities)	192.2	0.2	905.2	0.6
Germany	348.2	0.4	1,338.0	0.7
Japan	216.6 (1962)	1.2	1,757.4 (1969)	1.0
Netherlands (universities) . . .	134.0	0.3	435.5 (1969)	1.2
Norway	17.9	0.3	70.3	0.7
Sweden	35.0 (1960)	0.3	329.4	1.0
U.K. (England Wales univer- sities)	281.6 (1962)	—	800.4 (1969)	—
U.S.A.	5,800.0 (1959-60)	1.1	24,900.0 (1970-71)	2.5
Average		0.5%		1.3%

SOURCE: OECD, "Towards Mass Higher Education," tables on pp. 178-179.

TABLES

TABLE 14

EDUCATION BUDGET — FRANCE (1958-1977)
RELATIONS OF EDUCATION BUDGET
TO STATE BUDGET AND TO GNP
(in million francs)

Year	GNP	Total State Budget	Education Nationale Budget	Education Budget Expressed as Percentage of GNP	Education Budget Expressed as Percentage of State Budget	Higher Education Budget of State	Higher Education Budget Expressed as Percentage of Education Nationale
1958	244,700	46,990	4,521.4	1.84	9.62	—	—
1959	272,619	54,800	6,072.3	2.2	11.1	—	—
1960	301,578	58,011	6,946.8	2.3	12.0	—	—
1961	328,327	62,851	7,675.9	2.3	12.2	—	—
1962	367,172	69,196	8,802.2	2.4	12.7	—	—
1963	411,989	76,888	10,490.4	2.5	13.6	—	—
1964	456,669	86,313	13,278.7	2.9	15.4	—	—
1965	489,834	92,336	15,096.8	3.1	16.3	—	—
1966	532,529	100,994	16,764.6	3.1	16.6	—	—
1967	574,770	113,623	18,543.3	3.2	16.3	2,514.0	13.5
1968	630,012	124,581	20,519.5	3.3	16.5	—	—
1969	723,500	145,322	23,122.8	3.2	15.9	—	—
1970	809,200	154,422	26,106.2	3.2	16.9	—	—
1971	899,600	166,362	29,732.7	3.3	17.9	4,663.5	15.8
1972	1,001,900	176,836	32,507.3	3.2	18.4	5,198.2	16.0
1973	1,139,300	196,359	36,081.6	3.2	18.4	5,828.7	16.2
1974	1,283,200	218,971	40,667.8	3.2	18.5	6,474.3	15.9
1975	1,398,600	258,862	46,795.1	3.3	18.1	7,409.5	15.8
1976	1,656,284	293,172	54,984.0	3.3	18.8	8,375.7	15.2
1977	1,873,794	333,456	58,138.5	—	—	—	—

SOURCES: Guy Herzlich, "La préparation du budget," *Le Monde*, 3 October 1970; Kourganoff, *Face cachée*, p. 73; Asselain, *Budget*, p. 86; *Tableaux 1974*, p. 11; "Evolution du budget de l'éducation nationale," and *Tableaux 1976*, p. 15; France, secrétariat d'état aux universités," "Budget du secrétariat," m.s.; figures for the higher education budget were not available for 1977. The 58,138 million figure for éducation nationale did not include higher education as had been the case in earlier years.

237

TABLE 15

NUMBER OF SPACES IN STUDENT RESTAURANTS AND RESIDENCE HALLS, 1960-1977

Year	Spaces in Restaurants	Ratio to Total Student Enrollment	No. of Rooms in Residence Halls	Ratio to Total Student Enrollment
1960	16,500	1:13	11,000	1:19.5
1966-67	54,000	1: 8.5	43,000	1:10.7
1968-69	88,000	1: 5.7	89,000	1: 5.7
1969-70	88,138	1: 7.1	88,479	1: 7.1
1971-72	112,382	1: 6.2	98,773	1: 7.2
1972-73	117,264	1: 6.2	99,999	1: 7.4
1973-74	125,056	1: 5.9	100,327	1: 7.4
1974-75	125,845	1: 6.0	101,735	1: 7.5
1975-76	131,337	1: 6.2	104,132	1: 7.8
1976-77	138,682	1: 5.9	109,305	1: 7.5

SOURCES: Figures through 1968 taken from the Mallet report on student life, p. 32; for 1969-70 from "Résidences et restaurants universitaires," *Education*, no. 43 (30 October 1969), p. XII; for 1971-72 from Fontanet, 3rd séance, 9 November 1972, *Assemblée nationale, débats, J.o.* (10 November 1972), p. 4956; for 1972-77 from information provided by CNOUS, letter from J. Blondeau, underdirector of CNOUS to author, Paris, 12 May 1977; calculations for the ratios are based on student enrollments listed in table 1.

TABLE 16

PRICE OF MEALS IN STUDENT RESTAURANTS 1969-1977

Year	Price in Francs
1969	1.65
1970	1.75
1971	1.85
1972	1.95
1973	2.15
1974	2.45
1975	3.00
1977	3.30

SOURCES: *Le Monde*, 15 November 1973 and 24 September 1974; "Le budget moyen," *Dernières Nouvelles d'Alsace*, 21 April 1976.

TABLE 17

RESULT OF STUDENT POLL TO THE QUESTION:
WHICH OF THE FOLLOWING PROBLEMS
PREOCCUPIES YOU THE MOST?
(in percent)

	France	Paris	Provinces
Job Opportunities.................	66	59	71
Examinations....................	47	34	54
Finances........................	44	40	45
Leisure.........................	23	20	25
Loss of Time....................	22	28	18
Cost of Books/Xerox	19	22	18
Military Service.................	16	13	17
Housing........................	15	20	11
Health.........................	13	12	14
Boy-Girl Relations...............	11	16	8
Transportation..................	6	8	5
Food...........................	6	7	5
Library Access..................	2	4	1
No Opinion.....................	1	2	—

SOURCE: Soisson, *Six principes*, p. 21; since more than one answer was possible the total is higher than 100 percent.

240

TABLES

APPENDIX 1

A LISTING OF THE FRENCH UNIVERSITIES ABOVE AND BELOW THE AVERAGE SIZE OF 10,810 IN 1977

Universities above 10,810	*Universities under 10,810*
Aix-Marseille I	Amiens
Aix-Marseille II	Angers
Aix-Marseille III	Antilles-Guyane
Besançon	Avignon
Bordeaux I	Bordeaux III
Bordeaux II	Brest
Caen	Chambéry
Dijon	Clermont-Ferrand I
Grenoble I	Clermont-Ferrand II
Grenoble II	Compiègne
Lille II	Corsica
Lyon I	Grenoble III
Lyon II	I.N.P. de Grenoble
Montpellier I	La Réunion
Nancy I	Le Mans
Nantes	Lille I
Nice	Lille III
Paris I	Limoges
Paris II	Lyon III
Paris III	Metz
Paris IV	Montpellier II
Paris V	Montpellier III
Paris VI	Mulhouse (Haut-Rhin)
Paris VII	Nancy II
Paris VIII	I.N.P. de Nancy
Paris X	Orléans
Paris XIII	Pau
Poitiers	Paris IX
Rennes I	Paris XI
Rouen	Paris XII
Strasbourg I	Paris (I.E.P.)
Toulouse II	Paris (Observatoire)
Toulouse III	Paris (Ecole des haute études)

Tours

Perpignan
Reims
Rennes II
Saint-Etienne
Strasbourg II
Strasbourg III
Toulouse I
Toulon
I.N.P. de Toulouse
Valenciennes

SOURCES: *Note d'information* no. 77-07 (18 February 1977). The average was calculated on the basis of seventy-six universities, including centres universitaires and instituts d'études politiques, instituts nationaux polytechniques. The university of Corsica was not included since enrollment figures were not yet available. It opened in October 1977. Perpignon, Toulon and Valenciennes were transformed from centres universitaires to universities in 1978, *Le Monde*, 7 March 1978.

APPENDIX 2

UNIVERSITY STRUCTURES

The 77 French universities could be divided into twenty-one mono-disciplinary ones, twenty-six bi-disciplinary, eleven tri-disciplinary, and nineteen quadri-disciplinary.

Monodisciplinary universities — twenty-one

Science:

Compiègne
Institut national polytechnique:
Grenoble, Nancy, Toulouse,
Montpellier II
Paris (Observatoire)

Law:

Paris II
Strasbourg III
Toulouse I

Letters:

Bordeaux III
Corsica
Grenoble III
Lille III
Montpellier III
Paris (Institut d'études politiques)
Paris (Ecole des hautes études en sciences sociales)
Paris III
Paris IV

242

APPENDIX

Rennes II
Strasbourg II
Toulouse II

Bi-disciplinary universities — twenty-six

Letters-sciences:

Aix-Marseille I
Avignon
Chambéry
Clermont-Ferrand II
Mulhouse
Perpigan
Valenciennes

Law-sciences:

Aix-Marseille III
Bordeaux I
Lille I
Paris IX
Toulon

Letters-medicine:

Paris V

Law-medicine:

Clermont-Ferrand I

Law-letters:

Lyon II
Lyon III
Nancy II
Paris I
Paris VIII
Paris X

Sciences-health:

Lyon I
Nancy I
Paris VI
Toulouse III

Law-health:

Lille II
Montpellier I

Tri-disciplinary universities — eleven

Law-letters-sciences:

Grenoble II
Les Antilles
Le Mans
La Réunion
Orléans
Metz
Pau

Sciences-health-letters:

Bordeaux II
Grenoble I
Paris VII

Sciences-law-health:

Paris XI

APPENDIX

Quadri-disciplinary universities — nineteen

Law-letters-medicine-sciences:

Aix-Marseille II	Poitiers
Amiens	Reims
Angers	Rennes I
Besançon	Rouen
Brest	Saint-Etienne
Caen	Strasbourg I
Dijon	Tours
Limoges	Paris XII
Nantes	Paris XIII
Nice	

SOURCES: GARACES Report, p. 10; *Note d'information* no. 77-07 (18 February 1977) and *Tableaux statistiques 1976-77*, March 1977, pp. 32-33; for listing of all universities and UERs, see Association pour l'expansion de l'enseignement supérieur, "Les universités et leurs UER 1976," *Cahiers des universités françaises—Bulletin de liaison des universités françaises*, 13-15 no. special (1976).

APPENDIX

APPENDIX 3
PROPORTION OF STUDENTS AND FACULTY
IN DIFFERENT FIELDS OF
STUDY IN NINETEEN SELECTED UNIVERSITIES — 1975
(in percentage)

University	Total no. Students	Letters		Law/ Economics		Sciences		Technology		Medicine Dentistry Pharmacy Health	
		A*	B**	A*	B**	A*	B**	A*	B**	A*	B**
Amiens	8,940	29.0	21.0	21.7	11.4	14.0	29.0	9.0	14.2	25.0	24.4
Bordeaux I	14,030	—	—	64.0	29.6	26.0	54.1	9.3	16.3	—	—
Bordeaux II	13,225	13.5	6.0	—	—	2.3	2.3	—	—	82.5	91.7
Brest	6,927	24.0	20.0	19.3	5.5	15.8	31.8	23.9	29.0	16.9	13.7
Grenoble III	4,306	100.0	100.0	—	—	—	—	—	—	—	—
Limoges	6,881	21.6	14.5	21.7	10.6	13.6	25.8	14.2	22.6	28.7	26.5
Montpellier I	17,099	—	—	35.4	16.6	—	—	—	—	62.5	83.4
Montpellier II	7,118	—	—	2.7	0.7	71.4	73.4	25.9	25.9	—	—
Nantes	15,666	27.7	17.7	19.3	5.8	14.5	21.9	19.9	22.0	28.4	32.0
Orléans	5,151	21.8	12.5	28.2	14.4	32.5	47.9	17.5	25.2	—	—
Paris V	26,713	29.2	10.8	—	—	—	—	5.7	6.5	65.0	82.7
Paris X	21,174	57.3	63.3	39.8	26.4	—	—	2.8	8.3	—	—
Paris XI	19,267	—	—	17.4	3.3	41.9	55.3	10.0	15.0	30.6	26.4
Reims	10,498	21.6	15.0	23.4	6.9	11.2	28.8	14.3	21.9	29.5	27.4
Strasbourg I	11,031	9.2	3.5	9.2	3.2	26.5	41.3	—	—	53.5	52.0
Strasbourg II	6,527	100.0	100.0	—	—	—	—	—	—	—	—
Toulon	1,851	—	—	60.8	11.1	10.1	17.5	29.1	71.4	—	—
Toulouse II	10,088	99.4	95.6	—	—	—	—	—	—	—	—
Toulouse III	20,568	—	—	—	—	34.8	52.5	28.5	17.1	51.3	30.4

*A — refers to percentage of students.

**B — refers to percentage of faculty.

SOURCE: GARACES *Report of 1975*, p. 353; my calculations based on *Tableaux 1976*, pp. 320-325; in some cases the percentage of faculty and students does not add up quite to 100 percent because some were in fields other than those listed above.

245

APPENDIX 4

THE ORIENTATION OF HIGHER EDUCATION ACT,
no. 68-978.   November 12, 1968.

The National Assembly and the Senate have adopted, and the President of the Republic hereby issues the Act, the text of which follows :

Title I

The Aim of Higher Education

Article 1

The fundamental aim of the universities and institutions to which the provisions of the present Act will apply is the working out and the transmitting of knowledge, the development of research and the training of men.

The universities must strive to bring the advanced forms of culture and research to their highest level and to their best rate of progress, and to make them available to all those who have the necessary calling and ability.

They must meet the demands of the nation by providing it with top ranking personnel in every field and by taking part in the social and economic development of every region. In this task, they must comply with the democratic evolution made necessary by the industrial and technical revolution.

Concerning faculty and researchers, the universities must insure them the means of carrying out their teaching and research activity in an atmosphere of independence and calm, which is indispensable to intellectual reflection and creation.

Concerning students, the universities must make every effort to insure the means of their orientation and of the best choice of the professional field to which they intend to dedicate themselves and, towards this end, to give them not only the necessary knowledge but the fundamentals of a training.

The universities facilitate the cultural, sporting and social activities of the students;· this is an essential condition of a well-balanced and complete training.

The universities train teachers of national education, attend to the general uniformity of this training - without neglecting the specialization of the teachers to their respective tasks at their respective levels - and allow for the continuous improvement of pedagogy and the updating of knowledge and methods.

Higher education must be open to former students and to people who have not been able to pursue studies, in order to enable them, according to their abilities, to improve their promotion possibilities or to branch off towards another profession.

246

APPENDIX

The universities must contribute, by taking advantage, among other things, of the new means of transmitting knowledge, to making continuing education available to every segment of the population for all its possible uses.

Generally speaking, higher education - the diversified fields which follow secondary studies - contributes to the cultural promotion of society, and in so doing plays an important part in its evolution towards a greater responsibility of every man in regard to his own destiny.

Article 2

The universities and the national and regional institutions provided for in Title II are to take on, within the framework determined by the Government, the initiatives and to make the provisions necessary to organize and develop international university cooperation, particularly with universities which are partially or entirely francophone. Very close ties are to be estabed with universities of those countries which are members of the European Economic Community.

Title II

University Institutions

Article 3

The university is a public institution of a scientific and cultural nature; it is a legal person ("personnalité morale") with financial autonomy. Universities are grouped into education and research units (and the services common to them) and can receive the status of a public institution of a scientific and cultural nature. These units are to assume all the activities currently performed by the universities and faculties, as well as, with possible exceptions which could be decreed, the activities carried out by the institutes associated with the universities.

When education and research units are not public institutions, they have their own provisions for management and administration, resulting from the present Act and from the decrees made regarding its application.

Decrees issued after consulting the National Board of Higher Education and Research draw up the list of public institutions of higher education under the Ministry of National Education to which the provisions of the present Act will apply, with the adaptations which may be made necessary for each institution due to the particular assignment given it. Decrees determine which of these institutions will be attached to universities.

Article 4

Public institutions of a scientific and cultural nature are created by decree following consultation of the National Board of Higher Education and Research.

Education and research units which do not have the status of a public institution of a scientific and cultural nature are created by order of the rector of an "académie". (1)

Article 5

The universities and other public institutions of a scientific and cultural nature under the jurisdiction of the Ministry of National Education can agree to cooperate with other public or private institutions.

An institution can be joined to a university by decree upon the request of the institution and the proposal of the university, after the approval of the National Board of Higher Education and Research. Institutions which have been joined to a university retain their standing as a legal person ("personnalité morale") with financial autonomy.

247

APPENDIX

Article 6

One or more universities can be created within every "académie".

The universities are multi-disciplinary and must associate arts and letters with sciences and technical studies as much as possible. They can, however, have a dominant field of specialization.

Article 7

Several universities can create services or structures of joint interest. These creations are approved by the Minister of National Education with the consent of the National Board of Higher Education and Research. The deliberations resulting in the institution of these services or structures are considered as deliberations of a statutory order.

Article 8

A regional board of higher education and research is instituted by decree in each region.

These boards are made up of elected representatives of the universities and of elected representatives of institutions of higher education and research which are independent of the universities. One third of their composition is made up of laymen representing communities and regional activities.

Faculty and students representing the universities and the institutions of a scientific and cultural nature of a particular region under the jurisdiction of the Minister of National Education are elected by secret vote and by distinct electoral colleges composed of faculty and of students who are members of the university and institution boards. One half of the faculty thus elected will be chosen among those who perform the functions of professor or "maître de conférences". (2)

The decree which creates regional boards of higher education and research determines their composition and the conditions under which their members are to be designated or elected.

These boards contribute in their district to the planning, coordination and programming of higher education and research under the Minister of National Education. They are consulted on curricula and on requests for funds made by the universities and by other public institutions of a scientific and cultural nature in this district.

The boards insure all the links and coordination with the organizations which are responsible for regional development.

They advise on the choice of the categories of laymen called upon to serve on the university boards detailed in Article 13, below.

Article 9

A National Board of Higher Education and Research, which includes elected representatives of the universities, elected representatives of the institutions of higher education and research which are independent of the universities, and, for one third of its composition, laymen representing the important national interests, is created with the Minister of National Education as chairman.

Faculty and students representing the universities and the institutions of a scientific and cultural nature under the jurisdiction of the Minister of National Education are elected by secret vote and by distinct electoral colleges composed of faculty and of students who are members of the university and institution boards.

A decree determines the composition of the national board and the conditions by which its members are designated.

248

APPENDIX

The National Board of Higher Education and Research :

1. Plans the organization of higher education and research in relation with the organizations in charge of the recurrent national plans, taking these plans into account, and with a view towards a more long-term perspective;

2. Is consulted regarding curricula and requests for funds made by the universities and by other institutions of higher education under the jurisdiction of the Minister of National Education; must be consulted on the distribution of budget assignments among the various institutions;

3. Advises the Minister of National Education regarding the rectors' oppositions, in accordance with the following Article 10, during the deliberations of institution boards;

4. Makes all proposals and gives all advice on decisions pertaining to the coordination of the statutes of the various public institutions of a scientific and cultural nature, and assumes the general responsibility of coordination between the universities and other institutions;

5. Makes all proposals and gives all advice on decisions regarding the conditions of obtaining national degrees under the Minister of National Education and regarding rules common to all institutions on the pursuit of studies.

The National Board of Higher Education and Research performs all the functions currently assigned to the Board of Higher Education. It can hold sessions by sections and consider the advice of commissions representing various fields of study.

Article 10

In each "académie", the rector insures the coordination of higher education with the other branches of education.

As chancellor of the universities in his "académie", he represents the Minister of National Education before the statutory organizations of public institutions of a scientific and cultural nature under the jurisdiction of the Ministry of National Education, he attends their sessions or is represented, and he can suspend the outcome of deliberations for serious reasons, pending the decision of the Minister of National Education, who must make a ruling within three months after consulting the National Board of Higher Education and Research.

In the "académie", the rector represents the Minister of National Education at the regional board, and presides over this board.

Title III

Administrative Autonomy and Participation

Article 11

The public institutions of a scientific and cultural nature and the education and research units grouped with them determine their statutes, their internal organization and their ties with other university units in accordance with the provisions of the present Act and its application decrees.

Decisions concerning a change in statutes are made by the majority of two thirds of the members who make up the boards.

The statutes of the education and research units are approved by the university board, of which they are a part.

249

APPENDIX

Article 12

Public institutions of a scientific and cultural nature are administered by an elected board and directed by a president who is elected by this board.

The education and research units are administered by an elected board and are headed by a director who is elected by this board.

The number of members on these boards cannot exceed eighty for the institutions and forty for the units.

Article 13

A spirit of participation reigns on the boards, which are composed of faculty, researchers, students and non-teaching personnel. No one can be elected to more than one university board or to more than one education and research unit board.

The same attitude must prevail in statutes which provide for participation, on the boards of universities and of public institutions which are independent of the universities, by laymen chosen for their competence and especially for their part in regional activity. They cannot number less than one sixth nor more than one third of the total make-up of the board. Statutes can also provide for participation by laymen on the boards of education and research units. Provisions regarding this participation are endorsed by the university boards when they pertain to the universities and to the institutions of a scientific and cultural nature which are independent of the universities.

Representation by faculty who carry out the functions of professor, "maître de conférences", "maître-assistant", or functions similar to these, must be at least equal to the representation of students in student-teacher bodies, on boards and in other organizations in which students and faculty are associated. Representation in these organizations by teachers performing the functions of professor or "maître de conférences" must be at least 60% to 100% of all faculty, except under special circumstances approved by the Minister of National Education after consulting the National Board of Higher Education and Research.

The determination of research curricula and the distribution of the necessary funds are the exclusive responsibility of science boards composed of faculty performing the functions of professor, "maître de conférences" or, possibly, "maître-assistant", of researchers of the same level and of persons chosen for their scientific competence.

Regarding the administration of research centers and laboratories, only faculty and researchers who have published scientific material and third-cycle (3) students who are already engaged in research work can belong to, and be elected by, the electoral colleges of faculty, of researchers, and of students.

Article 14

The various representatives to the education and research unit boards, to the university boards, and to the boards of other public institutions of a scientific and cultural nature are periodically chosen by secret ballot and by distinct electoral colleges.

A decree will determine the conditions by which students who cannot personally vote will be able to cast a vote by proxy, or otherwise will not be included in calculating the quorum, as detailed in the following paragraph.

Student representatives are selected from a list of students by simple majority vote. There are no split or preferential votes and student representation is proportional. Provisions will be made to insure the regularity of the vote and the representativeness of those elected, particularly by prohibiting voting registration in two or more education and research units and by requiring a quorum of at least 60% of the enrolled students. If the number of voters is less than 60% of the enrolled students, the number of representatives is determined in proportion with the number of voters in relation to this figure.

250

APPENDIX

Elections for student delegates take place, inasmuch as possible, by distinct electoral colleges and by years or cycles of study.

The right to vote is reserved to those students who have satisfied the normal academic requirements for the preceding year. The percentage of first-year student representatives cannot exceed one fifth of all the student representatives when the unit requires more than two years.

Foreign students regularly enrolled in an institution of higher education have the right to vote. But only those foreign students from countries with which France has reciprocal agreements can be elected.

A decree will determine the composition of the electoral colleges and the means of appealing elections.

Article 15

The president of an institution assures its leadership and is its legal representative. He is elected for five years and cannot be re-elected immediately. Except in the case of a two-thirds majority decision by the board, he must have the rank of "professeur titulaire" of the institution and be a member of the board; if he is not a "professeur titulaire" his appointment must be approved by the Minister of National Education after consulting the National Board of Higher Education and Research.

The director of an education and research unit is elected for three years. Except in the case of a two-thirds majority decision by the board, he must have the rank of "professeur titulaire", "maître de conférences" or maître-assistant" of the institution and be a board member. If he is not a "professeur titulaire", "maître de conférences" or "maître-assistant" his appointment must be approved by the Minister of National Education, after consulting the university board of which the education and research unit is a part.

Article 16

Decrees can be issued to specify the particular administration conditions of services common to several education and research units or to several institutions.

Article 17

In an "académie", the rector cannot, at the same time, carry out the functions of president of a public institution of a scientific and cultural nature and of director of an education and research unit.

The president of a public institution of a scientific and cultural nature cannot, at the same time, carry out the functions of director of an education and research unit.

Article 18

In the case of a serious difficulty in the functioning of the statutory bodies or in the event that they do not fulfill their responsibilities, the Minister of National Education can, in such exceptional cases, take all the necessary measures, previously consulting the National Board of Higher Education and Research or, in the event of an emergency, informing it as soon as possible. Under these same circumstances, the rector has the power to take all conservatory measures.

Title IV

Pedagogical Autonomy and Participation

Public institutions of a scientific and cultural nature and the education and research units grouped within them determine their educational activities, their research programs, their pedagogical methods, and their methods for testing and verifying knowledge and aptitudes, within

251

APPENDIX

the limits of the provisions of the present act, of the statutes for the personnel called upon to carry out the functions of education and research, and of the regulations established after consulting the National Board of Higher Education and Research.

Article 20

The joint rules for the pursuit of studies leading to national degrees under the Ministry of National Education, the stipulations for obtaining these degrees, and the measures for protecting the titles which they bestow are determined by the Minister, on the advice or proposal of the National Board of Higher Education and Research.

Aptitudes and the acquisition of knowledge are tested by teachers regularly and continually. Final examinations provide an additional test of aptitudes and knowledge.

Doctoral titles are bestowed after a thesis is defended or several original scientific studies are presented and defended. This thesis and these studies can be individual or, if the field justifies it, collective; they can be already published or previously unpublished. If the thesis or the studies are the result of a collective work, the candidate must write and defend a report permitting a judgment of his personal part in it.

Article 21

When university authorities feel that it would be useful to verify the aptitudes of students who are newly enrolled in the education and research units (which are part of the universities) for the studies they are undertaking, they organize orientation periods for this purpose.

These periods are compulsory for all students for whom they have been planned. At the end of these periods, students can be advised to choose other studies in the same university or a shorter educational cycle adapted to a professional activity. If the student follows this advice, his new enrollment automatically follows. If he pursues his initial choice and if he completes unsuccessfully the academic year, he can be called, at the beginning of the following year, to attend another orientation period involving several fields of study. The results of this period will be conclusive.

With all the means at their disposal, the universities provide for the continuous orientation of students, particularly at the end of each study cycle.

Article 22

The Minister of National Education and the universities take all the measures which concern them in co-operation with the national, regional and local organizations qualified to inform and advise students regarding the job and career possibilities to which their studies can lead them.

The universities and the above-mentioned qualified organizations also take all the necessary measures, in keeping with their fundamental aim, in order to insure a reciprocal adaptation of professional openings and of the university subjects taught.

Article 23

The universities, having recognized an aptitude in people who are already engaged in professional life, regardless of whether they hold university titles, open educational training and improvement programs to them, thus enabling them to obtain the corresponding degrees. The educational contents, pedagogical methods, degrees, academic calendar and schedules are specially adapted.

Article 24

The universities provide for the organization of continuing education in the education and research units grouped within them, in the institutions attached to them, and in the services created by the universities for this purpose. This activity is organized in conjunction with regional and local communities, public institutions, and all other organizations involved.

252

APPENDIX

Article 25

The universities organize physical education and sports in conjunction with the qualified organizations. They facilitate teacher participation in, or association with these activities.

Title V

Financial Autonomy

Article 26

In order to reach their aim, public institutions of a scientific and cultural nature have at their disposal the facilities, personnel and funds allotted to them by the Government. They also have other resources, such as legacies, foundations and donations, remuneration for services rendered, funds and various subsidies.

Article 27

The Finance Act details the amount of the funds and equipment to be appropriated by the Government to all the institutions of a scientific and cultural nature under the jurisdiction of the Minister of National Education.

The distribution of salaries for personnel is detailed in the Finance Act, according to categories of teachers, as are the funds which the Act allots for scientific and technical research.

Having examined their programs, and in accordance with national criteria, the Minister of National Education, after consulting the National Board of Higher Education and Research, assigns among the universities and the public institutions of a scientific and cultural nature which are independent of these universities, the uses of the funds detailed in the Finance Act and allots to each a global appropriation for current expenditures.

The Minister also assigns among the various finance planning programs the funds necessary for their installation, having first consulted the National Board and, if necessary, the regional boards of higher education and research. For programs which are to be spread over a period of two years or more, he announces the entire program and the dates due for payments. However, a portion of the installation funds can be distributed among the various institutions and assigned to them, in accordance with the provisions of the preceding paragraph.

Every institution assigns among the education and research units grouped within it the institutions attached to it and its proper services, the use of funds assigned to it by the Finance Act, its allotment of working funds and, if need be, its allotment of installation funds.

Article 28

Every institution distributes under the same conditions the resources which do not come from the Government.

Article 29

Every institution votes on its budget, which must be balanced and made public. The university board approves the budgets of the institutions which are attached to it.

The appropriations for current expenditures specified above are used to cover the working expenses and the material needs of the institutions and their education and research units and can also be used to engage and remunerate personnel other than that provided for in the Finance Act. Installation funds are intended to cover capital expenses.

253

APPENDIX

Education and research units without a legal capacity have a budget of their own included in the budget of the institution of which they are a part. This budget is approved by the board of the institution.

The president of every institution has the power to authorize the collection of returns and to sanction expenditures within the limits of the funds voted.

The accountant of every institution is designated by the institution board from a list of qualified candidates approved jointly by the Minister of National Education and the Minister of Economy and Finances. He has the status of a public accountant.

The institutions are under the administrative control of the General Inspection of National Education.

Financial control is exercised *a posteriori*; the institutions are inspected by the General Inspection of Finance and their accounts come under the judicial inspection of the "Cour des comptes". (4)

A decree issued by the "Conseil d'Etat" (5) will indicate the circumstances and the conditions under which the budgets of institutions are to be submitted for approval. The decree will determine their financial regulations.

Title VI

Faculty

Article 30

Education in public institutions of a scientific and cultural nature under the Ministry of National Education is assured by government personnel, by associated teachers and by the contractual personnel of the various institutions.

These institutions can call upon researchers, laymen, and qualified students, if need be, for teaching purposes.

Notwithstanding the general regulations for public officials, teachers of foreign nationality can, under the conditions determined by a decree issued by the "Conseil d'Etat", be appointed to the teaching body of higher education.

Article 31

Personnel appointed by the Government to the universities and to the institutions attached to them must, unless they enjoy a special status, be declared to have met national requirements to exercise the functions for which they have been engaged.

The examination of individual questions regarding the hiring and the career of personnel, in each of the pertinent organizations, comes within the jurisdiction of representatives of faculty and assimilated personnel whose rank is at least equal to that of the person in question. No one can be elected for more than six years nor immediately re-elected in the government bodies designated for this examination.

Article 32

The choice of faculty exercising the functions of professor, "maître de conférences" or "maître-assistant" in an institution is the responsibility of bodies composed exclusively of faculty and assimilated personnel of at least equal rank.

Article 33

The provisions currently in effect regarding the granting of "chaires" to professors on a personal basis (6) are repealed, although this does not result in any other changes in the status of these professors nor in the rights and guarantees they enjoy.

254

APPENDIX

The assignment of teaching functions and research activities within an institution is periodically revised.

The teaching personnel who are the object of the preceding article have the exclusive power of effecting this assignment, of organizing tests of knowledge and aptitude, of designating examiners and of awarding titles and degrees. Only teaching personnel or, under officially stated conditions, qualified persons outside the institution, can serve on the examining board.

Only authorized heads of institutions or education and research units can hire and discharge the personnel under their jurisdiction, in accordance with the status of the latter.

The institutions determine the extent of the student guidance, council and orientation entailed in all university teaching and research, as well as the ensuing residence and attendance obligations. The institutions cannot be excused from all or part of this mission or these obligations except in exceptional circumstances and by a ruling by the Minister on the advice of the National Board of Higher Education and Research.

Article 34

Teachers and researchers enjoy complete independence and entire freedom of expression in the teaching and research activities within the limits imposed, in accordance with university traditions and the provisions of the present Act, by the principles of objectivity and tolerance.

Title VII

University Rights

Article 35

Teaching and research demand objectivity of knowledge and tolerance of opinions. They are incompatible with all forms of propaganda and must remain outside of all political influence.

Article 36

Students enjoy freedom of information in regard to political, economic and social matters, inasmuch as teaching and research activities are not interfered with, and provided this is not conducive to one-sided propaganda and public order is not disturbed.

The premises put at the students' disposal for this purpose will be, insofar as possible, distinct from the premises intended for teaching and research. They will be off hospital limits. The conditions of their use will be defined after consulting the board and they will be supervised by the president of the institution or by the director of the education and research unit.

Article 37

The presidents of institutions and the directors of education and research units will be responsible for maintaining order on university premises. They exercise this function within the framework of the laws, general rules and internal ruling of the institution.

Any action or incitation to action threatening to the freedoms defined in the preceding article or to public order on university premises is subject to disciplinary measures.

A decree issued by the "Conseil d'Etat" will determine the application conditions of the present article.

Article 38

Disciplinary power regarding faculty is exercised first by the university boards or by the boards of public institutions of a scientific and cultural nature which are independent of the universities, and in case of appeal, by the National Board of Higher Education.

255

APPENDIX

Jurisdictional matters are decided by a disciplinary section of the boards. The members of this section are elected from within the boards by elected representatives of the teaching body.

In judging every case, the disciplinary section, which can only include teachers of a rank equal to, or higher than that of the teacher being investigated, can be completed, according to the individual case, either by co-option of a member of the teaching body to which the teacher in question belongs, if this body is not represented, or by naming representatives of private institutions of higher education.

These jurisdictional sections, completed by an equal number of members elected from within the boards by elected student representatives, exercise disciplinary power regarding students.

A decree issued by the "Conseil d'Etat" will determine the applicable penalties and will specify the composition and the working order of these jurisdictional sections.

Title VIII

Implementing the Reform

Article 39

Before December 31, 1968, the Minister of National Education will establish, after consulting the pertinent groups, a provisional list of the education and research units which will make up the various universities. The categories of electoral colleges will be convened by the rectors on the basis of this provisional list in order to elect their delegates. The makeup of the electoral colleges, the voting conditions and the measures necessary to insure regularity and representativeness, especially as regards the quorum, will be specified by a decree, in accordance with the provisions of Title III of the present Act.

Article 40

Delegates thus designated are to :

1. Work out the statutes for the units to which they are attached : these statutes must be provisionally approved by the rector;

2. Designate the delegates of the unit to the provisional constitutuent assembly of the university.

The education and research units which have not adopted statutes in accordance with the provisions of the present Act by March 15, 1969, can be given provisional statutes established by decree.

In the event that the education and research units have not designated their delegates to the provisional constituent assembly of the university by this same date, faculty, students and other personnel of these units will designate directly their representatives to the provisional constituent assembly of the university.

Article 41

Representatives elected by the units, or elected directly, under the conditions defined in Article 40 will constitute the provisional constituent assembly of the university. They will work out university regulations, which must be approved by the Minister of National Education, and they will appoint their representatives to the national board.

The structure of the electoral colleges, the rules regarding the electorate and voting elegibility and conditions, and the composition of the assemblies will be determined by decree in accordance with the provisions of Title III of the present Act.

256

APPENDIX

Three months after the publication of the ministerial order designating the universities of an "académie", those universities which have not adopted statutes in accordance with the provisions of the present Act can be given regulations established by decree.

Universities regularly endowed with a legal status will become, by decree, public institutions of a scientific and cultural nature.

Article 42

Decrees issued by the "Conseil d'Etat" will administer the transfer of the rights and obligations of former institutions to the public institutions of a scientific and cultural nature created in application of the present Act. These decrees will administer as well the transfer of all property belonging solely to the former institutions.

Article 43

The National Board of Higher Education and Research can be validly constituted when universities which include half of all faculty and students in France have been able to adopt their statutes and designate their representatives. The Board of Education will then be eliminated.

Article 44

In order to facilitate the implementation of the institutions provided for in the present Act, and regardless of the legislative and statutory provisions currently in effect, decrees can determine all provisional measures designed to insure the administration of university institutions, the development of their education and research activities, and the transition between the former and the new institutions.

Title IX

Final Provisions

Article 45

As regards higher education leading to the medical and dental professions and related research, the provisions of Ordinance no. 58-1373 of December 30, 1958, and of the public health code remain applicable to the institutions and units defined by the present Act, contingent upon necessary modifications which will be decreed by the "Conseil d'Etat".

The Minister of Social Affairs will participate in all decisions concerning medical, pharmaceutical and dental education and related research.

Article 46

The provisions of the present Act regarding research apply solely to non-oriented research conducted in the universities and other institutions of higher education with a view towards maintaining education at the highest level of knowledge.

The provisions of the present Act are not aimed at modifying the mission of the "Centre National de la Recherche Scientifique", nor the conditions of the part it plays, nor the power of its subsidiary consultative organs, particularly the "Comité National de la Recherche Scientifique".

257

APPENDIX

The present Act will be executed as State Law.

Signed in Paris, November 12, 1968,

By the President of the Republic, C. de Gaulle,
The Prime Minister, Maurice Couve de Murville,
The State Minister of Social Affairs, Maurice Schumann,
The Minister of Economy and Finance, François Ortoli,
The Minister of National Education, Edgar Faure,
The Minister of Scientific Research and Atomic and Space Matters, delegated to the Prime Minister, Robert Galley.

Footnotes

(1) This term designates an educational district; each "académie" is headed by a rector and includes at least one university.

(2) The following is an explanation of the categories of teachers in French higher education : "Maître-assistant" - usually holds the "agrégation", has partially completed his doctoral thesis and is on the list of those who are qualified to teach in a university,

"Maître de conférence" - holds the "Doctorat d'Etat" and is waiting for a "chaire" (the highest professorial title - its holder has tenure) to be vacated;

"Professeur titulaire" - full professor.

(3) University studies are divided into cycles; the first cycle consists of the first two years of university study, the second cycle requires one to two years and is sanctioned by the "licence" or the "maîtrise" degree, and the third cycle represents all further studies and can be compared roughly with graduate studies in the United States.

(4) This is a national body in charge of verification of accounts which are under government jurisdiction.

(5) An administrative court of justice, the "Conseil d'Etat" pronounces judgment on certain government decrees, as well as on government bills. In a general sense, it has many of the same functions as the Supreme Court.

(6) "Chaires" are usually attributed in accordance with the number of them stipulated for a given field of study at a given university; they could formerly be created also on a personal basis - for instance, to honor the merit of a particular professor.

SOURCE: French Embassy Publication also found in Fomerand, "Policy Formulation," pp. 323-326.

258

APPENDIX

BIBLIOGRAPHY

"L'action syndicale contre l'asphyxie financière des universités." *Bulletin du SNE-Sup*, no. 54 n.s. (April, 1975), pp. 15-17.

Agnès, Yves. "Amertume chez les palois." *Le monde de l'éducation*, no. 26 (March, 1977), pp. 38-39.

_____. "Aspects de l'enseignement supérieur à Bordeaux." *Le monde de l'éducation*, no. 23 (December, 1976), pp. 27-34.

_____ et al. "Les universités dans leurs régions," *Le monde de l'éducation*, no. 29 (June, 1977), pp. 5-15.

Altbach, Philip C. *Student Politics in America. A Historical Analysis.* New York, 1974.

Alexandre, Philippe. *Chroniques des jours moroses, 1969-1970.* Paris, 1971.

Amestoy, Georges. *Les universités françaises.* Paris, 1968.

Antoine, Gérald and Passeron, Jean-Claude. *La réforme de l'université.* Paris, 1966.

Approches pour une régionalisation des universités. Paris, 1968.

Ardagh, John. *The New French Revolution.* New York, 1968.

Arditti, Catherine. "L'enseignement au féminin. I — Vocations et pis-aller. II — Une subtile hiérarchie des sexes. III — Un désequilibre néfaste." *Le Monde*, 3, 4, 5 May 1977.

Aron, Raymond. "La crise de l'université." *La revue administrative*, no. 123 (May-June, 1968), pp. 287-95.

_____. *La révolution introuvable. Réflexions sur les événements de mai.* Paris, 1968. [Transl. as *The Elusive Revolution: Anatomy of a Student Revolt*, New York, 1969]

Asselain, Jean-Charles. *Le budget de l'éducation nationale 1952-1967.* Paris, 1969.

Association d'étude pour l'expansion de l'enseignement supérieur. *Cahiers des universités françaises.* (1971-1976)

Association internationale d'information scolaire, universitaire et professionnelle (AIISUP). *Etudes supérieures en France.* Paris, 1974.

_____. *Informations universitaires et professionnelles internationales.* 1971, 1974-1978

Association pour l'étude et l'expansion de la recherche scientifique. "Le colloque national de Caen." *Revue trimestrielle*, no. 23-24 (May, 1967).

_____. "Recommandations du colloque national d'Amiens, 15-17 mars 1968." *Revue trimestrielle*, special no. (May, 1968).

"Au sujet des status des nouvelles unités d'enseignement et de recherche." n.d.

Ayache, Alain. *Les citations de la révolution de mai.* Paris, 1968.

Bacquet, Paul. "Réponse à deux démissionnaires." *Le monde de l'éducation*, no. 23 (December, 1976), pp. 39-41.

Barrau, Patrick and Ginoux, Jean-Claude. "Pour une méthodologie de la formation de formateurs 'travailleurs sociaux' à l'université." *Education permanente*, no. 27 (January-February, 1975), pp. 83-109.

Barre, Raymond and Boursin, Jean-Louis. "De l'enseignement secondaire à l'enseignement supérieure (expériences étrangères et problèmes français)." *La documentation française.* Paris, 1974.

Bartoli, Pierre. "L'université de Paris et son avenir," in Crémieux-Brilhac, Jean-Louis, ed. *L'éducation nationale* (Paris, 1964), pp. 539-46.

Bauchart, Philippe and Bruzek, Maurice. *Le syndicalisme à l'épreuve.* Paris, 1968.

Baudelot, Christian and Establet, Roger. *L'école capitaliste en France.* Paris, 1971.

Beaud, Michel. *Vincennes, An III. Le ministère contre l'université.* Paris, 1971.

Bernard, P. *et al.* "Les nouvelles universités." *Bulletin du SNE-Sup*, no. 194 (November, 1970), pp. 18-35.

Berstescher, Dieter and Hecquet, Ignace. "Coût et financement de l'enseignement universitaire," in Berstecher *et al.*, eds. *L'université de demain.* Brussels, 1974, pp. 99-145.

_____ *et al. L'université de demain.* Brussels, 1974.

Birnbaum, Pierre. *Les sommets de l'état, essai sur l'élite du pouvoir en France.* Paris, 1977.

Bisseret, Noëlle. *Les inégaux ou la sélection universitaire.* Paris, 1974.

_____. "La 'naissance' et le diplôme. Les processus de sélection au début des études universitaires." *Revue française de sociologie*, 9, special no. (1968), pp. 185-207.

_____. "La sélection à l'université et sa signification pour l'étude des rapports de dominance." *Revue française de sociologie*, 9 (1968), pp. 463-96.

Boggio, Philippe. "L'expérience de l'université de Vincennes. Part I. La peur du début de la fin." *Le Quotidien de Paris*, 28 October 1974.

_____. "L'expérience de l'université. Part II. La révolution du possible." *Le Quotidien de Paris*, 29 October 1974.

_____. "La géographie de la concertation. La carte universitaire de Jean-Pierre Soisson." *Le Quotidien de Paris*, 21 January 1975.

BIBLIOGRAPHY

Borel. "La démission est-elle une arme efficàce?" *Libération*, 22 October 1973.

Borrelly, Martine. "Des étudiants dans la cité." *Le monde de l'éducation*, no. 14 (February, 1976), pp. 38-39.

Bosc, C. "Les bourses d'enseignement supérieur," *Education et gestion*, no. 43 (1974), pp. 70-76.

Boudon, Raymond. "La crise universitaire française. Essai de diagnostic sociologique." *Annales, économies, sociétés, civilisations*, 24 (May-June, 1969): 739-64.

_____. "The French University since 1968." *Comparative Politics*, 10 (October, 1977): 89-119.

_____. *L'inégalité des chances*. Paris, 1973.

Bourcier, Paul. "Université: L'an II de la réforme." *Les nouvelles littéraires*, 18 June 1970, pp. 6-7.

_____. "Université: Les raisons du naufrage." *Les nouvelles littéraires*, 16 May 1968, pp. 6-7.

Bourdieu, Pierre. "Avenir de classe et causalité du probable." *Revue française de sociologie* 15 (1974): 3-42.

_____ and Passeron, Jean-Claude. *Les héritiers. Les étudiants et la culture*. Paris, 1964.

_____. *La reproduction: Eléments pour une théorie du système d'enseignement*. Paris, 1970.

_____. *Les étudiants et leurs études*. Paris, 1964.

_____. "L'examen d'une illusion." *Revue française de sociologie* 9, special no. (1968): 227-53.

_____ and de Saint-Martin, Monique. "Les catégories de l'entendement professoral." *Actes de la recherche en science sociale*, no. 3 (May, 1975), pp. 68-93.

Bourges, Hervé, ed. *The French Student Revolt: the Leaders Speak*. Paris, 1968.

Bourget, J.-M. "Les nouvelles universités de Paris: Projet déposé au ministère." *L'Aurore*, 11 March 1970.

Bourjac, Georges. "L'administration locale," in Crémieux-Brilhac, ed. *L'éducation nationale*, pp. 505-28.

Bourricaud, François. *Université à la dérive*. Paris, 1971.

Boussard, Isabel. "La participation des étudiants aux élections universitaires en France (1970-1973)." *Revue française de science politique* 24 (October, 1974): 940-65.

Boutmy, Emile. *Le baccalauréat et l'enseignement secondaire*. Paris, 1899.

BIBLIOGRAPHY

Bouzerand, Jacques. "Etudiants: La grande peur." *Le Point*, 25 September 1972, pp. 91-92.

Boyance. "L'université en ruines." *Revue des deux mondes*, 1 December 1969, pp. 528-34.

Brevanne, Gilles. "A bas la loi Faure." *Aspects de la France*, 12 March 1970.

Brown, Bernard E. "The Decision to Reform the Universities," in James B. Christoph and Bernard E. Brown, eds. *Cases in Comparative Politics*. Boston, 1976.

Bruges. Collège d'Europe. *Université européene; documents et conclusions du colloque international organisé par le Collège d'Europe et le Bureau universitaire du mouvement européen à Bruges du 4-7 avril 1960*. Bruges [Belgium], 1960.

Brunelle, Lucien, ed. *Pourquoi des examens; l'université en question*. Paris, 1968.

Bulletin du syndicat national de l'enseignement supérieur, 1968-77.

Burnier, Michel-Antoine and Kouchner, Bernard. *La France sauvage*. Paris, 1970.

Caire, Mireille. "Nanterre 1974." *Education et gestion*, no. 43 (1974), pp. 3-15.

Cairns, John C. *France*. Englewood Cliffs, N.J., 1965.

Callot, Jean-Pierre. *Histoire de l'école polytechnique*. Paris, 1975.

Calvet, Louis-Jean. "Sélection à toutes les étapes." *Politiques hebdo*, 3 May 1973.

Camilleri, Carmel and Tapia, Claude. *Jeunesse française et groupes sociaux après mai 1968*. Paris, 1974.

Capelle, Jean. *Education et politique*. Paris, 1974.

――――. *Tomorrow's Education. The French Experience 1945-1964*. [Transl. and ed. with an introduction by W. D. Halls.] London, 1967.

Caussade, Gerald. "Soisson: Le masque tombe; affaire de Toulouse." *Bulletin du SNE-Sup*, no. 50 n.s. (January, 1975), p. 16.

Centre de regroupement des informations universitaires. *Quelle université? Quelle société?* Paris, 1968.

Centre national d'étude des problèmes de sociologie et d'économie européennes. *L'université européenne. Colloque des 22 et 23 mars 1962*. Brussels, 1963.

――――. "Dans certains départements de Vincennes: Pas de diplômes nationaux." *Combat*, 16 January 1970.

Chabarol, D. "La commission de contrôle des élections universitaires." *La revue administrative*, no. 140 (March-April, 1971), pp. 159-63.

BIBLIOGRAPHY

Chapsal, Madelaine and Manceaux, Michèle. *Les professeurs pour quoi faire?* Paris, 1970.

Chardonnet, Jean. *L'université en question*. Paris, 1968.

Chalendar, Jacques de. *Une loi pour l'université avec le manuscrit inédit d'Edgar Faure*. Paris, 1970.

_____. "La loi d'orientation." *Etudes*, January, 1970, pp. 21-48.

Charrière, Christian. *Le printemps des enragés*. Paris, 1968.

Chateau, Jean. *L'étudiant périmé*. Paris, 1968.

Cheramy, Robert. *La fédération de l'éducation nationale. 25 ans d'unité syndicale*. Paris, 1974.

Chevallier, Jacques. *L'enseignement supérieur*. Paris, 1971.

Chevrolet, Daniel. "Les universités et l'éducation permanente ou la difficile survie des missions." *Education permanente*, no. 27 (January-February, 1975), pp. 11-29.

Chombart de Lauwe, Paul-Henry. *Pour l'université avant, pendant et après mai 1968*. Paris, 1968.

Citron, Suzanne. *L'école bloquée*. paris, 1971.

Clark, Burton R. *Academic Power in Italy*. Chicago, 1977.

Clark, Terry N. *Prophets and Patrons: The French University and the Emergence of the Social Sciences*. Cambridge, Mass., 1973.

Claustre, Henri. *Vivre dans l'université*. Grenoble, 1973.

Clavel, M. *et al. Que faisaient-ils en avril? Regards sur une révolte*. Paris, 1969.

Clignet, Remi. *Liberty and Equality. The Educational Process. A Comparative Sociology of Education*. New York, 1974.

Cockburn, Alexander and Blackburn, Robin, eds. *Student Power*. London, 1969.

Cohn-Bendit, Daniel and Granatier, H. *Les enragés de Nanterre*. Paris, 1968.

"Colloque franco-britanique. Problèmes d'administration comparée." *Education et gestion*, no. 35 (March, 1973), pp. 24-32.

"Les communistes et l'enseignement supérieur." *L'école et la nation*, no. 131 (August, 1964), pp. 3-23.

Conférence des présidents d'universités. [Les cahiers de l'INAS] Paris, 1975.

Conference on "Two Decades of Gaullism — The Impact of the Fifth Republic on France," June 9-11, 1978. State University of New York College at Brockport.

Cornec, Jean. *La fédération des conseils de "parendélèves" (FCPE). Pour l'enfant . . . Vers l'hommε*. Paris, 1972.

263

BIBLIOGRAPHY

_____ and Capelle, Jean. *Le baccalauréat. Pour et contre.* Nancy, 1968.

Council of Europe. Centre de documentation pour l'éducation en Europe. *Bulletin d'information*, 2 July 1974.

Conseil de la coopération culturelle. *Réforme et développement de l'enseignement supérieur en Europe.* Strasbourg, 1967.

_____. Conférence ad hoc des ministres européens de l'éducation. *L'explosion scolaire.* Strasbourg, September, 1967.

"Création à partir du ler décembre d'un corps de 'maîtres-assistants'." *Le Figaro*, 24-25 September 1960.

Coutin, A. *Huit siècles de violence au quartier latin.* Paris, 1969.

Crémieux-Brilhac, Jean-Lous, ed. *L'éducation nationale. Le ministère, l'administration centrale, les services.* Paris, 1965.

Crozier, Michel. *The Bureaucratic Phenomenon.* Chicago, 1964.

_____. *La société bloquée.* Paris, 1970.

_____. "France's Cultural Anxieties under Gaullism." Conference on "Two Decades of Gaullism." Brockport, N.Y., 1978.

Dalevèze, Jean. "Dans six ans la panique?" *Les nouvelles littéraires*, no. 1836 (8 November 1962).

Daniels, Mathé J. M. and Schowten, J. *L'éducation en Europe.* Series I — *Enseignement supérieur et recherche. La sélection des étudiants*, no. 8, Paris, 1970.

Delclaux, M. and Minot, J. "A propos des jurys." *Education et gestion*, no. 20 (April, 1970), pp. 17-23.

Delion, A. G. and Le Veugle, J. *L'éducation en France* [La documentation française.] Paris, 1973.

Département de formation continue de l'université des sciences humaines de Strasbourg. "Intervention dans l'entreprise." *Education permanente*, no. 27 (January-February, 1975), pp. 51-62.

Dhombres, Dominique. "Amiens, Angers, Marseille. Trois écoles de commerce saisies par le modernisme pédagogique." *Le monde de l'éducation*, no. 12 (December, 1975), pp. 28-30.

_____. "Qui peut être boursier?" *Le monde de l'éducation*, no. 5 (April, 1975), p. 47.

Didier, Paul. "La réconciliation inachevée." *Le monde de l'éducation*, no. 8 (July-August, 1975), pp. 34-37.

Dogan, Mattei. "Causes of the French Student Revolt in May 1968," in Stephen D. Kertesz, ed., *The Task of Universities in a Changing World.* South Bend, Indiana, 1972.

Dreze, Jacques and Debelle, Jean. *Conception de l'université.* Paris, 1968.

264

BIBLIOGRAPHY

Duchêne, Roger. *A la recherche de l'université*. Paris, 1972.

Dupeux, Georges. *La société française 1789-1970*. 7th ed. Paris, 1974.

Duprilot, J.-P. "Les IUT." *La Revue administrative*, no. 136 (July-August, 1970), pp. 401-11.

Dansette, Adrien. *Mai 1968*. Paris, 1971.

Darbel, A. "Inégalités régionales ou inégalités sociales? Essai d'explication des taux de scolarisation." *Revue française de sociologie* 8, special no. (1967): 140-66.

D'Artois, Robert. "La loi d'orientation et ses premières applications." *Revue de l'AUPELF* 6, 3 (1968): 43-49.

Dasté, Pierre. "Autopsie d'une commission. La commission de l'orientation du ministre de l'éducation nationale, Octobre 1968-Avril 1969." *Education et gestion*, no. 19 (January, 1970), pp. 11-23.

Daumard, Pierre. *Le prix de l'enseignement en France*. Paris, 1969.

"Dauphine à travers un entretien avec Bertrand Girod de l'Ain. 11 Octobre 1973." *Education et gestion*, no. 43 (1974), pp. 24-31.

"Dean Quits Riot-torn French University." *Herald Tribune*, 18 March 1970.

"Débats sur la loi d'orientation." *Bulletin du SNE-Sup*, no. 164 (October, 1968), pp. 6-9.

Debbasch, Charles. *L'université désorientée. Autopsie d'une mutation*. Paris, 1971.

Debeauvais, Michel. "Education et revenues." *Le monde de l'éducation*, no. 12 (December, 1975), pp. 31-32.

_____. *L'université ouverte: Les dossiers de Vincennes*. Grenoble, 1976.

Durond-Prinborgne. "Le recteur et les inspecteurs d'académie." *Education et gestion*, no. 44 (4 September 1974), pp. 52-58.

Duveau, Georges. *Les instituteurs*. Paris, 1966.

Ecole et la nation. 1974-75.

Ecole nationale d'administration (Promotion Léon Blum). *Rapport. Voie d'administration générale. La planification des enseignements universitaires*. Paris, 1974.

Education. 1968-76.

Education et développement. 1975.

Education et gestion. 1968-75.

Ehrlich, Stephane and Tronel, G. "Des professeurs jugent la réforme." *Le monde de l'éducation*, no. 17 (May, 1976), pp. 40-42.

Emmanuel, Pierre. *Pour une politique de la culture*. Paris, 1971.

Enseignement supérieur court. Tout sur les IUT. Instituts universitaires de technologie en 6 brochures. Paris, 1971.

Epistemon. *Ces idées qui ont ébranlé la France. (Nanterre, Novembre 1967-Juin 1968). Comprendre les étudiants.* Paris, 1969.

Equipe de chercheurs de l'institut de recherche sur l'économie de l'éducation de Dijon. "Coût et rendement de l'éducation." *Education et gestion*, no. 30 (June, 1972), pp. 3-18.

Erikson, Erik H. "Reflections on the Dissent of Contemporary Youth," in Graubard, Stephen R. and Balloti, Geno A., eds. *The Embattled University*. New York, 1970, pp. 154-76.

Ettori, J.-B. "Besançon: Ou le charme discret de l'université." *Education et gestion*, no. 43 (1974), pp. 33-39.

Etzioni, Amitai, ed. *Readings on Modern Organizations*. Englewood Cliffs, N.J., 1969.

"L'expérience de Dauphine." *Le monde de l'éducation*, no. 1 (December 1974), p. 49.

L'Express. 1968, 1974, 1976-77.

Fabre-Luce, Alfred. *Le général en Sorbonne*. Paris, 1968.

Faita, Daniel and François, Denise. "Formation continue — Trop tard pour apprendre." *Le monde de l'éducation*, no. 10 (October 1975), pp. 47-48.

Fargier, Marie-Odile. "Les centres universitaires expérimentaux. Antony ou le malentendu." *Combat*, 17 December 1968.

_____. "La constitution des universités parisiennes. Le doyen Zamansky publie son plan." *Combat*, 9 February 1970.

_____. "Vincennes huit jours après." *Combat*, 18 December 1968.

Fauconnier, Henri. "Orléans: L'université cherche un second souffle." *La Croix*, 6 July 1975.

Faure, Edgar. *L'âme du combat pour un nouveau contrat social*. Paris, 1970.

_____. *Ce que je crois*. Paris, 1971.

_____. *L'éducation nationale et la participation*. Paris, 1968.

_____. *Philosophie d'une réforme*. Paris, 1969.

_____. "Réponse à Jean-Paul Sartre." *Le Nouvel observateur*, 31 March 1969.

_____ et al. *Apprendre à être*. Paris, 1972.

Ferniot, Jean. *Mort d'une révolution*. Paris, 1968.

Fields, Belden A. *Student Politics in France*. New York, 1970.

Le Figaro. 1968.

Flacks, Richard. "Social and Cultural Meaning of Student Revolt," in Sampson, E. E. and Korn, H. A. *Student Activism and Protest* (San Francisco, 1970), pp. 117-42.

266

BIBLIOGRAPHY

Fohlen, Claude. *Mai 1968: Révolution ou psychodrame?* Paris, 1973.

Fomerand, Jacques. "Policy Formulation and Change in Gaullist France: The 1968 Orientation Act of Higher Education." *Comparative Politics* 8, 1 (October, 1975): 59-89.

_____. "Policy Formulation and Change in the Fifth Republic: The 1968 Orientation Act of Higher Education." Ph.D. dissertation, Political Science, City University of New York, 1973.

"Fonctionnement et innovation — Université de Paris IX Dauphine." *AUPELF*, 12 (Spring, 1974): 145-48.

Fontanet, Joseph. "Voici pourquoi nous réformons le bac." *Paris Match*, no. 1294 (23 February 1974), pp. 36-37.

"La Formation continue dans les universités membres de l'AUPELF." *AUPELF* 12, 1 (Spring, 1974): 98-142.

"Les formations de deuxième cycle à caractère professionnel." *Le monde de l'éducation*, no. 21 (October, 1976), pp. 42-49.

Fouchet, Christian. *Mémoires d'hier et de demain.* Paris, 1971.

Fournier, Jacques. *Politique de l'éducation.* Paris, 1971.

Fourrier, Charles. *Les institutions universitaires.* Paris, 1971.

France. Commissariat général du plan.

Préparation du VI° plan. Rapport de la commission éducation, 1971-1975 [La documentation française.] Paris, 1971.

_____. *Rapport de la commission éducation et formation* [La documentation francaise]. Paris, 1976.

_____. *Journal officiel, Assemblée nationale débats*, 1968-1976.

_____. *Journal officiel, Lois et décrets*, 1968-1976.

_____. *Enseignement supérieur. Loi d'orientation et textes d'application.* Paris, 11 April 1972.

_____. Ministère de l'économie et des finances. *INSEE* (Institut de la statistique et des études économiques). *Annuaire statistique de la France, 1974* (1974).

_____. Ministère de l'éducation nationale.

Budget voté de 1975. Education et universités. Paris, 1975.

_____. *Bulletin officiel de l'éducation nationale*, 1968-1976.

"La consultation des Francais sur les problèmes de l'éducation nationale." *Information rapides*, special issue (September, 1973).

_____. Bureau universitaire de statistique et de documentation scolaires et professionnelles. *L'entrée des non-bacheliers dans les facultés.* Paris, 1968.

_____. *Informations rapides*, 1973.

_____. Projet de loi de finances. *Présentation du budget de l'éducation sous forme de "budget de programmes." (1974-1977)*, 5 vols. Paris, 1973-76.

_____. Commission d'études sur la fonction enseignante dans le second degré. *Rapport* (The Joxe commission) [La documentation française]. Paris, 1972.

_____. Commission nationale paritaire de la vie de l'étudiant [The Mallet commission]. *Rapport de la commission plénière.* Paris, 1969.

_____. Groupes d'étude des formations supérieures. *Documents de travail*, nos. 1-8 (1971-1973).

_____. Institut national d'administration scolaire et universitaire (INAS). *Note d'information, enseignement supérieur.* 1973-1975.

_____. "Les nouvelles institutions universitaires." (Les cahiers de l'INAS). March 1973, March 1974.

_____. Fontanille, Henri. Les problèmes de la sécurité dans les universités françaises. [Cahiers de l'INAS, November 1973.]

_____. [Olivier Guichard.] "Conférence de presse," 11 and 28 March 1970.

_____. Institut national de recherche et de documentation pédagogiques (INRDP).

Le mouvement éducatif en France. 1971-1973. (Rapport présenté à la XXXIV° internationale de l'instruction publique.) Paris, 1973.

_____. L'organisation de l'enseignement en France. [Cahiers de documentation, no. 1 CD.] Paris, 1973.

_____. Service central des statistiques.

Statistiques des enseignements. Tableaux et informations, 1967-1975.

_____. L'éducation nationale en chiffres. Paris, 1971.

_____. Service central des statistiques et sondages. *Tableaux de l'éducation nationale, 1968-1976*, 8 vols. Paris, 1968-76.

_____. Université. *Paris VII. Enseignement 1973-1974.* Paris, 1973.

_____. Université de Paris. *Les universités de la région parisienne, rentrée 1973.* Paris, 1973.

_____. Ministère de l'éducation and secrétariat d'état aux universités. *Note d'information* (1970-1978).

_____. Service des études informatiques et statistiques. *Tableaux des enseignements et de la formation 1976.* Paris, 1976.

268

BIBLIOGRAPHY

_____. Ministère des affaires étrangères, Cultural Services of the French Embassy, New York. *Higher Education in France*. New York, 1974.

_____. Premier ministre. Groupe d'études. *Les conditions de développement, de recrutement, de fonctionnement et de localisation des grandes écoles en France*. [La documentation française, no. 45.] Paris, 1964.

_____. Secrétariat d'état aux universités.
Rapport de la commission chargée de proposer une meilleure répartition des crédits de l'état [Bienaymé commission]. *Le Financement des universités* [La documentation française]. Paris, 1976.

_____. "Les universités, les étudiants en quelques chiffres." Paris, 1974-75.

_____. Académie de Paris, université René Descartes.
Budget de l'université, exercice 1975. Paris, 1975.

_____. Conseil de l'université, minutes, 1974-1975. (Mimeographed.)

_____. Université de Paris I. *Guide de l'étudiant 1975-1976*. Paris, 1975.

_____. Baecque, Francis de. *La situation des personnels des universités, éléments de réflexion pour une réforme*. Paris, 1974.

_____. Groupe d'analyse et de recherche [GARACES]
Analyse et recherche sur les activités et les coûts des enseignements supérieurs. Paris, 1975.

_____. [Jean-Pierre Soisson.] "Conférence de presse," 30 October 1974 and 21 January 1975.

_____. Jean-Pierre Soisson. *Six principes et un projet politique*. Paris, 1974.

_____. Service central des statistiques et sondages.
Données statistiques sur le développement des effectifs de l'enseignement supérieur en France depuis 1960. [*Etudes et documents*, no. 31.] Paris, 1975.

_____. Service d'informations économiques et statistiques. *Tableaux statistiques*, 1973-1978.

_____. Université de Strasbourg III. *Guide des enseignements et des débouchés*, 1976-77. Strasbourg, 1976.

Fraser, W. R. *Education and Society in Modern France*. New York, 1963.

_____. *Reforms and Restraints in Modern French Education*. London, 1971.

Friglioni, J.-P. and Silvestre, Pierre. "Le nouveau visage démographique des académies." *Education et gestion*, no. 17 (July, 1969), pp. 33-37.

Gal, Roger. *Histoire de l'éducation*. Paris, 1969.

Gallant, Mavis. *The Affair Gabrielle Russier*. New York, 1971.

Galy, Philippe. "Le budget — Programme." *La revue administrative*, no. 140 (March-April, 1971), pp. 148-54.

Garnier, Maurice and Hazelrigg, Lawrence. "La mobilité professionnelle en France comparée à celle d'autres pays." *Revue française de sociologie* 15 (1974): 363-78.

————. "Father to Son Occupational Mobility in France: Evidence from the 1960s." *American Journal of Sociology* 80 (September, 1974): 478-502.

Gascar, P. *Quartier latin*. Paris, 1973.

Gaussen, Frédéric. "Non, l'égalité des chances n'existe pas." *Le monde de l'éducation*, no. 1 (December, 1974), pp. 14-19.

————. "Mme Alice Saunier-Seité. Les Universités doivent partir à la conquête des débouchés." *Le monde de l'éducation*, no. 16 (April, 1976), pp. 43-44.

————. "Enquête: Le palmarès des universités." *Le monde de l'éducation*, no. 19 (July-August, 1976), pp. 3-21.

————. "Michel Butor. L'université française est plus fermée sur elle-même aujourd'hui qu'avant 1968." *Le monde de l'éducation*, no. 14 February, 1976), pp. 35-37.

Géminard, Lucien. *L'enseignement éclate*. Paris, 1973.

Gentil-Baichis, Yves de. "Les facultés parisiennes regroupées en treize universités nouvelles pour octobre." *La Croix*, 22 March 1970.

————. "Les présidents d'université font le point. Après quatre années d'expérience, une séance de travail et de réflexion. 'Oui' à l'autonomie, 'non' à la concurrence sauvage." *La Croix*, 19 March 1975.

Gibson, Raymond. *Block Grants for Higher Education*. Dubuque, Iowa, 1972.

Gilli, Jean-Paul. "Pour une conception nouvelle des relations université-administration." *La revue administrative*, no. 139 (January-February, 1971), pp. 17-20.

Girod de l'Ain, Bertrand. "Une université expérimentale cinq ans après." *Education et gestion*, no. 43 (1974), pp. 24-31.

Giscard d'Estaing, Valéry. *Education et civilisation*. Paris, 1971.

Goblot, Edmond. *La barrière et le niveau* [1st ed. 1925]. Paris, 1967.

BIBLIOGRAPHY

Goguel, François and Grosser, Alfred. *La politique en France*. 3rd ed., Paris, 1964.

Graubard, R. Stephen and Ballotti, Geno, eds. *The Embattled University*. New York, 1970.

Grignon, C. "L'orientation scolaire des élèves d'une école rurale." *Revue française de sociologie* 9, special no. (1968): 218-26.

Guichard, Olivier. *Un chemin tranquille*. Paris, 1975.

_____. *L'éducation nouvelle*. Paris, 1970.

Guinat, J. *Le peuple devient perdant*. Rennes, 1967.

Gusdorf, Georges. *La nef des fous, Université 1968*. Québec, 1969.

_____. *L'université en question*. Paris, 1964.

Haby, René. "Pour une modernisation du système éducatif 1975." *Les cahiers français* (February, 1975). [La documentation française.]

Hallack, Jacques, *A qui profite l'école*. Paris, 1974.

_____. "Y a-t-il une limite à l'effort financier en faveur de l'éducation." *Revue française de pédagogie*, no. 15 (April-June, 1971), pp. 15-21.

Halls, W. D. *Society, School and Progress in France*. Oxford, 1965.

Hamilton, Richard F. *Affluence and the French Worker in the Fourth Republic*. Princeton, N.J., 1967.

Harmel, Claude. "La crise de l'enseignement supérieur en France." *Centre international de documentation et d'information* (INTERDOC). The Hague, 1970.

Heinz, Greta and Peterson, Agnes F. *The French Fifth Republic — Continuity and Change, 1966-1970. An Annotated Bibliography*. Stanford, Calif., 1974.

Herzlich, Guy. "Enquête: Les étudiants sont-ils de futurs chômeurs?" *Le monde de l'éducation*, no. 22 (November, 1976), pp. 4-14.

_____. "Les 'héros' du conservatoire des arts et métiers." *Le monde de l'éducation*, no. 14 (February, 1976), pp. 40-42.

Hoffmann, Stanley. "Participation in Perspective?" in Graubard, Stephen R. and Ballotti, Geno A., eds. *The Embattled University*. (New York, 1970), pp. 117-21.

_____ et al. *In Search of France*. New York, 1965.

_____. "Government and Society." Conference on "Two Decades of Gaullism." Brockport, N.Y., 1978.

Ikor, Roger. *L'école et la culture ou l'université en proie aux bêtes*. Paris, 1972.

Innocent, Georges. "Vincennes." *Bulletin du SNE-Sup.*, no. 184 (July, 1969), pp. 34-35.

271

BIBLIOGRAPHY

Internationale situationniste. *De la misère en milieu étudiant*. 2nd ed. Paris, 1976.

Isambert-Jamati, Vivien. *Crises de la société, crise de l'enseignement*. Paris, 1970.

_____. "Permanence ou variations des objectifs poursuivis par les lycées depuis cent ans." *Revue française de sociologie*, no. spécial (1967), pp. 57-79.

Jencks, Christopher and Riesman, David. *The Academic Revolution*. New York, 1968.

Jobert, Guy. "Une approche de l'éducation permanente en milieu universitaire." *Education permanente*, no. 27 (January-February, 1975), pp. 31-49.

Jullien, Claude-François. "Le blocus de Vincennes." *Le nouvel observateur*, 1 November 1971, pp. 46-47.

_____. *Les lycéens, ces nouveaux hommes*. Paris, 1972.

Keniston, Kenneth. "Sources of Student Dissent," in Sampson, E. E. and Korn, H. A. *Student Activism and Protest* (San Francisco, 1970), pp. 158-91.

Kerbouch, Jean-Claude. *Le piéton de mai*. Paris, 1968.

Kourganoff, Vladimir. *La face cachée de l'université*. Paris, 1972.

Labro, Philippe. *Les barricades de mai*. Paris, 1968.

_____ et al. *Ce n'est qu'un début*. Paris, 1968.

Lapassade, Georges. *Procès de l'université*. Paris, 1969.

"To the Left of the Maoists." *Times*, 20 April 1970.

Le Gendre, Bertrand. "Angers: Les grandes déboires d'une petite université." *Le monde de l'éducation*, no. 7 (June, 1975), pp. 40-42.

_____. "Le baccalauréat." *Le monde de l'éducation*, no. 18 (June, 1976), pp. 6-19.

Léon, Antoine. *Histoire de l'enseignement en France*. Paris, 1972.

Levine, Donald M. and Bane, M. J. *The "Inequality" Controversy: Schooling and Distributive Justice*. New York, 1975.

Lombard, Jacques. "Réflexion sur une crise. Nous n'avons plus confiance." *Le monde de l'éducation*, no. 18 (June, 1976), p. 37.

Luchaire, François. "Université: Le budget d'austérité doit se traduire par des réformes." *Le Quotidien de Paris*, 17 August 1974.

Majault, Joseph. *L'enseignement en France*. New York, 1973.

Malan, T. "L'évolution de la fonction de planification de l'éducation en France au cours des V° et VI° plans (1966-1975)." *Revue française de pédagogie*, no. 26 (January-February-March, 1974), pp. 23-37.

Mangenot, Marc et al. *Les jeunes face à l'emploi*. Paris, 1972.

BIBLIOGRAPHY

Markiewicz-Lagneau, Janina. "L'enseignement supérieur court en France." *Notes et d'études documentaires*, no. 4001 (29 June 1973).

Matthijssen, M. A. and Vervoort, C. E., eds. *Education in Europe. L'éducation en Europe* (European seminar on sociology of education). Paris, 1969.

Mayne, Margot. "Law School Forms own Police Force." *Guardian*, 30 November 1970.

Mazauriac, Claude. "Le SNE-Sup: 'La France n'a pas trop d'étudiants'." *L'unité*, 17-23 November 1972.

Mazliack, Paul. "Il faut 300 milliards aux universités. Soisson n'en a accordé que cinquante." *L'Humanité*, 16 January 1975.

Mendès-France, Pierre. *Pour préparer l'avenir*. Paris, 1968.

Menesson, Danielle. "Deux ans d'études pour les sept nouveaux diplômes (DEUG) dès la rentrée 73-74." *France-Soir*, 10 March 1973.

Michaud, Guy. *Révolution dans l'université*. Paris, 1968.

Minot, Jacques. "L'affaire des diplômes." *La revue administrative*, no. 153 (May-June, 1973), pp. 302-04.

_____. "L'année des mille réformes." *La revue administrative*, no. 130 (July-August, 1969), pp. 488-90.

_____. "CCU." *La revue administrative*, no. 151 (January-February, 1973), pp. 55-56.

_____. *L'entreprise éducation nationale*. Paris, 1970.

_____. "Former des administrateurs pour l'éducation nationale." *Education et gestion*, no. 16 (1969), pp. 3-10.

_____. *Les grands maîtres de l'université et les ministres de l'éducation nationale* [*Les cahiers de l'INAS*]. Paris, May 1974.

_____. *Lexique des termes en usage dans l'administration de l'éducation*. [*Les cahiers de l'INAS*], May, 1974.

_____. *L'organisation au ministère de l'éducation*. [*Les cahiers de l'INAS*]. Paris, January 1975.

_____. "Pour des universités bien administrées." *La revue administrative*, no. 125 (September-October, 1968), pp. 602-04.

_____. "Retour à la cogestion dans les oeuvres universitaires." *La revue administrative*, no. 137 (September-October, 1970), pp. 552-54.

_____. *Les théories générales de l'ensemble éducatif*. [*Les cahiers de l'INAS*]. Paris, January 1975.

_____ and Delclaux, M. *L'administration de l'éducation. Essai de bibliographie*. [*Les cahiers de l'INAS*, November 1974].

"La mise en place des nouvelles structures universitaires." *La revue administrative*, no. 134 (March-April, 1970), p. 164.

273

BIBLIOGRAPHY

Mitterrand, François. *Changer la vie, programme de gouvernement du P.S.* Paris, 1972.

Mockler, Tony. "Too little and too few for too many. The Paris universities." *Guardian*, 8 August 1970.

Le Monde. 1967-78.

Le monde de l'éducation, 1974-78.

Monneron, Jean-Louis *et al. Politique et prophétisme: Mai 1968.* [Centre catholique des intellectuels français, recherches et débats, no. 63]. Paris, 1969.

Monnerot, Jules. *Démarxiser l'université.* Paris, 1970.

———. *La France intellectuelle.* Paris, 1970.

Montlibert, Christian de. "Promotion et reclassement. Les élèves d'un centre d'enseignement par cours du soir à la recherche d'une promotion par un diplôme." *Revue française de sociologie* 9, special no. (1968): 208-17.

Morin, Edgar. "Culture adolescente et révolte étudiante." *Annales, économies, sociétés, civilisations* 24 (May-June, 1969): 765-76.

——— *et al. Mai 1968: La brèche. Premières réflexions sur les événements.* Paris, 1968.

———. *La prise de la parole, mai 1968.* Paris, 1968.

Mouchon, Jean-Pierre. *La crise estudiantine et les émeutes de mai 1968.* Paris, 1969.

Moulins, Jean-Pierre. "Metz: L'université asphyxiée." *L'unité*, 9 May 1975.

Najman, D. *L'enseignement supérieur, pour quoi faire.* Paris, 1974.

Natanson, Jacques, Prost, Antoine, *et al. La révolution scolaire.* Paris, 1963.

Nice, Université de. Centre d'études administratives. "Journée d'étude sur les relations université-administration, 9 mars 1970." Nice, 1970.

Niel, Mathilde. "A propos de la révolte de mai. Réponse à Raymond Aron." *Combat*, 26 June 1968.

———. *La crise de jeunesse.* Paris, 1965.

———. *Le mouvement étudiant ou la révolution en marche.* Paris, 1968.

Nouvel, Luc. "Rencontre avec le doyen Paul Ricoeur. Universités nouvelles: un périlleux apprentissage." *Réforme*, 28 February 1970.

Le Nouvel observateur. 1968-1977.

Organization for Economic Co-operation and Development (OECD). *Développement de l'enseignement supérieur 1950-67. Rapport analytique.* Paris, 1971.

———. *Educational Policy and Planning. France.* Paris, 1972.

274

BIBLIOGRAPHY

_____. *Educational Statistics Yearbook*. Vol. II. *Country Tables*. Paris, 1975.

_____. *Planification à long terme des politiques d'enseignement*. Paris, 1973.

_____. Centre pour la recherche et l'innovation dans l'enseignement. *L'éducation récurrente, politique et évolution: rapports pars pays, France*. Paris, 1976.

_____. *Programmes d'enseignement à partir de 1980*. Paris, 1972.

_____. *Etudes des coûts et des économies possibles — Etudes sur la gestion des établissements d'enseignement supérieur. Université de Bradford*. Paris, 1973.

_____. Boisot, Marcel. *Discipline, interdisciplinarité, programme interdisciplinaire*. Paris, 1970.

_____. Husén, Torsten. *Origine sociale et éducation: perspectives des recherches sur l'égalité devant l'éducation*. Paris, 1972.

_____. Conference on Policies for Educational Growth. [Paris, 3-5 June 1970.] *General Report, Educational Policies for the 1970s*. Paris, 1971.

_____. Conference of Future Structures of Post-secondary Education. *Towards Mass Higher Education. Issues and Dilemmas*. Paris, 1974.

_____. Conférence sur les structures futures de l'enseignement post-secondaire. *Rapport général. Politiques de l'enseignement supérieur*. Paris, 1974.

_____. Frankel, Charles. *Reviews of National Policies for Education. France*. Paris, 1971.

_____. Furth, Dorothée *et al. L'enseignement supérieur court, recherche d'une identité*. Paris, 1973.

_____. Comité du personnel scientifique et technique. *Examen des politiques nationales en matière d'éducation. France*. Vol. I. *La planification du système d'enseignement*. Paris, 1969.

_____. Grignon, Claude and Passeron, Jean-Claude. *French Experience before 1968 (Case Studies on Innovation in Higher Education)*. Paris, 1970.

_____. Study Group in the Economics of Education. *Organizational Problems in Planning Educational Development*. Paris, 1966.

_____. "L'orientation des élèves." *L'université syndicaliste*, no. 8 (14 December 1967), pp. 17-48.

"Paris de I à XIII. Les nouvelles universités." *Combat*, 21 March 1970.

"La participation." *Espoir*, no. 5 (December 1973-January 1974).

Paillet, Marc. *Table rase. 3 mai-30 juin 1968*. Paris, 1968.

Parti communiste français. *Propositions du parti communiste français*

275

pour une réforme démocratique de l'enseignement. 2nd ed. [*L'école et la nation,* special no. 185-186 (January-February, 1970)].

Passeron, Jean-Claude. "Les problèmes et les faux problèmes de la 'démocratisation' du système scolaire." *Education et gestion,* no. 28 (January, 1972): 10-23.

Paulhac, Jean. "Réflexion sur une crise. Une purulence secrète." *Le monde de l'éducation,* no. 18 (June, 1976), p. 36.

Perret, J. *Inquiète Sorbonne.* Paris, 1968.

Perrot, Michelle *et al. La Sorbonne par elle-même. Mai-juin 68.* [*Mouvement social,* no. 64 (July-September, 1968).]

Petitjean, Gérard. "Le vrai boulot d'Alice." *Le nouvel observateur,* no. 629 (29 November-5 December 1976), pp. 56-57.

Peyrefitte, Alain. *Le mal français.* Paris, 1976.

———. *Rue d'Ulm, chroniques de la vie normalienne.* Paris, 1963.

Philip, A. *Mai 68 et la foi démocratique.* Paris, 1968.

Pic, Pierre. "A propos de la création d'une troisième université à Aix-en-Provence. La sélection et le patronat pris à partie." *Les Echos,* 13 April 1973.

Pitts, Jesse. "Continuity and Change in Bourgeois France," in Hoffmann, ed., *In Search of France* (New York, 1963), pp. 235-304.

La planification d'après le V° plan." *L'université syndicaliste,* no. 8 (14 December 1967), pp. 37-40.

Poignant, Raymond. *L'enseignement dans les pays du marché commun.* Paris, 1965.

Le Point. 1976-1977.

Ponteil, Félix. *Histoire de l'enseignement 1789-1965.* Paris, 1966.

———. *Les institutions de la France de 1814-1870.* Paris, 1966.

Porscher, Louis. *Chemin dans le labyrinthe.* Paris, 1974.

"Problèmes de l'enseignement supérieur." *Bulletin du SNE-Sup,* no. 192 (October, 1970), pp. 5-47.

"Problèmes financiers des universités." *Education et gestion,* no. 43 (1974), pp. 57-63.

Prost, Antoine. *L'enseignement en France de 1800 à 1967.* Paris, 1968.

"Que faire avec le baccalauréat." *Le monde de l'éducation,* no. 40 (June, 1978), pp. 10-27.

Quermonne, Jean-Louis and Casadevall, André. "L'université abandonée." *Le monde de l'éducation,* no. 21 (October, 1976), pp. 3-11.

Le Quotidien de Paris. 1974-1975.

Rachou, Henri. "La direction des enseignements supérieurs," in Crémieux-Brilhac, ed., *L'éducation nationale,* pp. 371-78.

BIBLIOGRAPHY

"La réalité de l'orientation." *L'université syndicaliste*, no. 8 (14 December 1967), pp. 27-36.

"La réforme du deuxième cycle: Qu'est-ce qui va changer?" *Le monde de l'éducation*, no. 15 (March, 1976), pp. 42-43.

"La réforme du premier cycle des enseignements supérieurs et la création du diplôme d'études universitaires générales en France." *AUPELF* 11, 1-2 (Spring-Fall, 1973): 109-17.

"Dans les résidences universitaires." *Education et gestion*, no. 21 (July, 1970), pp. 33-44.

Rémond, René. *Vivre notre histoire*. [Interviewed by Aimé Savard.] Paris, 1976.

La revue administrative. 1968-1975.

La revue de l'AUPELF (Association des universités partiellement ou entièrement de langue française, Montréal). 1968-1975.

Revue de l'enseignement supérieur (Cahiers des universités françaises). 1969-1975.

Revue française de pédagogie. 1969-1975.

Richardot, Jean-Pierre. "Une semaine à Tolbiac." *Le monde de l'éducation*, no. 28 (May, 1977), pp. 36-45.

Ridard, B. "Toutes les universités de France (sauf Paris): un organigramme." *Science et vie* (November, 1970), pp. 138-47.

Rigaud, Jacques. "A propos de la loi d'orientation de l'enseignement supérieur." *France forum* (February, 1969), pp. 19-23.

Robert, Fernand. *Un mandarin prend la parole*. Paris, 1970.

Roig, Charles and Billon-Grand, F. *La socialisation politique des enfants*. Paris, 1968.

Rolant, Michel and Rivoire, Maurice. "Syndicat et patronat: Université, économie, éducation permanente. Conception de la CFDT." *AUPELF* 12, 1 (1974): 172-80.

Romilly, Jacqueline de. *Nous autres professeurs*. Paris, 1969.

Roszak, Theodore. *The Making of a Counter Culture*. New York, 1968.

Roulland, M. "L'évolution des charges administratives des universités." *Education et gestion*, no. 43 (1974), pp. 51-53.

Rousselet, Jean *et al*. *Les jeunes et l'emploi*. [*Cahiers du centre d'études de l'emploid*, no. 7]. Paris, 1975.

Saint-Martin, Monique de. "Les facteurs de l'élimination et de la sélection différentielles dans les études de sciences." *Revue française de sociologie* 9, special no. (1968): 167-184.

_____. *Les fonctions sociales de l'enseignement scientifique*. Paris, 1971.

Salais, Robert and Lionnet, Roger. "Enquête sur l'emploi de 1968 et 1969. Résultats détaillés." *Les collections de l'INSEE*, no. 79, 18 D. *Démographie et emploi*. Paris, January 1973.

Sampson, Edward E. and Korn, Harold A., eds. *Student Activism and Protest*. San Francisco, 1970.

Sauvageot, Marc and Geismar, Alain. *Le livre des journées de mai*. Paris, 1968.

Sauvy, Alfred. *La révolte des jeunes*. Paris, 1970.

———— and Girard, Alain. *Vers l'enseignement pour tous*. Paris, 1974.

Schnapp, Alain and Vidal-Naquet, Pierre, eds. *Journal de la commune étudiante. Textes et documents, Novembre 67-Juin 68*. Paris, 1969.

Schonfeld, William R. *Obedience and Revolt: French Behavior toward Authority*. Beverly Hills, Calif., February 1976.

Schreiner, Bernard. "Les problèmes restent posés." *Témoignage chrétien*, 19 March 1970.

Schwartz, Bertrand. "L'université, service public et ouverture sur l'extérieur." *Education permanente*, no. 27 (January-February, 1975), pp. 5-10.

Les secrétaires généraux d'académie face à leurs problèmes. *Education et gestion*, no. 19 (January, 1970), pp. 61-68.

Servan-Schreiber, Jean-Jacques. *Réveil de la France*. Paris, 1968.

Seys, B. and Lauthé, P. "Enquête sur l'emploi de 1976. Résultats provisoires." *Les collections de l'INSEE*, 48 D (November, 1976).

Silvestre, Pierre. "La réussite à l'agrégation." *Education et gestion*, no. 19 (January, 1970).

Singer, Daniel. *Prelude to Revolution France in May 1968*. London, 1970.

"Le SNE-Sup. et la loi d'orientation." *Bulletin du SNE-Sup.*, no. 170 (January, 1969), pp. 6-12.

"Springtime in France." Editorial. *Times* (London), 17 April 1976.

Suffert, Jacques and Lesieur, Jean. "Université: l'enlisement." *Le Point*, no. 242 (9 May 1977), pp. 115-22.

Suleiman, Ezra. "Industrial Policy Formulation in France," in Warnecke, Steven J. and Suleiman, Ezra N., eds. *Industrial Policies in Western Europe* (New York, 1975), pp. 23-42.

————. "The Myth of Technical Expertise — Selection, Organization and Leadership," *Comparative Politics* 10 (October, 1977): 137-158.

————. *Politics, Power and Bureaucracy in France — The Administrative Elite*. Princeton, N.J., 1974.

278

BIBLIOGRAPHY

_____. "Two-Track Education System Divides French." *Los Angeles Times*, 2 May 1976.

Syndicalisme universitaire. 1968-1975.

Talbott, John E. *The Politics of Educational Reform in France, 1918-1940.* Princeton, N.J., 1969.

Thuillier, Pierre. "Bonnes et mauvaises universités." *Le nouvel observateur*, 19 October 1970.

Todd, Olivier. "Sur plusieurs fronts Edgar Faure se bat contre tout le monde . . . sauf contre l'Elysée." *Le nouvel observateur*, 9 September 1968.

Tonka, Hubert. *Fiction de la contestation aliénée.* Paris, 1968.

Touraine, Alain. *Le mouvement de mai ou le communisme utopique.* Paris, 1969.

Tournoux, J.-R. *Le mois de mai du général.* Paris, 1969.

Touscoz, Jean. "Les universités insignifiantes et prophétiques." *Le monde de l'éducation*, no. 25 (February, 1977), pp. 38-40.

Union nationale des étudiants de France (UNEF). *Manifeste — Pour une réforme démocratique de l'enseignement supérieur.* Paris, 1967.

United Nations Scientific Educational and Cultural Organization (UNESCO). Conférence des ministres de l'éducation des états membres d'Europe sur l'accès à l'enseignement supérieur (Vienna, 20-25 November 1967). *Accès à l'enseignement supérieur du point de vue de l'origine sociale, économique et culturelle des étudiants.* Paris, 1967.

_____. *Accès à l'enseignement supérieur du point de vue des besoins actuels et prévisibles du développement de la collectivité.* Paris, 1967.

_____. *Document descriptif d'information sur l'accès à l'enseignement supérieur en Europe.* Paris, 1967.

_____. *Données statistiques comparatives sur l'accès à l'enseignement supérieur en Europe.* Paris, 1967.

_____. Deuxième conférence des ministres de l'éducation des états membres d'Europe (Bucarest, 26 November-4 December 1973). *L'enseignement supérieur en Europe — Problèmes et perspectives. Etude statistique.* Paris, October 1973.

_____. Hallack, Jacques. *The Analysis of Educational Costs and Expenditure.* Paris, 1969.

_____. International Institute for Educational Planning. Callaway, Archibald. *Planification de l'éducation et chômage des jeunes.* Paris, 1971.

279

BIBLIOGRAPHY

_____. Onushkin, Victor G. *La planification du développement des universités, I.* Paris, 1971.

_____. Rowley, C. D. *Les aspects politiques de la planification de l'éducation dans les pays en voie de développement.* Paris, 1971.

_____. Ruscoe, G. C. *The Conditions for Success in Educational Planning.* Paris, 1969.

_____. Le Gall, A. *et al. Le développement de l'enseignement supérieur. Problèmes actuels de la démocratisation des enseignements secondaire et supérieur.* Paris, 1973.

"L'université de Paris." *La documentation française illustrée,* no. 211-212 (November-December, 1975).

"L'université de Paris éclate." *La vie française,* 18 October 1968.

Université moderne. 1968-1973.

L'université syndicaliste. 1968-1975.

Valabrègue, Catherine. *La condition étudiante.* Paris, 1970.

Vermot-Gauchy, Michel. *L'éducation nationale dans la France de 1975.* Monaco, 1965.

"Vincennes: L'expérience continue." *Le monde de l'éducation,* no. 2 (January, 1975), p. 33.

Vinocur, John. "'Danny the Red' Homesick for France after 10-Year Exile." *The New York Times,* 3 April 1978.

Vion, Marc. "L'exemple américain." *Le monde de l'éducation,* no. 18 (June, 1976), p. 39.

"Vives critiques contre le projet de découpage des universités parisiennes." *Combat,* 17 March 1970.

Vivies, Jacques. "L'autonomie financière des universités." *Education et gestion,* no. 18 (October, 1969), pp. 63-67.

Vrain, Philippe. *Les débouchés professionnels des étudiants 1967-70.* Paris, 1973.

Vuillemin, J. *Rebâtir l'université.* Paris, 1968.

Wigg, Richard. "100,000 French Students Take to the Streets." *The Times* (London), 17 April 1976.

Wilson, Bryan, ed. *Education, Equality and Society.* London, 1975.

Zamansky, Marc. *Mort ou résurrection de l'université.* Paris, 1969.

Zegel, Sylvain. *Les idées de mai.* Paris, 1968.

Zeldin, Theodore. "Higher Education in France, 1848-1940." *Journal of Contemporary History,* 2 (1967): 53-80.

BIBLIOGRAPHY